Rural Education for the Twenty-First Century

Edited by

Kai A. Schafft and Alecia Youngblood Jackson

r e

Rural Education for the Twenty-First Century

2 1

Indentity, Place, and Community in a Globalizing World

The Pennsylvania State University Press
University Park, Pennsylvania

Library of Congress Cataloging-in-Publication Data

Rural education for the twenty-first century : identity, place, and community in a globalizing world / edited by Kai A. Schafft and Alecia Youngblood Jackson.

p. cm.—(Rural studies)

Includes bibliographical references and index.

Summary: "A collection of essays examining the various social, cultural, and economic intersections of rural place and global space, as viewed through the lens of education. Explores practices that offer both problems and possibilities for the future of rural schools and communities, in the United States and abroad"—Provided by publisher.

ISBN 978-0-271-03682-3 (cloth : alk. paper)

ISBN 978-0-271-03683-0 (pbk. : alk. paper)

1. Education, Rural—History.
2. Rural schools—History.
3. Rural poor—Education.
4. Education and globalization.
I. Schafft, Kai A., 1964– .
II. Jackson, Alecia Youngblood, 1968– .

LC5146.R82   2010
370.9173'4—dc22
2009044135

Dedicated to William L. Boyd, 1935–2008

Contents

Acknowledgments

This book was the result of a great deal of effort from many different people. Each of the chapters went through an initial internal and external review process. We would therefore like to thank each of the contributors for taking part in this review. We would especially like to thank external reviewers and readers. These include: Ted Alter, David Berliner, William Boyd, Tom Farmer, Constance Flanagan, Matt Foulkes, Stephan Goetz, Hobart Harmon, Jessica Hayes-Conroy, Dana Mitra, Nona Prestine, Esther Prins, Kristine Reed, Gretchen Schafft, Patrick Shannon, and Rachel Tompkins. The former editor of the Penn State Press Rural Studies Series, Clare Hinrichs, enthusiastically supported this project from the beginning. Clare then passed the responsibility on to current series editor, Steve Sapp, who saw it through a speedy yet thorough and incisive review process. The book has benefited strongly from the attentions of Clare and Steve. Erin McHenry-Sorber provided additional and valuable editorial support. Last but not least we remain deeply indebted to Trudi Haupt, who completed the Herculean tasks of helping to organize and manage the review and editing process, and who then read and copyedited each of the chapters with a careful eye—and with unflagging good humor throughout. We could not have done this without her.

INTRODUCTION:
RURAL EDUCATION AND COMMUNITY
IN THE TWENTY-FIRST CENTURY

Kai A. Schafft and Alecia Youngblood Jackson

The year 2008 marked the first time in human history that more of the world's population was located in urban rather than rural places (United Nations Population Fund 2007). In the United States as well as across the globe, the history of development has been largely one of urbanization, rural outmigration, and the subsumption of spatial peripheries into the social, cultural, economic, and political spheres of the urban core (Krannich 2008; Lipton 1977; McGranahan 2003; White 1998). This long, steady process has been deeply etched into the history of rural education, and in the United States and elsewhere it has to varying degrees been directly abetted by rural education (Corbett 2007; Theobald 1997; Woodrum 2004).

Well over one hundred years ago, school reformers in the United States began to talk about what came to be known as the "rural school problem" (Kannapel and DeYoung 1999; Tyack 1972). Rural schools, these reformers argued, were too inefficient for the demands of a rapidly changing, urbanizing, and globalizing society. At the heart of the "efficiency" problem was local control: people in rural communities, reformers believed, were simply ill equipped to run their own schools and prepare students to be economically competitive and productive in a modernizing world. As Elwood Cubberley (himself an urban educational reformer) wrote nearly one hundred years ago, "Managed as it has been by rural people, themselves lacking in educational insight, penurious, and with no comprehensive grasp of their own problems, the rural school, except in a few places, has practically stood still"[1] (1922, 102).

---

1. As Corbett (2007, 34) has aptly noted, "The 'rural problem' in contemporary educational theorizing effectively constructs the rural community itself as a problem."

The solution, reformers like Cubberley concluded, was to make rural schools look more like urban schools: larger, bureaucratized, run by educational professionals rather than locals, and informed by the latest pedagogical knowledge. This legacy is now manifested for urban and rural schools alike in the form of school consolidation, the standardization of curricula and assessment, and the increased reliance on business models of school management (Engels 2000; Jo 2005; Lyson 2002; Tyack and Cuban 2001). As Gruenewald and Smith (2008, xiv) have observed, "Today the seldom questioned underlying assumption about the purpose of schooling is to prepare the next generation to compete and succeed in the global economy." It is for these reasons that Corbett has argued that in rural areas schooling may be considered the "quintessential institution of disembedding" (2007, 251), as public education serves the economic imperative of capitalism by severing attachment to place and producing mobile, adaptable youth flexibly responsive to changing labor market conditions.

Simultaneously, increased political, economic, and cultural globalization has reshaped the global-local interface (Drainville 2004; Swyngedouw 1997) and, consequently, the identity of rural people and places (Bonanno and Constance 2003, 241). Rural people and places have likely never had the "closed" identities suggested by the community-based traditions, political and cultural conservatism, and generational discourses of sameness often described by rural community members (Bell 1992; Woods 2005). But as we enter the twenty-first century, the face of rural communities has nevertheless been radically transformed by the economic effects of multinational free trade agreements, the proliferation of mass media and information technology, and educational reforms such as No Child Left Behind that privilege standardized curricula and "high-stakes" accountability for test scores over accountability to the contexts of local people and places. These changes have presented new opportunities for rural people, as well as new challenges.

What does this mean for rural education? And what does this imply for the relationship between rural schools and the communities they serve? Historically, rural schools have served important roles as centers of social activity and cultural meaning, helping to maintain local traditions and particular identities of rural communities. They are sites of civic interaction and shared intergenerational identity and experience (Elder and Conger 2000; Lyson 2002; Peshkin 1978). Yet rural schools also paradoxically represent a direct *challenge* to local (rural) identity and community survival when embodying urban values and serving national-level economic agendas that largely dismiss the "inefficiencies" of rural places—and even the connection to place in general (Corbett 2007; DeYoung and Howley 1990; Edmondson 2001). This edited volume takes these issues as its point of departure and analyzes the multiple, competing discourses that vie for the identity of place—and therefore the institution of schooling—by exploring the practices that offer problems and possibilities for the futures of rural community members as well as the educational systems that serve them.

Organization of This Book

Our purpose in writing this book was to gather together in one volume a diverse set of voices and perspectives, including those representing educational theory and policy and educational leadership, but also scholars with backgrounds in sociology and rural sociology, demography, political science, and community development. While much contemporary educational research takes it as a given that the walls of the classroom or the school building largely describe the limits of the analytic focus, the work in this volume instead foregrounds the *interrelationship* between school and community, and how that interrelationship is shaped by the global-local context in which it is embedded. We believe that closely examining issues at the school-community interface demands an inherently multidisciplinary approach, one we have tried to model within the pages of this volume.

Readers will find that most of the chapter authors rely on qualitative methods (i.e., interviews, observations, and documents analyses) to examine school-community issues. We believe that one of the strengths of this edited collection is a focus on naturalistic inquiry "in the field" of rural places. Qualitative designs such as ethnography, case studies, phenomenology, narrative inquiry, and mixed methods are represented in the text. As such, many of the chapters in this volume build on the sort of critical scholarship instituted in educational research by the pioneering sociological work of Paul Willis (1977), who initiated the theoretically informed analysis of the micro-dynamics of life in and out of school in an urban British community. Several chapters draw explicitly or implicitly on the tradition of critical scholarship and resistance that Willis's work established. While we acknowledge the contributions of objective, quantitative research in describing large trends and explaining or comparing certain variables that make up rural life, the authors in this collection take seriously the experiences and perspectives of rural people; they emphasize rural peoples' views and voices as they are situated within their local places, while keeping an eye toward the global contexts in which rurality is constructed, experienced, and critiqued.

Finally, while the contributors to this volume focus primarily on rural school and community relations in the United States, also included are perspectives from Canada, sub-Saharan Africa, and Australia, among others, to introduce an international comparative focus, and to suggest some of the ways that global economic, social, and cultural change have reshaped the rural school-community relationship across multiple contexts.

Spaces of Identity

The volume begins with part 1, "Spaces of Identity." The chapters in this section explore how rurality itself comes to be constituted as a discursive space, how rural and community identities are produced and reproduced, and how relations of power at local and supra-local levels shape how rural identity is constructed, negotiated, and challenged. Within these chapters, close critiques of these constructions of place-bound identities consider ways that rural education might provide opportunities for rural students to redefine *place* as something other than local geography, to craft alternative identities other than those imposed on them, and to encourage them to imagine worlds beyond their own.

In the opening chapter, Theobald and Wood employ a historical analysis to examine the construction of rural identity through popular and mass media, looking in particular at the ways negative stereotypes of rural identity are formed, and how cultural messages reinforce the associations between rurality, backwardness, and deficiency. Though they argue that anti-rural biases have roots that stretch at least as far back as seventeenth-century Europe, these stereotypes and negative associations are only strengthened by the proliferation of mass media and the globalized production and distribution of goods and services. "Though some may possess the ability to dismiss these messages," they argue, "the very act of dismissing them becomes a part of the identity an individual builds. . . . Since the United States is synonymous with 'progress,' and progress is culturally defined as ever more urban growth and development, rural youth see themselves as nonparticipants in the American experience, at least until they leave their home and move to the city."

Howley and Howley extend this discussion in chapter 2, examining the stigmas associated with the intersection of rurality and class. They argue that globalization "undermines the local commons from which local community is

developed, creating conditions that make the social exclusion of already marginalized groups just that much more likely." Far from deficiency, Howley and
Howley argue that those generally identified as "the rural poor" are instead
characterized by resiliency and remarkable productivity in their capacity to
identify resources and manage their existence (see also Corbett, this volume).
And yet the "othering" that rural people, and especially rural poor people,
experience obscures this resiliency. Rural educators are positioned to help their
students, and by extension the broader community, imagine different possibilities, "but they must do so on very different terms than those prized by the
institution of U.S. schooling and the global political economy that increasingly
sponsors it."

The first two chapters are communitarian in their orientation insofar as they
emphasize the social and educational potential of fostering and (re)building
rural community. In each case the tension over rural community identity is
framed principally at the interstices of the local and the global—the ways in
which local (rural) actors negotiate individual and community identity in the
face of economic policies, educational reforms, and cultural discourse that
ignores, dismisses, or denigrates local and rural experience. The following two
chapters in this section, however, complicate the discussion by regarding the
tension over identity construction *within* community, examining how individual and institutional actors work to define the boundaries of local community
and identity as a way of determining who is included and who is excluded.

Groenke and Nespor's chapter explores how the use of racist language is
employed by rural youth as a mechanism for establishing the boundaries of
local identity—"from symbolically excluding outsiders and newcomers to the
area, to subverting school administrators' attempts to integrate the school discursively into the larger cosmopolitan school district by instituting a speech
code, to policing intra-group identity among peers." They argue that "rural
spaces and the identities of persons living in rural spaces are highly
contested. . . . These negotiations and struggles unfold not only between local
and global forces (the rural community and cultural and economic forces originating outside it), but among different factions within rural communities who
may appropriate 'global' tools or imagery as readily as they embrace more
familiar and 'traditional' local practices." The authors conclude by suggesting
that administrators cannot condone or ignore the use of racist language, but
must also be aware of how actions on their part may inadvertently galvanize
oppositional identities that draw directly on racist categories.

In chapter 4, Jackson, using a Foucauldian analysis of discourse, similarly critiques the ways that power and identity are constituted and locally negotiated. The analysis of power and discourse in the rural town of Garner is meant to reveal how the institution of schooling, which may be a site of powerful local control and autonomy, can also exist as a structure of exclusion. Jackson's main thesis is that rural schools cannot always escape the power effects of their own resistance to globalizing trends. While rural places may yearn to hang onto their traditional identities, doing so can be dangerous to people in the community and schools. The desire for control can lead to power effects that can be damaging to the ways students learn to value themselves and their communities. What is important about this type of discursive analysis is its emphasis not only on knowledge about rural schooling itself, but also on how that knowledge was formed, and how that knowledge functions within discourse to open up or limit the lives of people. In this way, meanings of "community" can be critiqued and reimagined. Such an analysis also moves the focus from individuals (such as students who "fail" within certain places) to a rigorous tracing of how problems become possible within discourse.

Placing Education

Part 2, "Placing Education," builds on the ideas in part 1, offering a collection of chapters that analyzes the purpose of education in rural places—and its impact on community—within the tensions and conditions of a changing nation and world. Contributors in this section grapple with questions such as: What are the effects of U.S. neoliberal economic policies and standardization on the purpose of education? What are the messages inherent in formal, standardized schooling that are transmitted to rural students? What does it mean to "be" a teacher in such shifting times and unstable places?

Schafft, Killeen, and Morrissey's chapter analyzes the tensions of place and the purpose of education in a shifting world, using a case study of a set of rural communities in upstate New York to examine the interconnections among rural economic change, increases in rural poverty, and the added challenges imposed on rural students and schools by the federal No Child Left Behind legislation (NCLB). They argue that across the United States many rural communities, especially those historically based around agricultural or manufacturing economies, have experienced the economic brunt of neoliberal economic policies encouraging free trade and government deregulation. This has led to the concentration of agriculture and industrial shutdowns as manufacturing is resited overseas where labor is cheaper and environmental regulations laxer.

They argue that NCLB also derives from a market-driven logic fully consistent with neoliberalism, emphasizing standardization and the threat of sanctions based around a set of accountability measures. In upstate New York, as in many other declining rural areas in the United States, accountability measures may operate as a "double jeopardy," penalizing schools not necessarily for under-performance of students as a consequence of inadequate teaching and adminis-tration, but, ironically, for student underperformance directly related to deepening local poverty conditions and the residential instability and academic dislocation that so often results.

Michael Corbett's work in chapter 6 broadly addresses the clash between the generalizing discourse of formal education (especially its tendencies toward standardization of both curricula and assessment, and its translation of the specificity of locality into a placeless global) and the particularizing discourse of locality and community. As Corbett has written elsewhere (2007, 48), "These two competing spaces stand in resistance to one another; each creates its own criteria of intelligence and legitimate ('real') work and each sets up its 'own' as the people who have the 'natural gifts' to do the work that is done by 'people like us,' because each is considered to be 'naturally' suited to a particular hab-itat."

Corbett's many years of teaching and extensive ethnographic research in a Nova Scotia coastal fishing community raise important questions about these two "competing spaces": the multiple, informal institutions of community deeply embedded in local history and culture on the one hand, and the institu-tion of the school on the other hand, an instrument of the state and a purveyor of formal knowledge fundamentally constituting "a story about somewhere else." What does formal schooling have to say, implicitly or explicitly, about local experience? In this chapter Corbett reflects on his teaching experiences in a Nova Scotia elementary school and how these two competing spaces—and the tensions and ambivalences they create—help to shape the identities and future trajectories of rural people and the communities in which they live.

The community-global dynamic and its impact on rural education is further explored in chapter 7 by Giroux, Jah, and Eloundou-Enyegue as they look at rural education in the context of sub-Saharan Africa. Their chapter examines trends in rural-urban inequalities in educational attainment and labor market mobility. They observe that while the process of globalization has often been optimistically described as an equalizing force, facilitating the flow of ideas, information, communication, and opportunities across divergent spaces; com-pressing space; and reducing inequality, this process has been uneven at best.

In the African context, inequalities between countries have decreased overall, but inequalities within countries—and in particular between rural and urban areas—have increased, especially as the process of urbanization in developing countries continues. Because of this they investigate the extent to which rural communities experience economic marginalization as a consequence of globalization, and if so, whether this is primarily due to differences in human capital attributes. Their findings suggest that in the case of Cameroon, while rural-urban differences in educational attainment have decreased, human capital attributes appear to have less effect on outcomes than before.

Similar to chapter 7, in chapter 8 Edmondson and Butler look at the role of education in the context of economically declining postindustrial rural communities in Pennsylvania. Like Corbett, these contributors inquire into what it means to be an educator in a rural context, particularly one in which local economic opportunities have been markedly limited by rural economic change. The authors discuss prevailing ideological discourses—conservative, neoconservative, neoliberal, and liberal—how these discourses translate into coherent teaching practice, and what this implies for rural people, schools, and communities. They argue that none of these discourses provides direction for resolving the problems faced by rural communities, problems that require active local engagement and democratic deliberation.

Teaching Communities

After a consideration of issues of identity, place, and education, the book concludes with part 3, "Teaching Communities," a section that includes critical yet hopeful accounts of programs and partnerships that offer support for different ways of being "rural" in educational communities. Chapters argue for approaches such as indigenous education, culturally based pedagogies, interactive distance learning, and critical pedagogies for English Language Learners and special education students. The authors in this section advocate for rural education that may potentially shift the relationships among identity, place, and community in positive, productive ways.

In chapter 9, Faircloth and Tippeconnic note that while in popular culture "globalization" is a relatively recent notion, for indigenous tribes and communities globalization has been a reality for at least five hundred years, beginning with European contact and colonization. Despite the threats posed by disease, poverty, and concerted efforts to eradicate their cultures and languages, Native communities not only continue to persist (Schafft, Faircloth, and Thompson

2006), but use institutions like the tribal colleges to preserve traditional language and culture. They argue that tribal colleges do this both "through locally derived curricula, programming, and instructional practices [that] make tribal colleges spaces within which both Native and non-Native students can thrive intellectually and culturally," and also by taking specifically global approaches to higher education, developing multiple worldwide partnerships across educational institutions serving Native persons.

A broader discussion of higher education access for youth is the focus of chapter 10. Like the chapters by Corbett and by Edmondson and Butler, McDonough and colleagues similarly address the disconnects between formal education and the lived experience of rural students. They note that while rural K–12 schools are marked by their closeness to community, this does not extend to higher education, which has historically been unresponsive to rural contexts and the needs of rural students. While rural schools typically have higher graduation rates than urban schools, college enrollment of students from rural areas lags behind the national average, and especially behind rates of enrollment for urban students. Using an earlier published study of rural northern California, the authors argue that these graduation rates can at least be partially explained by the cultural disconnect between higher education and the lived experience and cultural contexts of rural students. Using Pierre Bourdieu's concept of habitus, they argue that rural areas like the Northstate area of California embody social and cultural practices that may militate against college attendance, such as attachment to community and locality as well as the prevalence of labor markets that historically have not required college degrees for gainful employment (though this is changing). The authors argue that to increase educational opportunities for rural students, institutions of higher education need to more fully engage with rural communities, and in so doing gain a deeper understanding of and appreciation for rural heritage, traditions, and the lived experiences of rural students.

Australia poses unique challenges for engaging rural students and building connections within and across localities given the sparsely settled population across the vast continent. In chapter 11, Crump and Twyford describe how these challenges are being met through a system of interactive distance e-learning that expands the reach of educational services for school-aged and adult learners. They describe how this system builds connections both to and between rural and isolated Australian communities via broadband Internet technology, "reducing the tyranny of distance, and reaffirming the sense of place that helps bind and hold rural communities together."

The next two chapters focus on programs and partnerships that support particular rural student populations. In the United States, one of the more notable demographic trends in rural areas has been the in-migration of international immigrants seeking employment (often in agriculture or in meat processing plants) or affordable, safe places to live. In certain cases in-migration, often shaped by family and acquaintance networks, can dramatically alter the ethnic composition of a community and place new strains on the resources of small schools required to accommodate new English Language Learner (ELL) populations. In their chapter, Bustamante, Brown, and Irby note that rural ELL teachers "often find themselves on the front line of changing demographics" within rural communities. They describe a program designed to enable local educators and administrators to improve ELL reading instruction while simultaneously acting as agents of change in their schools and communities.

Butera and Costello also focus on a specific set of students in their discussion of special education in the rural context, where the proportion of special-education-classified students is nearly twice the national average (NCES 2007). This is significant given that most preparation programs for special educators focus on urban contexts. These programs are therefore not well-placed to train educators to identify the particular assets of rural communities that may aid in the provision of special education. Butera and Costello describe a professional development course emphasizing parent partnerships and focusing on how biography and place affect teaching practice. The authors argue that the professionalization of education and its transformation into a standardized technology for content delivery has undermined the school-community connection. The program they describe provides an important opportunity to "deprofessionalize" the relationship between educator and parent, and in so doing to diminish the distance between school and community.

The volume concludes with a discussion by Schafft regarding how educational accountability has over time aligned directly with the economic imperatives of the state, assuming market models and fundamentally weakening the relationship between school and community. This has led, Schafft argues, to a shifting of educational allegiances within schools away from a broader accountability to community and society, in favor of accountability to sets of abstracted institutional and bureaucratic mandates, raising troubling questions about not only the nature of accountability, but the nature of education itself. Schafft argues, however, that community engagement and educational improvement are not only complementary but fundamentally interconnected priorities, and represent critical components of a necessary education for the twenty-first century and the challenges that lie ahead.

Conclusion: Looking Back, Thinking Forward

The chapters in this volume offer historical and contemporary critiques of the ways that rural places, their people, and their schools have experienced cultural hybridity in the wake of capitalism, globalization, immigration, economic shifts, NCLB, violence, war, and the proliferation of media and technology. The contributors have explored these competing interests and have analyzed the problems and possibilities of rural people having to rethink their entire ways of living, being, and educating their children. We hope that the analyses in this collection suggest the closely entwined fates of rural schools and communities as well as the multiple ways in which place *matters*. Place emerges not as a fixed, bounded, authentic site but as an articulation of social relations and cultural and political practices that are paradoxical, provisional, and constantly in the process of becoming. Rural places are dynamic and fluid, and as such are inseparable from broader networks of power and globalization; thus the twenty-first century will almost certainly pose new challenges for rural schools and communities. Global climate change, environmental degradation, peak oil, as well as new economic and demographic shifts, will all have significant, if as yet not completely known, effects on rural well-being (Klare 2002; Speth 2008). We offer these chapters not as blueprints for how to respond to these challenges, but as evidence of the complexity and resiliency of rural people and places, and what that might mean for the practice and meaning of education— and alternatives for living—as we forge our way into this new century.

References

Bell, M. 1992. The fruit of difference: The rural-urban continuum as a system of identity. *Rural Sociology* 57 (1), 65–82.

Bonanno, A., and D. H. Constance. 2003. The global/local interface. In D. L. Brown and L. E. Swanson, eds., *Challenges for rural America in the twenty-first century*, 241–51. University Park: Penn State Press.

Corbett, M. 2007. *Learning to leave: The irony of schooling in a coastal community*. Halifax: Fernwood Publishing.

Cubberley, E. P. 1922. *Rural life and education: A study of the rural-school problem as a phase of the rural-life problem*. Boston: Houghton Mifflin.

DeYoung, A. J., and C. B. Howley. 1990. The political economy of rural school consolidation. *Peabody Journal of Education* 67 (4), 63–89.

Drainville, A. C. 2004. *Contesting globalization: Space and place in the world economy.* London: Routledge.

Edmondson, J. 2001. *Prairie town: Redefining rural life in the age of globalization.* New York: Rowman and Littlefield.

Elder, G. H., and R. D. Conger. 2000. *Children of the land: Adversity and success in rural America.* Chicago: University of Chicago Press.

Engels, M. 2000. *The struggle for control of public education: Market ideology versus democratic values.* Philadelphia: Temple University Press.

Gruenewald, D. A., and G. A. Smith. 2008. *Place-based education in the global age.* New York: Lawrence Erlbaum Associates.

Jo, T. 2005. Neoliberalism as a social ideology and strategy in education. *Forum for Social Economics* 35 (1), 37–58.

Kannapel, P. J., and A. J. DeYoung. 1999. The rural school problem in 1999: A review and critique of the literature. *Journal of Research in Rural Education* 15 (2), 67–79.

Klare, M. T. 2002. *Resource wars: The new landscape of global conflict.* New York: Holt.

Krannich, R. S. 2008. Rural sociology at the crossroads. *Rural Sociology* 73 (1), 1–21.

Lipton, M. 1977. *Why the poor stay poor: Urban bias in world development.* London: Temple.

Lyson, T. A. 2002. What does a school mean to a community? Assessing the social and economic benefits of schools to rural villages in New York. *Journal of Research in Rural Education* 17 (3), 131–37.

McGranahan, D. A. 2003. How people make a living in rural America. In D. L. Brown and L. E. Swanson, eds., *Challenges for rural America in the twenty-first century,* 135–51. University Park: Penn State Press.

National Center for Education Statistics (NCES). 2007 (July). *Status of education in rural America.* Retrieved October 7, 2007, from http://nces.ed.gov/pubs2007/2007040.pdf.

Peshkin, A. 1978. *Growing up American: Schooling and the survival of community.* Chicago: University of Chicago Press.

Schafft, K. A., S. C. Faircloth, and N. L. Thompson. 2006. Assessing the state of the knowledge: American Indian and Alaska Native rural early childhood education. In *Proceedings of the Rural Early Childhood Forum on American Indian and Alaska Native Early Learning, July 28–29, 2005, Little Rock, Ark.* (Rural Early Childhood Report No. 2), 1–11. Starkville: Mississippi State University Early Childhood Institute.

Speth, J. G. 2008. *The bridge at the end of the world: Capitalism, the environment, and crossing from crisis to sustainability.* New Haven: Yale University Press.

Swyngedouw, E. 1997. Neither global nor local: "Glocalization" and the politics of scale. In K. R. Cox, ed., *Spaces of globalization: Reasserting the power of the local,* 137–66. New York: Guilford Press.

Theobald, P. 1997. *Teaching the commons: Place, pride, and the renewal of community.* Boulder: Westview.

Tyack, D. B. 1972. The tribe and the common school: Community control in rural education. *American Quarterly* 24 (1), 3–19.

Tyack, D., and L. Cuban. 2001. *Tinkering toward utopia: A century of public school reform.* Cambridge: Harvard University Press.

United Nations Population Fund. 2007. *State of the world population 2007: Unleashing the potential of human growth.* New York: United Nations Population Fund.

White, S. E. 1998. Migration trends in the Kansas Ogallala region and the internal colonial dependency model. *Rural Sociology* 63 (2), 272–91.

Willis, P. 1977. *Learning to labor: How working class kids get working class jobs.* New York: Columbia University Press.

Woodrum, A. 2004. State-mandated testing and cultural resistance in Appalachian schools: Competing values and expectations. *Journal of Research in Rural Education* 19 (1), 1–10.

Woods, M. 2005. *Rural geography.* London: Sage.

1

SPACES OF IDENTITY

1

LEARNING TO BE RURAL:
IDENTITY LESSONS FROM HISTORY, SCHOOLING,
AND THE U.S. CORPORATE MEDIA

Paul Theobald and Kathy Wood

Though we teach in an urban institution of higher education, it is one that nevertheless views service to area rural schools as a part of its mission. As a result, we recently convened a group of administrators, teachers, students, and community members from eighteen rural school districts for a day of conversation about rural education: what it is for, what it might aspire to, and what ends it currently serves. We orchestrated role-alike discussions, cross-role discussions, and large group reporting in a pastoral setting in western New York. There was a particularly poignant moment toward the end of the day when a precocious adolescent serving as a spokesperson for the students shared before the large group (some eighty individuals, mostly adults) that as rural youth they were "well aware that we don't have the best schools, we don't get the best teachers or the best education. We know that we're going to have to catch up when we go to college."

What was amazing about this moment for us was that these remarks should have been at least mildly insulting to the many rural teachers and administrators in the audience. But there was no protest, no rebuttal that followed these statements. In fact, judging by the response of the adults in the room, it seemed as if they themselves found this sentiment accurate. Somewhere along the way, rural students and adults alike seem to have learned that to be rural is to be sub-par, that the condition of living in a rural locale creates deficiencies of various kinds—an educational deficiency in particular.

How do people learn to be rural? How do people learn that if they want the best of anything they must go to the city to find it? The questions are similar to the kinds of identity issues that stem from racial, ethnic, and religious memberships—but in the case of many rural dwellers, deficit identities are learned by individuals possessing the privilege of white skin (Atkin 2003). Others, of course, must deal with the stigma of being nonwhite and rural. It should be noted that the individual construction of identity is a complex process. Many forces play a role in that process, and the circumstance of being rural is merely one. We will argue that it is a significant one, however, and that despite the fact that rural dwellers possess differing levels of intellectual leverage over cultural messages, differing levels of a sense of self-efficacy or agency, and differing kinds of familial and community upbringing, all rural dwellers are nevertheless recipients of the messages from the dominant culture regarding what it means to be rural. Though some may possess the ability to dismiss the messages, the very act of dismissing them becomes a part of the identity an individual builds. The reality is that the messages are ubiquitous and therefore cannot fail to influence the way rural people come to think of themselves.

In this chapter we will explore the cultural connection between being rural and being considered or defined as backward, uncouth, and unsophisticated—a hayseed, hillbilly, cracker, yokel, hick, or country bumpkin. Further, we will reveal some of the ways these lessons are taught to all Americans—rural, urban, and suburban alike—and we will examine some of the consequences of these lessons. To accomplish this, we believe it is necessary to examine the historical roots of these cultural lessons, and to do that we must go back in history to a point before the United States was even established—all the way back to feudal Europe, in fact.

Constructing Rurality: European Historical Precedents

Getting to the bottom of our cultural conceptions of what constitutes rurality, or what defines rural life and living, is not an easy undertaking. The idea of rurality is not something that developed in the past few years or even decades, for we can actually trace the development back a few centuries. And even beyond this, there were moments in classical and medieval history when sizable urban population growth created a kind of rural versus urban contest of political influence. The struggle for this kind of power, for the upper hand in social, political, economic, even educational decision making, is likely most to blame for the development of cultural conceptions of one sort or another. A contemporary example might help to clarify what we mean. During the 1980s and early 1990s conservative politicians and strategists seeking control over the U.S. policy arena launched a campaign to impugn "liberal" politicians as the source of the nation's problems. Liberals were chastised as irresponsible spenders with other serious shortcomings, such as a propensity for letting hardened criminals out of jail. As late as 2001, Reverend Jerry Falwell publicly blamed the 9/11 attacks on "liberals and homosexuals."

Now imagine what kinds of cultural conceptions might be created if the struggle for control in the policy arena was between urban and rural interests. This is difficult for us from our twenty-first-century vantage point, because it seems inconceivable that rural interests might be able to muster the kind of power necessary to compete for influence at that level. But this wasn't always the case. In fact, throughout most of recorded human history, rural interests had the upper hand in terms of political decision making. The prolonged feudal era in Europe serves as perhaps the best example. For about one thousand years power and control over how affairs would be conducted in communities and neighborhoods across the continent rested in the hands of large aristocratic landowners—including the royal family. But things changed. In fact, the birth of the United States was a pivotal part of the unfolding story of how urban interests emerged and eventually usurped the centuries-long political control of the rural aristocracy.

The key ingredient in this usurpation was the gradual development of the bourgeoisie, the ever-growing middle group in late feudal society—the emerging bankers, insurance dealers, shipping magnates, skilled craftsmen, and factory owners who were increasingly wealthy and urban, yet powerless in the policy arena. They wanted a seat at the table. The early nineteenth-century debacle known as the fight over the "corn laws" in England represents a good example of why they wanted that seat.

England was rapidly industrializing by the dawn of the nineteenth century. Factories of all kinds, but especially textile factories, sprung up across the country. Factory owners employed tens of thousands of former peasants, and in the process England became the leading manufacturing nation on earth. Wages paid to these factory workers were tied closely to the cost of food, for workers had to be able to buy enough of it to make it worth the effort to return to work the next day. As a consequence, cheap food was highly desirable from the point of view of England's industrialists. When they got together to discuss this, they came up with the idea of importing food from the United States and other countries to get around the high cost of food in England. Of course, importing cheap grain had the immediate affect of reducing the price of English grain. The nation's rural interests, therefore, used their slim advantage in England's Parliament to pass the "corn laws," that is, tariffs on imported grain.

Spokespersons for England's industrialists were outraged. David Ricardo, widely recognized as the leading economist of the first half of the nineteenth century, was one such individual. In 1815 Ricardo published a pamphlet documenting the fact that a rural landlord's "situation is never so prosperous as when food is scarce and dear." He went on to explain that by contrast, "all other persons are greatly benefited by procuring food cheap" (Sraffa 1953, 4:21). This essay was the start of a decades-long contest between the economic interests of agricultural landowners and emerging industrialists. Ricardo clearly believed that society needed to move in the direction represented by industrial interests and at least attempt to wrest away the policy hegemony of England's rural landowners.

As the century progressed, the struggle for control gradually tipped in favor of the industrialists. Increasingly, those involved with manufactures and trade, the "captains of industry," so to speak, were elevated to a high status while the status of farmers and rural dwellers dropped precipitously. William Cobbett, England's fiery journalist and advocate of parliamentary reform during the first three decades of the nineteenth century, remarked that he had witnessed the transition in the status of rural dwellers during his own lifetime: "By degrees beginning about 50 years ago the industrious part of the community, particularly those who create every useful thing by their labour, have been spoken of by everyone possessing the power to oppress them in any degree in just the same manner in which we speak of the animals which compose the stock upon the farm. This is not the manner in which the forefathers of us, the common people, were treated" (Hammond and Hammond 1912, 211).

Identifying the switch from the use of the reference "the commons of England" to such phrases as "the lower orders," frequently used by David Hume and countless other elites, Cobbett blamed this development on "tax-devourers, bankers, brewers, and monopolists of every sort." He noted further that one could hear these sorts of pejorative designations not only from the wealthy in urban English society, but also from "their clerks, from shopkeepers and waiters, and from the fribbles stuck up behind the counter" (Hammond and Hammond 1912, 211). It is significant to note that by the second half of the nineteenth century this rural-urban status reversal was nearly complete. It was accepted as fully by Karl Marx as it was by mainstream English intellectuals like Ricardo and John Stuart Mill. Said Marx, "The bourgeoisie has subjected the country to the rule of the towns. It has created enormous cities, has greatly increased the urban population as compared with the rural, and has thus rescued a considerable part of the population from the *idiocy of rural life*" (Marx 1848, 208; emphasis added).

The ascendancy of urban political and economic power in subtle ways legitimated the increasingly popular view that the rural agrarian world was a thing of the past. Those who lived in rural areas were "living in the past." They were backward, unwilling to change with the times, too ignorant to play a role in the formation of policy.

Historical Perspectives Related to Rural Life: The American Story

The United States was not immune to this cultural development. The very same urban industrial–rural agrarian contest occurred here, probably best described using the careers of two of the nation's most famous statesmen: Alexander Hamilton and Thomas Jefferson. Hamilton was a New York lawyer and one of the chief architects of the U.S. Constitution, and also served as the nation's first secretary of the treasury. Hamilton was determined to follow the English example by creating a commercially oriented republic anchored by a national bank. Prior to the Constitutional Convention in 1787, he even lobbied for the creation of a limited monarchy of the sort occupied by George III.

Thomas Jefferson, on the other hand, was a planter from Virginia and author of the Declaration of Independence. He did not take part in the Constitutional Convention because he was in Paris serving as the U.S. ambassador to France. Had he been in Philadelphia that summer, it is possible that our constitution might have looked somewhat different. Jefferson went on to become the third U.S. president partially on a platform to abolish Hamilton's national bank. While Jefferson three times tried to pass laws to create free schools for children, Hamilton's only references to youth concerned the role they could play "at a tender age" in the nation's new factories (Cooke 1964, 131).

As in England, citizens in the young United States were divided about what the country was to be. While the careers and beliefs of Hamilton and Jefferson exemplify the division, the ramifications of the ultimate choice went considerably beyond the realization of one or another's ideal vision for the nation. There were real costs and benefits associated with the nation's path, and they were apparent from the outset. In fact, one development that clearly highlights the division occurred before the Constitution was created (and was a catalyst to calling for the Constitutional Convention in the first place). It happened in western Massachusetts in the fall of 1786 and spring of 1787. When laws were passed in Boston demanding that debts be repaid in specie (gold) rather than tender (farm commodities), many farmers were put in a precarious position. This was followed by a wave of foreclosures and imprisonment for indebtedness until farmers began to unite under the leadership of Daniel Shays, a captain during the Revolutionary War. The farmers took over courtrooms to stop foreclosures and also seized a state militia armory in Springfield (Szatmary 1980).

The national government, then operating under the Articles of Confederation, was unable to put an army in the field to oppose the rebel farmers. Consequently Boston merchants created their own and sent them to Springfield. The farmers were dispersed, and the crisis gradually ended. But many pointed to the inability of the national government to respond to this insurrection and demanded a convention to amend the Articles or create a new government. Shays' Rebellion marks the start of a pattern in which urban commercialist interests carried the day in the policy arena at the expense of rural agrarian interests. The pattern is not without some interruptions—as when Jefferson was elected in 1800 and abolished the first national bank, or when Andrew Jackson was elected in 1828 and abolished the second one.[1] But the point is that from our first days as a nation, urban and rural interests differed, the differences created struggle, and the struggle created a culture marked by mutual suspicion—and in some cases outright antipathy.

Two nineteenth-century developments went a long way toward exacerbating rural-urban and industrial-agrarian tensions: policy related to (1) tariffs and (2) the money supply. In keeping with Hamilton's plan for building a commercially oriented republic, the United States frequently imposed high tariffs on imported manufactured goods. This tax had the effect of raising the prices of foreign products to the point where the United States' infant industries could have an edge over the established producers of Europe. The problem with this strategy was that the nation's farmers, the largest consumers of these manufactured goods, were forced to pay higher prices than they would have if no tariff existed. This circumstance was considered especially egregious by agricultural

1. Interestingly, Andrew Jackson was known as "Old Hickory," and this, combined with the fact that he was most popular with Americans in the West on the rural frontier, has led some to speculate that the term "hick" derived from the overwhelmingly rural supporters of Old Hickory.

interests in the South, and those parties used it to build an argument for seces-
sion. But the larger point here is that the tariff question further exacerbated
already growing tensions related to urban/industrial versus rural/agrarian
policy.

When the South did secede, it was followed by the bloodiest war in our
nation's history. And while rural and urban dwellers in both the North and
South generally agreed on the reasons for the war, they differed strenuously on
the question of how to rebuild the nation's economy after the war. The immediate crisis was to combat war-driven inflation. Throughout the antebellum
years the nation's money supply had been held consistent with available gold
reserves. But the financial exigencies of Civil War created the need to "suspend"
the gold standard and issue paper bills that came to be known as "greenbacks."
The inflation that occurred by the war's end meant that greenback dollars were
worth considerably less than a dollar. The drive to return to "sound money
policy" was begun by the northern banking community at the war's end. Having loaned the government millions in dollars worth say, fifty cents, they were
eager to receive repayment in dollars worth a full dollar.

But an immediate contraction of the money supply, though it would have
been a great boon to the nation's financial interests, could have created so
much immediate hardship for the nation's debtors that it was deemed to be a
socially dangerous policy option. In the end it was decided that the money
supply would be held constant while population and the economy grew. This
had the effect of dragging out the pain associated with money contraction over
a long period of time. It also ensured that the money-supply question would
be the primary political issue for the remainder of the nineteenth century
(Goodwyn 1976). This policy option was still very favorable to the nation's
lenders, but it was a grievous burden to the nation's debtors—mostly farmers.
Every year of a farmer's mortgage meant that he was paying back his debt
with dollars worth more than those he received with the original loan. This
circumstance created great hardship not only for farmers, but also for factory
laborers in the nation's cities who struggled to repay home mortgages.

These circumstances became a catalyst to the growth of political parties (the
Greenback Party, the Socialist Party, the Populist Party, etc.) and occupational
unions (the National Labor Union, the Knights of Labor, the Farmers Alliance,
etc.). The intensity of the growing divide over the "money question" led to a
pronounced schism between capital and labor. It was at this point that attempts
were first made to join the interests of rural farmers and urban laborers, and
while such attempts would continue right through the Depression of the 1930s,

they were never very successful. There were too many long-standing cultural obstacles to overcome, and these were further complicated by issues like race, ethnicity, and religion.

It should be clear that there was a certain utility, from an urban commercialist perspective, in a culture that came to look at rural residents as backward, behind the times, fundamentally subpar. It was a way to legitimate urban control of the policy arena. Years later, when television scriptwriters came up with the idea of poking fun at rural "hillbillies" suddenly transplanted to Beverly Hills, they were capitalizing on a cultural conception developed centuries ago. It was a virtually unquestioned part of the modern mind-set. That kind of cementing, that kind of near-total acceptance of a mere cultural conception, required reinforcement over the years, one dimension of which turned up in our nation's literary history.

Reading Cultural Messages

In an era defined by ubiquitous forms of electronic media, the absence of "news" is culturally difficult to imagine. But if you were to go back to the very beginning of the twentieth century you would find a world devoid of electronic media. People in those days didn't sit around a television or even a radio to find out what was going on in the world. Fortunately, however, technological improvements in the printing industry meant that mass-produced publications could be obtained at an affordable cost. The first quarter of the twentieth century witnessed a veritable explosion in the number of available magazines and daily newspapers. Comic strips mimicking ignorant hayseeds, like *Li'l Abner* and *Snuffy Smith*, were an extraordinarily popular part of these periodicals for decades. Magazines and newspapers proved to be an invaluable agent of cultural transmission—transmitting the already old message that the future was certain to be urban, not rural.

The literary career of Hamlin Garland played a key role in this. Born in West Salem, Wisconsin, Garland grew up in rural Iowa. At the age of twenty-four he traveled to Boston determined to carve out a career as a writer. His first breakthrough came in 1891 when he published a widely popular collection of short stories called *Main-Travelled Roads*. The stories all shared a similar theme of lead characters leaving the countryside on well-traveled roads headed for the city—much as he had done. His first novel, *Rose of Dutcher's Coolly*, published in 1895, is the story of a young farm woman from rural Wisconsin and her struggle to leave her rural community and go to college. In 1899 Garland tried to recapture the success of *Main-Travelled Roads* by publishing what he called a "companion piece," *Prairie Folks*, once again a collection of short stories documenting the attempt by young rural dwellers to escape the ostensible drudgery of farm life.

It is likely impossible to overestimate the extent of Garland's contribution to elevating a desire to leave the countryside to the status of cultural common sense. His stories were published in countless magazines of the day: *Ladies Home Journal*, *McClure's*, *Harper's Bazaar*, *Women's Home Companion*, *Vogue*, and many others. He was the John Grisham of the first decade of the twentieth century.[2] In fact, the popularity of Garland's work may well have been a significant contributor to the decision by president Theodore Roosevelt to convene what he called the Commission on Country Life in 1907.

The task of the commission was to solve what was popularly referred to as the "rural problem." Although definitions of this problem varied, a central theme in all of them was the need to stop the migration of rural youth to the city, or, as one country life spokesperson put it, "to keep a standard people on our farms" (Carney 1912, 2). This should strike the reader as counterintuitive, since larger cultural messages suggested that leaving the countryside was the thing to do. The problem, according to Roosevelt's commissioners, was that the nation's cities were filling up with immigrants from southern and eastern Europe; seven million came through Ellis Island in 1907 alone. Steeped in the heavily social Darwinist milieu of the Progressive Era, leading intellectuals warned of ominous consequences if rural farm youth mixed with "the dregs of humanity." The end result would certainly be a diminished mean IQ for the nation. In an era when eugenics societies all across the country called for "racial purity," it shouldn't be surprising that there was considerable sentiment to keep a "standard people" on the farms.

The country life movement was short-lived, however, though it did result in improved rural roads, the establishment of rural free mail delivery, and even some venerable institutions, such as 4-H and the Future Farmers of America. But nevertheless out-migration continued unabated, and the work of Hamlin Garland certainly encouraged this exodus. As Rose from *Rose of Dutcher's Coolly* explained to her father, who objected to her leaving, "You must let me

---

2. It should be noted that in later years Garland began to question his earlier views, looking back more critically at the rural experiences of his youth and seeing positive attributes in the world he chose to leave. His semiautobiographical *A Son of the Middle Border* (1917) represents a good example of his amended outlook.

go. I must go out into the world. I want to see great people" (Garland 1895, 176). Great people, at least according to conventional wisdom, lived in the city.

Other rural novels continued to hammer this theme. Glenway Wescott's *The Grandmothers* (1927) and Geoffrey Dell Eaton's *Backfurrow* (1925) painted grim portraits of life in the rural U.S. heartland. But in time this literary trend created a backlash of sorts, as young writers produced work that took a balanced approach, recognizing many redeeming features in rural life. O. E. Rolvaag, Willa Cather, and Paul Corey could be counted among this group. Yet even these sophisticated novelists were forced to deal at some level with migration to the city. If the lead character stayed, a dear family member or the love of that character's life left.

In any event, by the 1920s U.S. literary taste had moved in a new direction. There were now urban novelists who wrote about life in the city, who defined what it meant to be cosmopolitan, to be chic, to be with the times. Though some had rural roots, and some, like Sinclair Lewis, sometimes set novels in small towns, they were clearly urban authors. F. Scott Fitzgerald, Ernest Hemingway, John Dos Passos, and Lewis captured the literary imagination of the American public. Though great rural literature continued to be written, it took a backseat to the work of these individuals. For example, William Faulkner produced outstanding rural novels, but the American public wasn't much interested; all were out of print before 1940.[3] When in 1930 the Nobel Prize in Literature was awarded to Sinclair Lewis, the first American ever to receive that honor, Lewis himself admitted that it should have gone to the rural novelist Willa Cather instead. But that was not to be.

A few rural novels became best sellers during the 1930s and 1940s, but not many. John Steinbeck's success with *Of Mice and Men* (1937) and *The Grapes of Wrath* (1939) represent exceptions. It is interesting to note, however, that these novels were critiques of the capitalist system and the devastation that system wrought during the Great Depression; they were not particularly penetrating portraits of rural life. If anything, they reinforced typical cultural messages about backward rural dwellers. The Joads, after all, were merely illiterate tenant farmers. While there probably were illiterate farm families in Oklahoma during the 1930s, such families would have been a rare exception rather than the rule. In 1960 Lois Phillips Hudson published *The Bones of Plenty*, depicting the expe-

---

3. The literary critic Malcolm Cawley is credited with "saving" Faulkner through his 1946 publication *The Portable Faulkner*. In this work, Cawley explicated the highly nuanced nature of Faulkner's prose, making his work more accessible to readers. Faulkner's popularity rebounded as a result, and he went on to receive, like Hemingway and Lewis, the Nobel Prize in Literature.

rience of a North Dakota "Okie" family forced to migrate to the Pacific Northwest. This family was educated and highly articulate—the exact opposite of the Joads. Though literary scholars praised *The Bones of Plenty* as perhaps the quintessential Depression-era novel, the American public showed little interest.

Of course, 1960 brings us up to a new era, one in which Americans began to leave behind the written word as their source for news, their cue for comprehending cultural conceptions about how the world works. Before turning to the contribution of electronic media regarding what it means to be rural in the United States, however, we will first explore some of the cultural lessons related to rural life delivered in our nation's public schools.

School Curriculum and Rural Identity

A big part of the state-sponsored endeavor of public education is to teach American youth that the United States is a great country, one that rarely makes mistakes, one that is always on the side of justice. A quick glance at elementary school textbooks is all that is needed to reveal this effort: *A Nation Grows*, *America: Pathways to the Future*, and *America: The Story of Progress*, are two salient examples. Since the United States is synonymous with "progress," and progress is culturally defined as ever more urban growth and development, rural youth see themselves as nonparticipants in the American experience, at least until they leave their home and move to the city. If there is a rural version of progress at all, it is defined as a quick transition from family farms to large, corporate-controlled "agricultural complexes," as one school book referred to them (Weisberger 1966, 7). Textbook companies, of course, try to maximize sales, meaning they need to appeal to as many people as possible. Since there are four urban and suburban students for every rural student in this country, one rarely finds much reference to rural life except in history and social studies texts. And then rural life is portrayed as a past condition that we have left behind.

The story is the same when the focus shifts to the "global community," when students are exposed to information about other countries around the world. It goes like this: because of technology, fewer people are needed to work in rural areas, so they move to the city to take jobs. In this story, technology is a force unto itself. Its development is predictable and the results of its deployment are always good (McKibben 2007). If rural people are displaced, students learn the correct cultural response: "That's the price of progress; they will be better off in the city anyway." The fact that people come together to make policy decisions related to how people ought to farm or fish, or if they should farm or fish at all, never comes up in school textbooks. Students are simply taught that the farm-to-city or fishing-village-to-city trend is a "natural," inevitable progression.

The point, of course, is that the curriculum in U.S. schools tends to feed the cultural assumption that suggests that in all cases, bigger is better. Big cities are better than small towns. Big farms are better than small farms. Big schools are better than small schools. Students from big schools are better than students from small schools. Freshmen survey data reported by the Higher Education Research Institute at UCLA indicate that rural students attending a publicly supported comprehensive college in Nebraska perceive their academic ability and their self-confidence to be significantly lower than their peers at similar institutions across the country (Higher Education Research Institute 2002).

Many teachers measure their success by the size of the school in which they come to be employed. The tacit assumption is that I am better than those who teach in small schools by virtue of the fact that I was hired to teach in a large one. Sometimes students exiting teacher education programs compete to see who will receive a position in a large urban or suburban district versus those who are only able to find a job in a small rural school.

Anti-rural bias frequently comes out in textbooks commonly used in teacher preparation programs. Most often it exists merely as omission; the idea that some schools are small and rural never emerges as a topic for study or discussion. But sometimes it is more obvious and insidious. In one social foundations of education text, for example, immigration into the United States was discussed. According to the authors, "The refugees came from all strata of society. Some were wealthy; others were poverty stricken. Some were widely traveled and sophisticated; others were farmers and fishing people who had never before left their small villages" (Sadker and Sadker 2003, 488). The obvious implication is that sophisticated individuals do not farm or fish for a living. We routinely accept this stereotype because it is deeply engrained in our culture. We give no consideration to how this colors the aspirations of rural youth, despite the fact that this generalization does not stand up to even minimal scrutiny.

The Era of Radio, Television, and Cinema

The advent of radio put the first dent in the United States' near-total reliance on print media. It became an increasingly powerful cultural force in the years between 1920 and the advent of television in the early 1950s. Taking its cues from what people enjoyed in newspapers and magazines, radio allowed people to listen to stories and comic strips without having to actually read them themselves. In this way *Lum and Abner*, starring two stereotypical hillbillies, became an enormously popular radio show, running from 1931 until 1954. While these kinds of shows have disappeared from contemporary radio, the medium's power to deliver anti-rural imagery remains in full force.

Not long ago an auto body shop in Lincoln, Nebraska, ran a radio advertisement just prior to the beginning of the college football season. It went like this: A graceful, polished voice announced to listeners that it was the start of Cornhusker football season and, as a result, Lincoln residents needed to be on guard, "since you never know who will be in town for the big game." Then, in a feigned hillbilly voice, a man said to his wife, "Golly! Look ma, a stoplight!" Next came the sound of automobiles crashing. The graceful voice returned to let Lincoln residents know that if their car is hit by rural hillbillies, they can get it fixed at the auto body shop.

Making rural residents the butt of jokes is completely permissible in American society. Anyone—not just rural dwellers themselves, but literally anyone—can poke fun at cousin-marrying hicks from the sticks. In fact, it is particularly in vogue today to poke fun at rural residents through the use of what has come to be called "redneck humor." The comedian Jeff Foxworthy built a career doing this, and many others have followed in his footsteps. While it would be unfair to say that there is no resistance to this brand of humor, the resistance that exists is inconsequential, in part because it comes from rural people. In the eyes of the dominant culture, redneck humor is "all in good fun."

Television, of course, has been the most egregiously shameful with respect to images of rural people. A recent television advertisement in Des Moines, Iowa, for example, features the owner of a used car lot who dresses as a backwoods rural resident so ignorant that he sells cars for much less than they're worth. While this sort of stereotyping's prevalence is hit-and-miss, think about the consistent portrayal of various rural characters on television shows that continue to be rebroadcast daily: Mr. Haney from *Green Acres*; Barney Fife from *The Andy Griffith Show*; Larry, Darryl, and Daryl from *The Bob Newhart Show*; Uncle Joe and Mr. Drucker from *Petticoat Junction*; Gomer Pyle from *Gomer Pyle–USMC*; Boss Hogg in *The Dukes of Hazzard*; and Jethro and Elly May from *The Beverly Hillbillies*. Additionally, the long-running variety show called *Hee Haw* was a parody on rural life depicting slow-moving, dim-witted characters without ambition or sophistication. Ostensible rural ignorance was funny to the urban United States, and it has remained so.

The contemporary reality show called *The Simple Life* starring Paris Hilton and Nicole Richie opens with a theme song with these lyrics:

> Let's take two girls, both filthy rich
> From the bright lights
> Down to the sticks

Playing themselves, the show focuses on Paris and Nicole's unscripted reaction to the simple and simplistic rural residents they encounter in small towns all across the country. Even the animated comedy *The Simpsons* has a recurring rural character, Cletus Spuckler, otherwise known as the "slack-jawed yokel." For years the long-running comedy *Saturday Night Live* ran a skit called "Appalachian Emergency Room" depicting inept rural medical personnel.

As late as 2003 CBS began production of a reality show called *The Real Beverly Hillbillies*. The central thrust of this show was to take "real" rural people and put them in spectacular housing in Beverly Hills and then film their inept attempts to negotiate life in a cosmopolitan urban setting. To the great surprise of everyone at CBS, this project actually generated considerable protest from rural groups as well as politicians representing rural constituencies. CBS cancelled the project. Of course, the old *Beverly Hillbillies*, not to mention *Green Acres, Petticoat Junction,* and others, are still broadcast daily as reruns all across the country, and they continue to be watched by millions of Americans.

The cinema has made its cultural contribution, too, by making rural residents the butt of jokes beginning as early as the 1940s. The enormously popular film *The Egg and I* (1947) launched the career of the rural characters known as "Ma and Pa Kettle." The success of this film led to the creation of a series of Ma and Pa Kettle movies, all comedies poking fun at rural lifeways. There are many contemporary examples of movies that use rural people as a catalyst for humor, such as *For Richer or Poorer* (1997), *Joe Dirt* (2001), and *Witless Protection* (2008). But the cinema has also featured a dark rural element, a kind of twisted perversion ostensibly existing in rural locales, captured in the phrase "cousin marrying." *Deliverance* was one such movie, but there have been many others that featured evil rural dwellers, especially rural police from the American South. This side of rural stereotyping occasionally comes out even in rural comedies like *The Dukes of Hazzard*, when Bo and Luke must save Daisy from being forced to marry into a family of sociopathic hillbillies.

Conclusion

"We are well aware that we don't have the best schools, we don't get the best teachers or the best education. We know that we're going to have to catch up when we go to college." Obviously, this assessment of growing up rural was learned. In this chapter we have tried to delineate some of the historical antecedents to the contemporary purveyors of this lesson. Rural equals backward is an old cultural message, but its age hasn't diminished its utility. The message legitimates policy measures that are demonstrably unfair to rural locales. School consolidation is the best, and most ubiquitous, example. Consolidation doesn't actually need to save tax dollars, as long as it appears as if it will. That's why consolidations continue to take place without an evidential base to support the practice. And it need not stop with schools. Government agencies, rural hospitals, newspapers, and all manner of necessary services can be consolidated. It is OK to do these things, for the future is urban, and rural residents can either "get with the times," move to the city, or accept the "price of progress"—even if they alone must pay that price.

It would be much more difficult to do these things if we hadn't already culturally defined rural as deficient in various ways. We can take virtually any policy action, no matter how demonstrably unfair to rural places, and legitimate it on the basis of rural shortcomings, or on the fact that only a few people live in rural areas. There should be little wonder why the students at our "rural schools day" expressed their belief that they have second-class schools and teachers, and that rural students everywhere go to college less confident of their academic preparation than they should be.

When schools operate in ways that deliver the message that success in life means migrating to the city (e.g., the successful ones will "go far"), they also send a message in reverse, saying in effect that staying rural means failing on some level (Corbett 2007). These pronouncements are vacuous, of course, merely empty cultural constructions, but that doesn't prevent them from exerting force on the lives of rural individuals. It contributes to a tendency among new teachers and administrators to be constantly on the lookout for their chance to work in urban and suburban schools after paying their dues in rural schools. One can witness this phenomenon among other professional groups as well, such as doctors, lawyers, and even clergy. None of this goes undetected. Rural youth see it and internalize the message it sends. Some reject the message and stay. Others accept it and leave the countryside behind. In either case, the social capital, or the wherewithal of rural communities when it comes to improving their circumstances, is negatively affected.

These kinds of internalized messages may wield more power given the dramatic growth in the trend toward globalizing the production and distribution of goods and services. We live in a "flat" world, we are told, meaning that rural youth must be made aware of the fact that their competition in life goes well beyond American urban and suburban youth to the perhaps two billion age-mates who live somewhere else on the planet. Still, while it is hard to be optimistic about the fate of rural youth and rural places in an increasingly globalizing economy, it is not a given that present trends will continue; it is not a certainty that rural areas will continue to be passed over as places with few economic opportunities, places where messages related to what constitutes success are inextricably tied to leaving.

The world is running out of the Paleolithic sunlight we call fossil fuels. Prior to the economic meltdown in 2008, the daily demand for oil had begun to exceed our daily pumping capacity (Daly 2005; Mouawad 2007). With an economic recovery, we will likely encounter that circumstance in short order once again. In the face of this reality, many cling to the hope that some as yet unforeseen technology will appear that will enable us to maintain our current lifestyle well into the future. But absent such a development, it seems quite certain that human economic activity will of necessity cease to be global and will become, once again, local. In particular, food and energy production will become local matters, and in the process rural regions of the globe will move from being passed over to being pivotally central to human life on a fossil-fuel-free planet. All of our cultural conceptions about a leisurely urban future will disappear and the cultural trend to degrade rural dwellers as backward or behind the times will likely undergo something approaching a complete reversal. At least that is one scenario. There are certainly others.

A good deal more research is needed if we are to make progress exposing the forces contributing to cultural lessons about rural life and the ways these lessons are learned. The chapters in this volume represent an excellent start on this project.

References

Atkin, C. 2003. Rural communities: Human and symbolic capital development, fields apart. *Compare* 33 (4), 507–18.

Carney, M. 1912. *Country life and the country school*. Chicago: Row, Peterson.

Cooke, J., ed. 1964. *The reports of Alexander Hamilton*. New York: Harper and Row.

Corbett, M. 2007. *Learning to leave: The irony of schooling in a coastal community*. Halifax: Fernwood Publishing.

Daly, H. T. 2005 (September). Economics in a full world. *Scientific American*, 100–107.

Garland, Hamlin. 1895. *Rose of Dutcher's coolly*. Chicago: Stone and Kimball.

Goodwyn, L. 1976. *Democratic promise: The populist moment in America*. New York: Oxford University Press.

Hammond, J. L., and B. Hammond. 1912. *The village labourer, 1760–1832*. London: Longmans, Green.

Higher Education Research Institute. 2002. *First-time, full-time freshmen at Wayne State College, 2001–2002*. Los Angeles: Higher Education Research Institute.

Marx, K. [1848] 1983. Manifesto of the Communist Party. In *The portable Karl Marx* (E. Kamenka, ed. and trans.), 203–41. New York: Penguin.

McKibben, B. 2007. *Deep economy*. New York: Times Books.

Mouawad, J. 2007 (October 9). A quest for energy in the globe's remote places. *New York Times*, A1.

Sadker, M. P., and D. M. Sadker. 2003. *Teachers, schools, and society* (6th ed.). New York: McGraw-Hill.

Sraffa, P., ed. 1953. *The works and correspondence of David Ricardo*. 12 vols. Cambridge: Cambridge University Press.

Szatmary, D. P. 1980. *Shay's rebellion: The making of an agrarian insurrection*. Amherst: University of Massachusetts Press.

Weisberger, B. A. 1966. *Captains of industry*. New York: Harper and Row.

2

POVERTY AND SCHOOL ACHIEVEMENT IN RURAL COMMUNITIES: A SOCIAL-CLASS INTERPRETATION

Craig B. Howley and Aimee Howley

"The rich are not like you and me."
"Yes, they have more money."

Introduction

In this chapter we discuss the relationship between social class and achievement, examining rural identity and rural community among those called "poor" across two related contexts—the global society and the local community.[1] A continuous experience of living in impoverished rural places among "the rural poor" gives us a certain outlook on the work of this chapter and this book. Our aim is to interpret the school performance of impoverished rural children in the context of differences among rural communities.

The organization of our chapter proceeds as follows. We begin by considering what we call the "othering" of the poor, with the rural poor particularly in mind. Rural people in general—and also rural commitments, ideals, and practices—are also "othered" (e.g., Howley 1997; Howley and Howley 1999; see also Theobald and Wood's chapter, this volume), but the rural poor suffer the most from this diminution. We examine how "othering" is shaped by the contradictory impulses of community and globalization—the place-valuing of community and the *dissolving* of place and community in the service of a

---

1. This exchange is apocryphally attributed to F. Scott Fitzgerald and Ernest Hemingway (Keyes 2006, 179).

hyper-mobile global economy. Globalization, in our view and experience, undermines the local commons from which local community is developed, creating conditions that make the social exclusion of already marginalized groups just that much more likely, further abetting the destruction of community. These processes are strongly shaped by broader economic regimes and ideologies. We are not trying to define the elements of what constitutes the "best" community. Rather, we believe that communities should, in fact, be as different as human individuals, and that education should cultivate these differences.

Our discussion then examines the way poverty is constructed—or viewed—in different types of rural communities. We draw on our own qualitative research in rural schools (Howley, Howley et al. 2006; Howley, Howley, and Burgess 2006), supplemented by the related scholarship of others. We find the common rendering of poverty as inferiority highly problematic, and we are troubled that deficiency remains the prevalent construct for describing and justifying cultural work in rural places (see, e.g., Corbett 2007; DeYoung 1995; Williams 1973). In our experience, rural people who know how to get by ("the rural poor") are astoundingly productive ("self-provisioning"). The chapter concludes with an interpretation of the dubious contribution of schools—in light of "othering" and community difference—to the formation of rural identities among the (rural) poor.

Many Ways of "Othering" the Poor

People called "poor" are diminished. Our rural students and neighbors say, "I grew up poor, but I didn't know it until . . ."—that is, "until I went to school," or "until we moved to town." Such confessions may strike residents of the metro- or cosmopolis as odd. The imposition of deficiency is very much the issue, even if one argues that some or many cosmopolitans or suburbanites understand the rural confession.

Because we consider identity as contextualized by the processes of community, on the one hand, and the processes of globalization, on the other, we begin with a consideration of what *being* is like among the rural poor. What does it mean to *be* poor and rural? Accepting, at least for the sake of argument, that poverty is socially constructed, it makes sense to investigate the contexts in which "the poor" learn who they *are* and thereby accept poverty as a marker of their identities. Community and society represent two critical and different contexts for shaping identity in this way because humans in our contemporary world are simultaneously lodged, to varied degrees, in both community and society—in *globalized* society (an abstraction) and in *localized* communities (actual places).[2] Prior to engaging the central discussion, therefore, we problematize the work of community, society, and global(izing) society.

Exclusion and Inclusion in Community and Society

One well-known account of community contrasts it with society: in community humans remain together despite their differences, whereas in society humans remain separate despite their commonalities (Nisbet 1966). This account is important because it shows that the social priority in community is *mutual interdependence* whereas the social priority in society is *unilateral independence*. On such a view, the difficulty with society is precisely the want of community, and, indeed, many social theorists have articulated just this complaint about the modern world (see, e.g., Bellah et al. 1985; Kraybill and Olshan 1994; Putnam 2000; Theobald 1997).

But what do such theorists mean by "community"? We think three senses of the word fit their (and our) view of the concept: (1) the everyday, local lifeworld of important meanings that are constructed in a particular place; (2) the ideal of a locally constructed common good; and (3) an indeterminate group of people in a place who engage the project of constructing the common good in a way that reflects but also redefines important local meanings.[3] Our preferred scope disqualifies cities, nations, and the whole world as communities. It also disqualifies narrowly affiliated social groups (virtual communities, learning communities, communities of practice, etc.).

As theologian Martin Buber (1949, 145) observed many years ago, "A real community . . . must consist of people, who precisely because they are comrades, have mutual access to one another and are ready for one another." Because the priority for community is "remaining together despite difference," the great work of community is to adjudicate the degree of difference to be tolerated. Community of this sort builds on family, whereas society tends both

2. As a modernist form of organization, society, almost by definition, works to erode the localities where community most "naturally" exists (see, e.g., Giddens 1990). Globalization—the postmodern extension of economic and cultural modernity—intensifies the rate of erosion, as sociologist Zygmunt Bauman (1998) suggests in his discussion of the process of "localization" that accompanies globalization.

3. See Howley and Howley (2007, 126–27) for the range of meanings attributed to community, and for the recent (1984) U.S. origin of communitarianism as an ideology.

to fragment the ideal of community and to contract the circle of family itself to an isolated "nuclear" core (e.g., Selznick 1995; Theobald 1997; Tönnies 1899). Arguably, community has the immediacy and functionality that society—because of its expanding scale, its increasing tendency to propagate isolation and alienation, and its intensifying abstraction—can never approach.

Perhaps community remains an advantage for rural people (see, e.g., Franzese 2002; Kuznets 1955; Orfield 1997)—in the sense that social distinctions, especially those status distinctions related to class and material welfare, could be less hatefully constructed when the common good is engaged on local ground. Hypothetically, belonging to the third sort of community—one that engages the local common good actively and successfully—would make it more difficult for one to *be* poor, that is, to regard oneself as inherently inferior or deficient. This insight, in fact, informs much of the American (as opposed to the European) work on "social capital" (e.g., Putnam 2000; cf. Bourdieu and Passeron 1990).

Rural Communities and the Place of the Poor

Under the regime of globalization, the ultimate standard for calling people "poor" (inferior and deficient) is the standard prevailing among the moderately affluent in world class cities—Paris, London, New York, Hong Kong, Singapore, Tokyo. On such a basis, nearly all humans can be called poorer, and most can be classified as abjectly poor—*inferior* indeed from the heights of cosmopolitan well-being.

Rural communities, by virtue of their (albeit quite partial) ability to define themselves culturally and to determine rules of inclusion and exclusion, hypothetically offer a generative alternative to globalized *society*, that is, in accord with rural commitments to land, family, and nature. Such an outlook on community and rural place might well be viewed as naïve, except for the fact that half the world continues to live in rural places (United Nations 2004). One might indeed assert that such a world is exactly the one that globalization has intended to ruin on the strength of an ideology that associates global free trade with global improvement.

In the meantime, however, rural communities worldwide are still being sustained *almost exclusively* by people who are called poor even by prevailing national (not just global) standards. In the United States, though, the way resources are distributed among members of rural communities varies sharply, and, as a result, the dynamics between "rich" and "poor" may be more varied than is the case in many other parts of the world. Whether the dynamics of rural class relations can be understood in terms of systematic patterns and the role schools might play in shaping such dynamics are issues as yet unresolved (cf. Duncan 1999). Nonetheless, the discussion in the next section of the chapter draws on available evidence to argue for an interpretation in which community type—determined historically and economically—does in fact have a bearing on the construction of "rich" and "poor" and on schools' role in that social construction.

Community Type and the Social Construction of Rural Poverty

In this section we consider the nature of place and impoverishment in three different types of rural communities. The categories in use here perhaps owe most to the evolving economic typology of the USDA's Economic Research Service (ERS) (e.g., Cook and Mizer 1989; Economic Research Service 2005). Our three rural (as compared to the ERS's six[4]) community types are: (1) durable-agrarian communities, (2) resource-extraction communities, and (3) surburbanizing rural communities. The types are useful for two reasons, one theoretical and one practical.

First, agriculture-based economies and resource-extraction economies are the two most characteristically rural economic types according to the ERS, whereas suburbanization is related to these two types because it is the process by which such "typically rural" places are converted to something else (cf. Hobbs and Stoops 2002). Suburbanizing rural places are also the antithesis of a central ERS policy type[5]: persistent-poverty counties. Empirical warrant for

4. The 2004 revision of the ERS typology changed "resource-dependent" to "mining-dependent," and, for the first time, analyzed all U.S. county units. Of the 3,142 county units assigned these types in 2005, 2,052 were rural (nonmetropolitan), meaning that 65 percent of all counties are rural. Farming and mining are the types that disproportionately represent rural as opposed to non-rural counties. The ERS's six mutually exclusive economic types currently comprise: (1) farming dependent (92 percent nonmetro); (2) mining-dependent (88 percent nonmetro); (3) manufacturing-dependent (65 percent nonmetro); (4) nonspecified (65 percent nonmetro); (5) federal-and-state-government-dependent (58 percent nonmetro); and services-dependent (34 percent nonmetro).

5. The seven policy types are not mutually exclusive: (1) population loss (89 percent nonmetro); (2) persistent poverty (88 percent nonmetro); (3) low employment (86 percent nonmetro); (4) low education (80 percent nonmetro); (5) retirement destination (63 percent nonmetro); (6) housing stress (56 percent); and nonmetro recreation counties (334 counties; by definition only rural). Far more nonmetro than metro counties (88 percent of all such counties

the three community types is evident. Second, much of our own recent work has taken place in just these sorts of communities (e.g., Howley et al. 2007; Howley, Howley, and Burgess 2006; Howley et al. 2006). This scholarly experience gives us a firsthand familiarity that amplifies our living in such communities for the past thirty-five years.

Durable-Agrarian Communities

Despite massive changes in the nature of agricultural production, rural communities persist in which farming is an economically important enterprise (Jackson-Smith and Gillespie 2005). In these communities, particularly when population shifts are minimal, income inequality tends to be relatively low (Nielsen and Alderson 1997; Parrado and Kandel 2006). Few recent case studies describe social relations in communities of this type (cf. Goldschmidt 1978), but some quantitative research does suggest that structural features of agricultural business along with individual characteristics of farmers have an influence on the character of social participation in rural communities (e.g., Jackson-Smith and Gillespie 2005).

In our recent study of economically disadvantaged but comparatively high-achieving schools in Ohio communities (Howley et al. 2006), we investigated one school where community residents—many of whom were Amish—saw agricultural production as a focus of economic life.[6] The combination of Amish values and an agrarian ethos coincided with social relations that were far more egalitarian and communal than we observed in the other school districts in the study or, for that matter, in any place in which we have ever conducted a study.

Our interviews—not only those with teachers and school administrators but also those with parents and nonparent community members—revealed shared commitments to academic engagement, civility, and religious observance. Interviewees described adult residents of the Amish community as reserved, respectful, industrious, and helpful to one another. Moreover, our observations

---

nationwide; Economic Research Service 2005) are assigned to the persistent-poverty type. Of the 340 rural persistent poverty counties, 68 percent are *also* classified *both* as low-education and low-employment counties. In the 46 metro persistent-poverty counties, by comparison, the overlap is 48 percent. (Proportions calculated by authors with data retrieved from http://www.ers.usda.gov/Data/TypologyCodes/2004/all_final_cod es.xls.)

6. Amish schools were first built in 1925 as the "English" school-consolidation movement began to close rural public schools (Dewalt 2006). In the school we studied, a change in principals brought Amish *back* into this public school. In Holmes County, Ohio, home to the largest Amish settlement in the United States (Amish population ca. thirty thousand), one-third of Amish children attend "English" schools (McConnell and Hurst 2006).

revealed that the Amish students who attended the school exhibited the qualities valued by their culture. The children—especially the girls—were more reticent than their "English" counterparts, showing high levels of deference to adults and little inclination to distinguish themselves as individuals on the basis of school performance. Hard work, cooperation, and learning were valued; high academic performance ("achievement") for its own sake was not.

Our informants also indicated that the cultural norms of the Amish children seemed to exert an influence on the non-Amish children in the school—an influence thought by informants to be salutary. As a sixth-grade teacher put it, "I think the Amish children help our English students learn about tolerance and acceptance." Moreover, informants intimated that the values of the community as a whole seemed to reflect the Amish influence. One community member asserted, "We are a farming community with simple values. We believe in helping one another, being honest and trustworthy, and having respect for one another. . . . You can see that in most of our students. The Amish are certainly a factor. . . . The Amish children mirror these qualities that they see in their parents."

Reflecting and responding to community expectations, the school also exhibited a culture of cooperation and support. A close correspondence between school culture and community culture—what we observed and what we heard about—apparently had existed for a long time in the more distant past but had been eroded in the recent past. Notably, according to most accounts, a former principal sought to impose a "professional" distance between the school and the community. Nevertheless, for the four years preceding our study, a new principal had been helping the school and community reclaim earlier connections and commitments.

The school's new mission statement seemed to reflect these traditional community values: "United Effort, United Responsibility, United Success." In keeping with this mission, educators encouraged children to help one another by working in pairs or small groups to complete projects and assignments in class. Teachers also shared ideas with and provided help to one another, and they convened as a committee of the whole to make decisions about curriculum and other academic policies. The family-like ethos of the school matched community norms, described succinctly in one informant's characterization: "We are a very close-knit community—almost like a very large family. People are generous with their help. . . . If we need new [fire] equipment, the entire community pitches in to raise the money."

The community's ethos and practices also appeared to support cooperation across groups. Amish families helped "English" families and vice versa. As a consequence, students saw many examples of cross-group cooperation in their homes and in the local town. Many of the teachers, moreover, were native to the community or had grown up in similar communities in the surrounding area, and they too had been socialized to contribute their efforts toward a common good. The cooperative, even communal, spirit of social life extended to class relations in this community as well. In contrast to informants from the other communities included in the study, the informants in this community used words like "poor" or "poverty" only when prompted to do so by an interviewer's explicit questions about social class. One community member's response is characteristic of the prevailing egalitarian perspective: "There's not a difference between the rich and the poor, I mean, you can have a club and you've got poor . . . it doesn't make a difference. . . . Especially with the Amish, you need help with something, they're right there to help. . . . It's not just the Amish . . . anybody in the community would do almost anything for you."

Resource-Extraction Communities

In such rural places as the Appalachian communities portrayed by Duncan (1999) and Gaventa (1980), social-class relations are sharply different from those that prevail in certain durable-agrarian communities (e.g., Fisher 2001). The legacy of a local economy based in the extraction of coal, oil, or timber has seemed to some authors, Duncan and Gaventa notable among them, to predispose these communities to develop rather stark class divisions, with the separation reinforced ideologically. Often serving the interests of absentee owners, a cadre of managers, bankers, and attorneys forms a local elite that controls the community's economic fate (Duncan 1999; Gaventa 1980).

With the exception of Duncan's and Gaventa's work, most studies of such dynamics have used quantitative methods to explore the relationship between resource dependence and poverty, as well as the economic circumstances mediating that relationship (e.g., Freudenburg and Gramling 1994; Frickel and Freudenburg 1996). Beyond these studies, qualitative analyses of such dynamics in rural communities appear almost exclusively in the scant literature on rural communities in countries other than the United States (e.g., Elmhirst 2001; Gray 1991).

In our experiences (including formal empirical investigation) in resource-dependent Appalachian communities, we see dynamics similar to those reported by Gaventa and Duncan. Like Duncan (1999), moreover, we find that the schools in such places tend to reproduce long-standing community power relations by categorizing, stereotyping, and ultimately disabling "poor" students. Many teachers and school administrators in resource-dependent communities seem eager to establish, and exploit, a *determining* association between poverty and low achievement, so that poverty is not merely associated with, but caused by low achievement.

Located in a rural community with an eroding economy based in timbering, one of the schools in our study seemed to illustrate the process just described. In this community, 60 percent of households had annual incomes below thirty thousand dollars, whereas fewer than 20 percent of households—representing a comparatively less numerous local elite—had incomes above sixty thousand dollars. Despite the relatively high performance recorded for the year preceding our visit, achievement data from subsequent years disclosed two patterns: (1) markedly lower achievement among students classified as economically disadvantaged in comparison to students not classified as economically disadvantaged, and (2) achievement scores consistently below those of other schools in the state with similar demographic characteristics. The qualification of this district as serving impoverished students well had been an anomaly—a predictable anomaly, given what we heard there.

One teacher distinguished her experience working with students in this community from other teaching experiences: "We probably have more students at this school—maybe because of its demographics—that are unable to handle anything above and beyond a much reduced level of expectations or unable to necessarily fulfill the state standards . . ."

The consensus among educators, in fact, was that "generational poverty" limited personal and institutional horizons to such a degree that social mobility was beyond the school's capacity to address. One teacher's testimony exemplifies this perspective: "You know we have, in some cases, fourth-generation welfare. They are not ambitious. . . . You do not have to go out and get a job, necessarily, to get by. So they do not have any real ambition in life to try to go to college and whatever."

Other comments conveyed the pervasive sense of fatalism that most of the school's educators echoed: "We feel like we're fighting a losing battle where we are dealing with parents and generational welfare." "Their parents just stay on welfare . . . and nine times out of ten . . . the same thing is going to happen to them." "Parents sit at home and making more than we make here as teachers, and do nothing other than simply receiving their checks in the mail."

Life for these educators, however, was not uniformly grim, because they also had the chance to work with the children of the local elite. As one teacher noted, "You have good kids and good families, and they are really, really good." But a community member who saw herself, and was seen by others, as an "outsider" was critical of the educators' elitism, saying, "I think they need to pay more attention to students in the middle, not just the kids from important families." And students also commented on the favoritism that teachers showed toward some students and their punitive stance toward others: "Sometimes [teachers] let other students get by with more than other students. They have their favorites. . . . Some students they don't like; some students that get into so much trouble [the teachers] just don't care [about them] anymore."

Suburbanizing Communities

Distinct from both durable-agrarian and resource-extraction communities, rural places that are undergoing suburbanization appear to develop social structures in which preexisting class relations form a substrate over which a new social structure is built (e.g., Salamon 2003). Part of this change entails what the U.S. mainstream regards as improvement, but for rural communities it constitutes a sort of improvement that eventually destroys rural identity. Because of an ideological progression from arguably objective ("outmoded") to flatly dismissive ("ignorant"), the transition involved with suburbanization means that, in the end, the loss of rurality ceases to become an issue of concern to anyone in the community whose opinion counts.

In the meantime, the emerging social structure, into which newcomers of whatever social classes come to be incorporated, resembles the original for a while, in part because suburbanites do not immediately play an active or visible role in rural community life. They often live in separate enclaves at some distance from longtime residents, and they tend to earn and spend money in other places (Salamon 2003). Eventually, however, the social structure and the cultural features of the place change (Theobald 1988). A significant feature of such change is loss of community diversity and accommodation to the requirements of a homogenized national culture (Salamon 2003).

In our study of low-income but high-achieving rural schools, we spent time in three schools (an elementary, middle, and high school) located in a community in which suburbanization was just beginning to occur and in which longtime community members and recent transplants were starting to cocreate a shared system of values. These values were shaped by an agrarian legacy strongly evident among locals, but to some extent they were also influenced by aspirations for upward mobility that the newcomers brought with them (and which the locals we interviewed did not view as inappropriate).

The prevailing view supported a middle-class ethos that seemed to valorize both the traditional practices of longtime residents and the more materialistic orientation exhibited by the newcomers (see, e.g., Bushnell 1999). One might argue that this convergence was made easier by the consumerist vision deployed to everyone by global neoliberalism. The evolving cultural hybrid, however, also incorporated conservative political and religious values, a belief in the inherent virtue of hard work, and most notably a commitment to civic engagement.[7]

A third group also existed in the community: low-income residents whose cultural values and practices were not well understood and were certainly not endorsed by either the long-time residents or the upwardly mobile newcomers. Middle-class members of the community tended to regard this group with distrust, doubting the competence and good intentions of the low-income adults but nevertheless investing hope in their children. This response fueled a construction of poverty as *an adult vice* that children could avoid by accepting help from middle-class sponsors such as teachers and ministers. The schools became primary sites for delivering this help, modeling middle-class virtues, and ultimately "saving" these children from the "unsavory" influence of their own families.

In our more extensive discussion of these dynamics (Howley et al. 2006), we characterize the response of educators and other adult sponsors in this community in terms primarily of three themes: (1) acting in loco parentis, (2) teaching middle-class values, and (3) extolling the virtues of a college education. Educators in this community justified their efforts and constructed their work in terms of fulfilling their responsibilities as members of the community. One teacher gave this assessment: "It seems like the kids who don't have parents who care . . . another adult . . . steps up and takes the kid under their wing. . . . I think the community overall is a very caring and loving community and tries to help out when they see a need."

Educators used two strategies for "saving the children of the poor": molding the children's behavior to middle-class norms and insisting on academic

---

7. The important dilemma in such a synthesis is whether the old middle class of smallholders or the corporatist "middle class" of managers and professionals eventually dominates (Howley et al., 2006). Local actors, in our experience, often understand the serious and long-term consequences of what outsiders might regard as a subtle distinction (Howley et al., 2006; Woodrum 2004).

engagement. The pervasive civility of the school environment was a testament to their success. Students were cordial and respectful both to teachers and to peers, showing particular deference to adults. As one teacher commented, "They come in, they do what they're supposed to do. . . . When we take them . . . on field trips, I'm always impressed with the way our students behave as compared to what I see other schools' kids doing." Showing respect for students helped educators win trust and elicit respectful behavior in return.

This approach, though, also meant that educators viewed low-income parents as negligent or abusive: "[The children] don't have somebody. . . . They get barked at enough at home. Sometimes they need somebody to listen to them instead of yelling at them." Similarly, teachers also developed derogatory generalizations about low-income parents as a way to justify efforts to engage children in meaningful academic work: "You know, they're here all day and we try to provide an educational climate for them and encourage them to go beyond the classroom and go to the library and work on projects outside of the classroom and so forth, and to do things on their own. And to watch . . . PBS specials and that sort of thing. But when they go home . . . it's quite difficult. . . . We have our share of alcoholism and different things. It has to have a depressing effect on them."

The need to see themselves and their families as morally superior to low-income adults in the community led teachers to conflate pressure for achievement with parental love: "My mom didn't even go to college, but she set out with the idea that both of her kids were going to go to college, and now we're both teachers. And that's what I mean: It doesn't take a college-educated person to push someone to do well. It takes someone who cares enough . . . to want them to do better than they did." That such constructions required children to choose between their families and their teachers evidently didn't occur or didn't matter to these teachers.

Some community members, however, recognized and had explicit opinions about these dynamics. One young parent, who requested that her exact words not be quoted, talked about her experience of feeling negatively labeled and treated at the school for being poor. Others, such as the community member quoted below, endorsed the approach that the educators were taking: "I think you have, I guess like in all schools, you have kids who have problems, different type of family situations. And I think they [i.e., the educators] handle that real well. It's hard because you have emotional problems, discipline problems, there are parents that don't care; but I think you have that everywhere."

Community, Social Class, and Achievement
of Rural Identity

Identifying oneself as "rural" is problematic for many Americans. Indeed, schooling itself often makes rural places seem less attractive to rural people themselves. One can argue that the Amish, a concertedly rural white population, realized this fact early on, when, as their English neighbors began to close rural schools, they began their decades-long enterprise to build—and to defend the legitimacy of—their own rural schools. The criticism of rural schooling along these lines is hardly the exclusive province of the Amish, of course: prominent rural scholars have suggested that rural schools are the principal institutions in which young people learn *authoritatively* to leave rural places (e.g., Corbett 2007; DeYoung 1995; Theobald 1997). In Appalachia we have often worked with educators in resource-extraction communities who regard the local place as somewhere to leave. Although this psychological dynamic is particularly notable in resource-extraction communities, it is still evident, we would argue, in most rural communities.

Schools facilitate out-migration, in part, by shaping *identities* that willingly embrace departure. Entire realms of knowledge, experience, and affection are abandoned by the once-rural individual as part of the loss. Successful students and educators strive for achievement scores and other academic distinctions that will prove them up to the standards of other places and, indeed, of other societies. Children from impoverished rural families are doubly burdened by this scheme. Schooling denies them identification with the (bad) places where they are and simultaneously excludes them from the (good) places they hear about in school. Exceptions are rare indeed.

In the best circumstances, perhaps, such schooling may create bicultural middle-class adults who can "choose" to stay away or return. Some of our work (e.g., Howley and Harmon 1997) has reported on an Appalachian school district (formerly an extraction community) where the idea of middle-class return was explicit. Middle-class rural students learn to aspire to a permanent elsewhere, but youth from impoverished families are confined to a place they learn from their schooling is *no place to be*. In most cases, rural schooling avoids pushing back against the state, federal, and world-class standards that embed rural deficiency as if it were an existential certainty. It too often fails rural communities, families, and students—so far as we have been able to see in thirty-five years of rural work.

The possibility of repudiating such "standards" is perhaps at lowest ebb in suburbanizing rural communities. In these "rural" places, the inherent values of frugality, stewardship, enjoyment of work, and communality come increasingly to be viewed as unsavory—backward, conservative, and irrelevant—a native anathema to be eradicated. (The suburbanizing rural community discussed above was perhaps just beginning this change.) In the end, there will be no rural place to which young people might return, and sadly their schooling will not prepare them to undertake rural lives elsewhere—a mission of preparation that some rural writers have advocated (e.g., Jackson 1996; Orr 1995).

The durable-agrarian rural community that we studied stands as an emblem of an alternative sort of schooling precisely because it does value frugality, stewardship, and enjoyment of work, and because it helps to sustain a vision of the common good, locally lived. One senses, in visiting such rare schools and communities, that an authentic education is underway. Here, the issue for the formation of rural identity hinges less on a necessary departure and return, and more on a realization of the immediately valuable life possibilities that confront people locally. Few durable agrarian communities remain in the United States, and so the practical question is whether the commitments that animate such communities really are relevant in other types of rural communities. We think they could be, and should be. As Zygmunt Bauman reminds us, "One of the most seminal consequences of the new global freedom of movement is that it becomes increasingly difficult, perhaps altogether impossible, to re-forge social issues into effective collective action" (1998, 69).

The damage remains noticeable in rural places, whereas elsewhere, especially in the suburbs but even in the world-class cities (see Williams 1989), the damage is managed so as to keep it out of sight and out of mind. The damage simply becomes part of the unremarked fabric of life: frequent moves, divorce, and antidepressants become not liabilities, but signs of the good life. The rural values noted—frugality, stewardship, enjoyment of work, and communality—are widely needed in globalizing society precisely because their active repudiation under neoliberal rules is doing such widespread damage. The recent global economic collapse may harbor new opportunities for acknowledging this truth. Time will tell.

In the meantime, more rural educators might help students and communities imagine local possibilities for living well, but they must do so on very different terms than those prized by the institution of U.S. schooling and the global political economy that increasingly sponsors it. This work is tremendously difficult, and because of ideological bad habits, rural educators tend thoughtlessly to embrace the mission of creating "global citizens." They have no critique ready at hand to support them in acting otherwise. Perhaps for this reason few rural educators grasp the fact that caring for plants and animals in a self-provisioning mode is a curriculum already available to them.

References

Bauman, Z. 1998. *Globalization: The human consequences*. New York: Columbia University Press.

Bellah, R. N., R. Madsen, W. M. Sullivan, A. Swidler, and S. M. Tipton. 1985. *Habits of the heart: Individualism and commitment in American life*. Berkeley and Los Angeles: University of California Press.

Bourdieu, P., and J. Passeron. 1990. *Reproduction in education, society, and culture* (R. Nice, trans.). Thousand Oaks, Calif.: Sage.

Buber, M. 1949. *Paths in utopia* (R. F. C. Hull, trans.). Boston: Beacon Press.

Bushnell, M. 1999. Imagining rural life: Schooling as a sense of place. *Journal of Research in Rural Education* 15 (2), 80–89.

Cook, P. J., and K. L. Mizer. 1989. *The revised ERS county typology: An overview*. Washington, D.C.: U.S. Department of Agriculture, Economics Research Service.

Corbett, M. 2007. *Learning to leave: The irony of schooling in a coastal community*. Halifax: Fernwood Publishing.

Dewalt, M. W. 2006. *Amish education in the United States and Canada*. Lanham, Md.: Rowman and Littlefield.

DeYoung, A. 1995. *The life and death of a rural American high school: Farewell, Little Kanawha*. New York: Garland.

Duncan, C. M. 1999. *Worlds apart: Why poverty persists in rural America*. New Haven: Yale University Press.

Economic Research Service. 2005. *Measuring rurality: 2004 county typology codes*. Retrieved September 29, 2007, from http://www.ers.usda.gov/Briefing /Rurality/ Typology/.

Elmhirst, R. 2001. Resource struggles and the politics of place in North Lampung, Indonesia. *Singapore Journal of Tropical Geography* 22 (3), 284–307.

Fisher, D. R. 2001. Resource dependency and rural poverty: Rural areas in the United States and Japan. *Rural Sociology* 66 (2), 181–202.

Franzese, P. A. 2002. Does it take a village? Privatization, patterns of restrictiveness, and the demise of community. *Villanova Law Review* 47 (3), 553–93.

Freudenburg, W. R., and R. Gramling. 1994. Natural resources and rural poverty: A closer look. *Society and Natural Resources* 7 (1), 5–22.

Frickel, S., and W. R. Freudenburg. 1996. Mining the past: Historical context and the changing implications of natural resource extraction. *Social Problems* 43 (4), 444–66.

Gaventa, J. 1980. *Power and powerlessness in an Appalachian valley*. Urbana: University of Illinois Press.

Giddens, A. 1990. *The consequences of modernity*. Stanford: Stanford University Press.

Goldschmidt, W. 1978. *As you sow: Three studies in the social consequences of agribusiness*. Montclair, N.J.: Allanheld, Osmun.

Gray, I. 1991. *Politics in place: Social power relations in an Australian country town*. New York: Cambridge University Press.

Hobbs, F., and N. Stoops. 2002. *Demographic trends in the Twentieth century*. Washington, D.C.: U.S. Census Bureau, U.S. Department of Commerce.

Howley, A., and C. Howley. 1999. The transformative challenge of rural context. *Educational Foundations* 14 (4), 73–85.

———. 2007. *Thinking about school administration: New theories and innovative practice*. Mahwah, N.J.: Lawrence Erlbaum Associates.

Howley, A., W. Larson, S. Andrianaivo, M. Rhodes, and M. Howley. 2007. Standards-based reform of mathematics education in rural high schools. *Journal of Research in Rural Education* 22 (2). Retrieved March 1, 2008, from http://www .jrre.psu.edu/articles/22–2.pdf.

Howley, C. 1997. How to make rural education research rural: An essay at practical advice. *Journal of Research in Rural Education* 13 (2), 131–38.

Howley, C., and H. Harmon. 1997. *Sustainable small schools: A handbook for rural communities*. Charleston, W.Va.: AEL.

Howley, C., A. Howley, and L. Burgess. 2006 (March). Just say no to fads: Traditional rural pathways to success often bypass what some view as "best practice." *The School Administrator*, 26–33.

Howley, C., A. Howley, C. Howley, and M. Howley. 2006 (April). Saving the children of the poor in rural schools. Paper presented at the annual meeting of the American Educational Research Association, San Francisco, Calif. Retrieved September 30, 2007, from http://www.eric.ed.gov/ERICWebPortal/content delivery/servlet/ERIC Servlet?accno = ED495031.

Jackson, W. 1996. *Becoming native to this place*. Washington, D.C.: Counterpoint.

Jackson-Smith, D., and G. W. Gillespie. 2005. Impacts of farm structural change on farmers' social ties. *Society and Natural Resources* 18 (3), 215–40.

Keyes, R. 2006. *The quote verifier: Who said what, where, and when*. New York: St. Martin's Press.

Kraybill, D., and M. Olshan. 1994. *The Amish struggle with modernity*. Lebanon, N.H.: University Press of New England.

Kuznets, S. 1955. *Economic growth and structure*. New York: Norton.

McConnell, D. L., and C. E. Hurst. 2006. No "Rip van Winkles" here: Amish education since Wisconsin v. Yoder. *Anthropology and Education Quarterly* 37 (3), 236–54.

Nielsen, F., and A. Alderson. 1997. Income inequality in U.S. counties, 1970 to 1990. *American Sociological Review* 62 (1), 12–33.

Nisbet, R. 1966. *The sociological tradition*. New York: Basic Books.

Orfield, M. 1997. *Metropolitics: A regional agenda for community and stability*. Washington, D.C.: Brookings Institution.

Orr, D. 1995. *Earth in mind: On education, environment, and the human prospect*. Washington, D.C.: Island Press.

Parrado, E., and W. Kandel. 2006 (September). Hispanic population growth and rural income inequality. Paper presented at the annual meetings of the American Sociological Association and the Society for the Study of Social Problems, Montreal, QC.

Putnam, R. D. 2000. *Bowling alone: The collapse and revival of American community.* New York: Simon and Schuster.

Salamon, S. 2003. From hometown to non-town: Rural community effects of suburbanization. *Rural Sociology* 68 (1), 1–24.

Selznick, P. 1995. Thinking about community: Ten theses. *Society* 32 (5), 33–37.

Theobald, P. 1988. Districts on the edge: The impact of urban sprawl on a rural community. *Research in Rural Education* 5 (2), 9–15.

———. 1997. *Teaching the commons: Place, pride, and the renewal of community.* Boulder: Westview.

Tönnies, F. [1899] 1963. *Community and society* (C. P. Loomis, trans.). New York: Harper and Row.

United Nations. 2004. *World urbanization prospects: The 2003 revision.* New York: United Nations. Retrieved October 15, 2007, from http://www.un.org/esa/population/ publications/wup2003/2003WUPHighlights.pdf.

Williams, R. 1973. *The country and the city.* New York: Oxford University Press.

———. 1989. *The politics of modernism.* London: Verso.

Woodrum, A. 2004. State-mandated testing and cultural resistance in Appalachian schools: Competing values and expectations. *Journal of Research in Rural Education* 19 (1), 1–10. Retrieved September 16, 2007, from http://www.umaine.edu/jrre/19–1.htm.

3

"THE DRAMA OF THEIR DAILY LIVES": RACIST LANGUAGE AND STRUGGLES OVER THE LOCAL IN A RURAL HIGH SCHOOL

Susan L. Groenke and Jan Nespor

Introduction

Rural places are experiencing the effects of neoliberal globalizing forces, seen in the "hollowed-out" farming communities (Davidson 1996) created by the loss of farmland[1] and wetlands to agribusiness, and the development of suburb-like neighborhoods for elite baby boomers seeking the pastoral idyll (Brown, Fuguitt, Heaton, and Waseem 1997; Cloke and Little 1997; Flora, Flora, and Fey 2003; Gorelick 2002; Johnson and Howley 2000). For working-class rural residents, the accompanying shift from agricultural and manufacturing economies (as manufacturing jobs move offshore) to service industries (e.g., Wal-Mart) has resulted in lower wages and higher unemployment rates (Castells 1998; Sassen 1998; Dempsey 2007). Ensuing tensions are compounded by a breakdown in traditional forms of worker solidarity (Haas 1990; Tarca 2005), a rise in production and use of the drug methamphetamine[2] in rural communities (resulting in high incarceration rates and "meth orphans") (Council of State Governments 2004), and a rise in immigration of foreign-born persons

---

1. Kimmel and Ferber (2006) explain that the United States has lost nearly 750,000 of its small- and medium-sized family farms since 1982.
2. A growing body of evidence points to meth abuse as one reason substance abuse is higher among rural youth compared to their urban counterparts.

following job opportunities created by agribusiness or seeking "a better life" than can be had in metropolitan or urban areas.[3]

Rural schools are not immune to such forces: the incentives rural areas offer for economic development (e.g., lower taxes, tax breaks, subsidized infrastructure) deplete the fiscal resources of already underfunded rural public schools (Gaventa, Smith, and Willingham 1990; Moore 2001). In addition, out-migration of rural persons (especially young persons) to metropolitan areas in search of job opportunities (Johnson 2006) or as military recruits[4] (Tyson 2005) results in declining birth rates and thus low school enrollments[5] (Haas 1990; Heminway 2002); further, the difficulties of small rural schools in meeting federal education regulations (e.g., the 2001 No Child Left Behind Act's requirement of "highly qualified" teachers in all subjects) have resulted in the consolidation or closure of small rural schools[6] (Kannapel and DeYoung 1999; Reeves 2003; Rural School and Community Trust 2004). Finally, as rural communities experience increasing diversity, so too do their schools, sometimes with ensuing tensions (Riehl 2000; Tarca 2005).

Articulating the Rural

How such large-scale economic and cultural shifts play out in rural settings depends on a complex politics of articulation in which different groups struggle to define themselves in terms of particular versions of "rural" or "local" life. As Appadurai (1996) suggests, the local isn't a given or naturally bounded unit but a "project," or more accurately, the site of competing projects. The "local knowledge" that defines a rural place is best viewed, in Kalb's (2006, 583) words, "as the contingent product of a complex and dynamic field of power relationships, both among locals as well as between locals and their external

3. As Johnson (2006) explains, between 2000 and 2004, immigration accounted for 31 percent of the overall population increase in rural areas. In 297 U.S. rural counties, the foreign-born populations exceeded 5 percent for the first time in 2000.

4. Tyson (2005) reports more than 44 percent of U.S. military recruits come from rural areas. In contrast, 14 percent come from major cities. Youths living in the most sparsely populated zip codes are 22 percent more likely to join the army, with an opposite trend in cities. Regionally, most enlistees come from the South (40 percent) and West (24 percent).

5. Most school funding formulas are based on either average daily enrollment or cost per pupil. Faced with declining enrollments, schools must cut expenses or raise revenues.

6. Of all the school consolidations between 1986 and 1993, 59 percent were in small rural districts (Bickel and Howley 2000).

interlocutors. It is a negotiated project or program rather than an empirical fact" (583).

Rural spaces and the identities of persons living in rural spaces are highly contested, "negotiated" projects (Cloke and Little 1997), and given the confluence of forces outlined above, these negotiations and struggles unfold not only between local and global forces (the rural community and the cultural and economic forces originating outside it), but among different factions within rural communities who may appropriate "global" tools or imagery as readily as they embrace more familiar and "traditional" local practices.

For young people, schools are key sites in these negotiations—central community institutions and meeting places where rural youth encounter people, processes, and ideas from outside the area. Rural researchers (cf. Arnot 2004; Dempsey 2007; Panelli 2002) suggest that to understand how rural youth craft identities in such settings we must attend to the play of race, class, and gender. We argue in this chapter that language and imagery must also be considered integral to rural youths' identity negotiation processes (Baumann and Briggs 1990; Blot 2003; Kroskrity 2004; Silverstein 2003), as they are a key part of the larger cultural politics involved in defining the "rural."

Our focus in this chapter—based on Susan's ethnographic research on students' literacy practices at "Rivertown High" (Groenke 2003)—is on how language and race, or more precisely racist language, worked as a medium for contesting definitions of rural identity in a three-hundred-student rural high school in a southern U.S. state. Data for the study included participant observation from 2001 to 2002 (Hammersley and Atkinson 1995; Emerson, Fretz, and Shaw 1995), and interviews (Seidman 1998) with the English teacher, a school aide from the local community, and students in the English class. Student writings were collected (and used to structure some of the interviews), as were materials used in the English class.

In what follows, we analyze the racist speech of a small group of white male students, and show how, in Bakhtinian fashion, the boys "[borrowed] from other voices" (Scollon, Tsang, Li, Yung, and Jones 1998)—often the global or extra-local voices of the popular media, but also binary formations of race and space historically used in rural construction and categorization processes (e.g., black/white; urban/rural) (Agyeman and Spooner 1997; Kurtz 2006)—to deal with the changing economic and cultural organization of the area. In particular we show how racist speech served multiple uses, from symbolically excluding outsiders and newcomers to the area, to subverting administrators' attempts to integrate the school discursively into the larger cosmopolitan school district by instituting a speech code, to policing intra-group identity among peers.

Against simple equations of southern rural masculinities with racist attitudes, we suggest that racial language needs to be understood in terms of its uses and the conditions and contexts in which it's employed. In particular, we suggest that racial categories and racist speech have complex performative and micro-political uses that cannot be understood outside the larger cultural politics of the struggle over the definition of the rural community.

"Towelheads" and "Sandniggers"

Although the geographical area served by Rivertown High remains rural by most definitions—low population density, little developed land, and no large settlement areas or factories—it was part of a county school district that included two midsized towns and a large state university, and it was cut through by a state highway that was the site of a several convenience stores, a local restaurant, two gas stations, and a number of larger trailer parks, which housed a sizable proportion of the area's population.[7] The school population, then, was drawn from the poorest region of a school district politically and economically dominated by larger (and somewhat more ethnically diverse) towns.[8]

And it was a relatively homogeneous population in terms of ethnicity. Unlike many of the settings of research on racist speech, and unlike other schools in the district with larger (though still small) African American populations, Rivertown High had an almost exclusively European American enrollment—only four students in the school were African Americans and there were no Latino or Asian American students at the time of the study.

Along with the economic underdevelopment of the Rivertown area, this ethnic homogeneity meant that in contrast to the urban situation studied by Thomas (2005), where the school was a meeting place for black and white

---

7. As Cloke (2005, 19) notes, definitions of rurality sometimes also include as a criterion "cohesive identity based on respect for the environmental and behavioural qualities of living as part of an extensive landscape." The criterion would seem to potentially exclude many people who live in the countryside and in unmistakably rural areas; further, as Cloke argues, rural areas are diverse and dynamic, with mass media and mobility in many ways blurring urban-rural boundaries, or "hybridizing" the two (20).

8. Per capita income for Rivertown was $13,785. Almost half (120) of the 300 students attending Rivertown High School received free or reduced lunch at the time of the study.

students who did not interact with each other outside it, Rivertown High students encountered ethnic difference almost exclusively outside the school—in stores, workplaces, and the popular media. For example, one of the most symbolically prominent local manifestations of the kinds of globalizing processes described above had been the movement of Indian American families into the area economy by buying and operating most of the convenience stores and motels along the main highway linking this community to the outside world. As Donald and Jason, two eleventh graders, explained:

Jason:	We've only got like five stores in Rivertown and they own three out of the five.
Donald:	They own all of them down through the main drag and the hotel, and they live in the hotel.
Susan:	Do people pretty much leave them alone?
Jason:	There's a lot of people give 'em . . . [a hard time].
Donald:	Well, everybody used to go to the stores, you know, around here a lot, because they were owned by people who lived right in Rivertown, now they just you know, these people took it over, they don't want to go. And uh, well, there's one store left and that's that country store. (Personal interview, September 24, 2002)

One way the boys symbolically managed these changes was through a loose set of national and racial terms that defined categorical boundaries excluding the Indian Americans from membership in the community:

Donald:	All the stores are owned by a bunch of guidos.
Susan:	What do you mean "guidos"?
Jason:	Towelheads.
Susan:	Towelheads?
Donald:	Arabs, let's just go that way.
Susan:	OK.
Jason:	Arabs, I don't know. They all from Egypt or something.
	. . .
Susan:	Do people who aren't born in this area get treated differently than people who are born here?
Donald:	I don't treat them differently. I won't be extra nice to them, but I'll be courteous to them as long as they're courteous to me.

Susan: Do your parents go in the local stores?

Jason: Not all the time. Just when it's convenient. I live directly across
            from the Rivertown food mart. The store's—on your right. I
            live on the left and so they know me by name there. So I'm up
            there saying "Raj," he's an old sandnigger or something, I don't
            know. But he's cool as hell, he's got this big golden loop in his
            ear and shit. I'm like, "What's up, Raj?" and he's like, "What's
            up, Jason?" (Personal interview, September 24, 2002)

The September 11 terrorist attacks, events only a year old at the time of this
fieldwork, added another layer to the discourse, mixing with older myths about
immigrant store owners:

Susan: What about since 9/11? Have things changed since then?

Jason: Oh man, you don't even. I'd hate to be one of the store owners
            around here, man, you know how much business they've lost? I
            know people who will drive all the way to Reedsville from here
            even though there are ten stores around here just so they won't,
            you know, Arabs and shit.

Donald: They come here from their country, get U.S. citizenship, and
            they don't have to pay taxes for four years. And they get a no-
            interest loan from the government to buy up businesses. And
            guess what? I can't even get a loan to buy a car but they can get
            a loan to buy a couple of stores. That's pretty shitty. (Personal
            interview, September 24, 2002)

In these conversations the boys draw on global or extra-local discursive
resources to promote their particular construction of the local. The accusations
about "tax breaks" and "no-interest loans" for immigrants are what have been
labeled (inaccurately) "urban" legends.[9] As the boys use them, they imply that
the national government unfairly discriminates against native-born citizens—in this case rural citizens—by favoring cosmopolitanizing immigrants.

    In a different kind of borrowing, the assortment of labels the boys use to
characterize the store owners and clerks appears to have been appropriated
from the popular media. "Guido" is a term used for Italian American males in

---

    9. These "urban legends" (rural, too, it seems) date back to the 1960s. See http://www
.snopes.com/business/taxes/immigrants.asp.

New Jersey—possibly borrowed from the popular television series *The Sopranos*. Legitimate if inaccurately deployed labels like Arab and Egyptian are mixed in with racist terms like "sandnigger" and "towelhead," both of which seem to have come into popular usage following the first Gulf War. The serial substitution of terms allows the boys to emphasize the foreignness of the clerks and symbolically exclude them. But the racist terms have a special force. An Egyptian would be someone from Egypt, but a "sandnigger" would seem to be something fundamentally alien and inferior.

Folding the Rural into the School District

While the students in Rivertown were trying to categorize their store clerks, other kinds of diversity-related tensions were coming to a head in the larger, more diverse towns of the school district. The local NAACP lodged a complaint about the disproportionate number of suspensions of black students (which gave rise to the creation of a "diversity forum"). At about the same time, a controversy emerged in the district's most affluent town over dropping a Native American name for its school mascot. Finally, there were infrequent but well-publicized and racially inflected fights in the schools. A local newspaper provided this account of one of the latter from the year prior to the fieldwork: "A female sixth-grader said Thursday that four students—white and black—physically assaulted three others, one of whom wore a shirt that said: 'This shirt is 100 percent cotton and your momma picked it.' According to a male eighth-grader several students called a black student involved in the fight 'the N word' at one point. They also used a slur against the girlfriend of another person in the brawl. . . . [The school superintendent] does not believe there is a racial problem at the school" (Hoffman 2001, A1, A2). In response to the complaints and incidents, the county devised a "Six-Year Plan" that called for a student code of conduct that upheld the new mission of the district, which was to "ensure respect for the dignity of children, families, and all employees" ([County] Student Code of Conduct, 3). To carry out this mission, the school board outlined rules of conduct for student behavior, including rules regarding student dress and "verbal abuse" (7).

It was in the context of this "Six-Year Plan" that Rivertown High School introduced rules to increase tolerance of diversity, in particular penalties for the use of racist language. The principal, Mr. Simmons, explained, "We should be raising the *awareness* level, we should be raising the *conscience* level, we should be challenging students to think about how they treat humanity" (italics added):

> Inappropriate language could have to do with sexual harassment or bullying, or it could be as simple as using the "n word," but our tolerance level with that is very low. In other words, we're saying to students it's inappropriate, we've worked with you long enough, it's in the code of conduct, and you know it's a type of hateful speech and/or action/language that's unacceptable from anyone of any race, it's not just black and white. Uh, you know it could be red and yellow, it could be whatever, but it's a type of language we're not going to deal with. We just try to say to students we're not going to tolerate it. If it's hurtful, or else it's hate speech to someone else, then there's going to be disciplinary action. I remember a kid saying to me, "You can't suspend me because of that." I can't remember what the word was, but I said, "Sorry, but you've just been, you're gone, you're out." We've just been pretty much hard core, hard-line, saying, "No, you're not going to use that kind of language here." (Personal interview, February 17, 2003)

This policy and its enforcement seemed to surprise at least a small group of boys in the school who persisted in using racist terms and were suspended as a result:

Matt: Well, this year I got suspended like a day, two days for saying "nigger."

Susan: Did you say it in a particular class or outside of class or—?

Matt: I got in an argument with one of the girls who's dating one, another one. In the lunchroom, and then like my freshman year, I got suspended for saying "jigaboo."

Susan: So it's the teachers hearing it?

Matt: My freshman year a teacher heard me say it and then I got wrote up because she heard me say it. And then down there, when I was arguing with that girl, Mr. Knapp heard me say it so he was like, he took me to the office and he said I've got to suspend you for all that. (Personal interview, October 12, 2002)

In part, the boys seemed to read the language policy as an unexplained and unjustified change. As Donald remarked, "We have been able to walk around for, like ninth grade we used to go walk and say 'nigger' whenever we want to and nobody cared, there weren't no one around to say anything" (personal interview, October 12, 2002). But both the policy and the boys' flouting of it can also be viewed as parts of competing projects for reconstructing the rural in relation to broader processes. The policies themselves code collective spaces by officially proscribing certain words and discourse forms. They are political and cultural performances that symbolically integrate the school into the more affluent bordering town's cosmopolitan self-image by defining and regulating which knowledge, values, and behavior are considered legitimate, and what can be thought or said (Ares and Buendía 2007; Gusfield 1986; Lipman 2002; Ozga 2000; Smith, Heinecke, and Noble 1999). As Mayo (2004) suggests, speech policies such as this one help school districts appear "cultivated" and "sensitive": "By gaining a sense of . . . having currency with issues of diversity, [dominant people] maintain the veneer of a cosmopolitan person in the know, a kind of tourist of inequality" (35).

Hall (1997) reminds us, however, "it is when a discourse forgets that it is placed that it tries to speak for everybody else" (36). "Placing" the policy in this context means situating the students' language practices it seeks to suppress in a larger context, in this case one in which there have been few African Americans and the students' experience of African Americans has been almost entirely mediated through the school and popular culture. Thus boys like Donald parsed and reorganized even the most long-established binaries—"white" and "black"—in relation to multiple borrowed voices. In a conversation with Susan about a black teacher who had previously worked at Rivertown, Donald and Jason try to distinguish between the "black people" they knew and images of "niggers" from the popular media:

Donald:	He was whiter than half us here.
Susan:	What do you mean by that?
Donald:	He's black but he acted white.
Jason:	There's a difference between black and white.
Susan:	What does it mean to "act black"?
Donald:	Act black or act white?
Susan:	Well, you said that he acted white. What does that mean?
Donald:	He was more white.
Jason:	It's a whole point of attitude. You see [white] guys walking around here with their pants to their ass, they act thuggish and shit. And he was straight. Wore straight pants.

Donald: Wore ties all the time. He was clean-cut.

Susan: So, what you're saying, are white guys with their pants hanging
            down and stuff, are they "acting black"?

Donald: Look. You got black people, you got niggers. Black people are
            the kind of people live off Allentown Road, sit on the front
            porch every evening, wave at everybody, go to church every
            Sunday. They're real nice. Some people got their cars like this
            high off the ground, got their pants to their knees, and five
            hundred Mr. T–looking chains on their neck.

Susan: People like that go to school here? Live here?

Donald: Nah, they won't, they get, nah. (Personal interview, September
            24, 2002)

The boys did not single out any of the black students in the school as "niggers":

Matt: We got three black people here and they don't act like a nigger.
            They just act like a black person, a normal black person.

Susan: What's a normal black person?

Matt: You know, not a gangster.

As Pollock (2004) found in her fieldwork in a multiethnic California high
school, "when talking to one another *about racial classification* . . . students
almost always wound up contesting easy accounts of race group membership"
(36). Distinctions like the one the boys made between "black people" and "niggers" are readily available in the popular media (e.g., the well-known routine
by the comedian Chris Rock, quoted in Kennedy 2002, 41–43; Asim 2007, 209),
while the idea of "niggers" as "gangsters" may have actually been provided or
reinforced by the school itself, which the previous year had brought in an African American motivational speaker, a self-proclaimed former "gangster" (he
raised his shirt to show old bullet wounds) now counseling young people that
there is no "black race" or "white race," but only a "human race."

   Without denying the pernicious effects of terms like "nigger" in any context,
we want to suggest that policies that treat its use as a simple manifestation of
racist attitudes are problematic. The speech policy at Rivertown High treated
language as a marker of underlying beliefs, with the implication that such
beliefs are products of unreflexive cultural norms or irrational antagonisms
(i.e., that "racism" is a problem *inside* students—an infection caught from a
local "culture"). The speech policy located agency and the sources of racism in

individuated actors. Punishments were thus intended to make individuals reflect on their words (the "awareness" function) and the pernicious effects of their speech (the "conscience" function). The hope, presumably, is that the underlying individual beliefs will change.[10]

Yet as we've seen, the boys who used the term most had complex (or at least muddled) conceptions of race, which the policies do nothing to address or clarify. Moreover, as McCarthy (1995) suggests, by portraying white students as "flawed protagonists" (27) in their relations with blacks and other nonwhites, such policies ignore the fact that, as at Rivertown, racist language is common among exclusively European American groups of students (e.g., Peshkin 1978; Kiesling 2001), and the key functions of such language may be to shape relations *among* whites.

Finally, the hate-speech policy as implemented at Rivertown High can be viewed as parts of administrative projects to produce the rural as a "representation of space," in Lefebvre's (1991) sense of a "conceptualized space"—a space conceived and ordered according to abstract, generalized formulas (in this case regarding diversity and language) (38). In this respect, the policies ignore the likelihood that students' lived experiences of the spaces will conflict with such plans, and that students as a result may attempt to subvert administrative constructions or overlay them with their own imagined spaces (Lefebvre 1991, 39).

The Boys' Rural?

Some of the boys quoted above provide an example of this kind of overlaying of projects in their appropriation and subversion of an eleventh-grade English assignment. After her students had read Arthur Miller's *The Crucible* (1953) and researched acts of persecution throughout American history (e.g., Salem witch trials, McCarthyism) as part of a unit on American Puritanism, Mrs. Taylor, the eleventh-grade English teacher at Rivertown, asked the students to write skits that demonstrated an act of persecution and the idea that "history repeats itself": "Although we should learn from history, somehow we don't and we

---

10. One additional problem with hate-speech policies is the way they draw attention away from institutional racism. Brown and colleagues (2003), for example, note that "a focus on obvious bigotry, crude verbal performance, and political practices may make American 'nonracists' feel better about themselves. But it also produces a false sense of security. Because it ignores culturally acceptable sophisticated forms of racism, this perspective is unable to detect the 'non-racist' ways that being white works to the advantage of European Americans" (55; see also Gates 1994, 47).

keep making similar errors. The *Crucible* was so much about persecution, so that was to be the theme of [the students'] own skits. We talked at length about the saying, and that is the main reason we did the drama: to look at persecution closely and see what could possibly lie ahead if we did not pay attention to our historical mistakes now" (personal interview, May 28, 2003).

The text of one of the skits, written by three European American males— Jason, Alan, and Matt, and performed with the help of various classmates—is presented below verbatim:

Narrator:	(*The year is 2020*). Jamal and Jill are your ordinary happy couple. Well, I wouldn't exactly use the word ordinary, see, Jill is white and well, Jamal he's black. They are sitting together in the park when two people out for a walk pass by their bench.
Walker 1:	(*Chris*) Dude, that's nasty.
Walker 2:	(*this is me idiots LoL*) Yeah it is.
Walker 1:	I wonder what her daddy says about that?
Walker 2:	I don't know, but I *do* know I wouldn't allow it.
Jamal:	(*sounds angry* AND black) Yo what they say? They talkin bout us?
Jill:	Don't worry about it hun, they're gone now.
Narrator:	A few moments later Frank (a friend of Jill's brother Joe) is walking by when he recognizes Jill.
Frank:	Jill! What in the world are you doing with him? Does your family know about this?
Jill:	Ugh! Don't worry about it Frank, just go on some where.
Jamal:	Yeah fa real yo. You gotta problem or sumptin?
Frank:	(*walks away and laughs when he says*) Nah man looks like yall are the ones with problems.
Narrator:	As Frank continues his walk he sees his buddy out.
Frank:	Hey man what's up?
Joe:	Hey Frank Nuttin man just walkin around.
Frank:	I hate to burst your bubble and all man but you wouldn't believe who I seen your sister cuddled up with.
Joe:	Who?!?
Frank:	Well I don't know his name or anything but it was some black guy.
Joe:	WHAT!?! There's no way you are being serious.

Frank: As a heart attack.

Narrator: Joe storms off to find his sister.

Frank: Hey! Wait up man!

Pause for a few seconds

Joe: JILL!! (*okay Matt say what you would to your cousin. No
            Cussin!!!*)

Jill: But Joe, I care about him, and he treats me well!

Joe: I don't care! (*finish it up Matt*)

Immediately following the skit performance, a visibly upset European American female student, Jenny, stood up, left the room, and did not return. Mrs. Taylor followed her out, returned, and then began making announcements to the students about group evaluation rubrics and upcoming test dates. She then gave the students the last few minutes of class to "talk quietly among yourselves" (field notes, September 23, 2002).

The skit could be considered a "racist event" (Feagin and Vera 2004), and the teacher considered it as such, blaming the incident on the students' "ignorance" and "culture": "These guys are a buncha, they're a bunch of rednecks. They're ignorant. A lot of kids down there are like that. And I think a lot of it comes from the culture, from the background" (personal interview, May 28, 2003). The relatively short and classroom-specific relations of teachers to students, especially in cases where the former live far (socially or geographically) from the latter, favor explanations of student action similar to those espoused in the hate-speech policy: racist speech reflects students' internal beliefs, which reflect their rural cultures. But as LeCouteur and Augoustinos (2001) claim, consistent with our earlier discussion, "The language of contemporary racism is flexible, ambivalent, and contradictory. . . . Categorization and stereotyping are not . . . internal cognitive processes but, rather . . . discursive practices that are flexibly articulated within specific social contexts in order to construct particular versions or accounts of reality" (215).

If we consider the skit instead as a "ritual of racism"—a "repetitive and formalized" action that "[defines] socially acceptable practices and socially relevant knowledge for the community, including its youth" (Feagin, Vera, and Batur 2001, 48)—and treat "ritual" as a "busy intersection" where multiple agendas intersect (Rosaldo 1989, 20), we can begin to interrogate this use of racist imagery as part of a "version" of the "rural" that the boys were attempting to construct and police.

In this instance, rather than borrowing from popular media, the students drew on historically constructed binary formations of race and space, often reanimated in the media (e.g., black/white; urban/rural) (Kurtz 2006; Agyeman and Spooner 1997), to associate the category "black person," in particular "black male," with speech, deportment, and sexualities coded as deviant. They used mock African American vernacular (Ronkin and Karn 1999) to make Jamal "sound black," and situated the skit in an alien, urban construct (there were no parks in Rivertown). They also seemed to draw on imagery of the "White man" as the "self-designated protector of White womankind, defender of nation/territory" (Frankenberg qtd. in Kiesling 2001, 104; cf. Weis 2003, 77).

As Agyeman and Spooner (1997) suggest, for white people "ethnicity" is seen as being "out of place" in the countryside: "In the white imagination, people of colour are confined to towns and cities, representing an urban, 'alien' environment, and the white landscape of rurality is aligned with 'nativeness' and the absence of evil or danger. The ethnic associations of the countryside are naturalized as an absence intruded upon by people of colour" (199).

But the skit is not just a spasmodic expression of such beliefs, or of a generalized hostility toward African Americans. As we have argued throughout, the language must be understood in terms of specific localized uses. In a conversation with Susan, Jason—one of the skit writers—explained his group's reasons for writing the skit:

Jason: Did you know what our skit was about yesterday?

Susan: I want you to tell me more about that.

Jason: About . . . white women with white men (laughs). We couldn't put what we wanted. Matt, his cousin, Jenny, Jenny's dating a black guy and Matt don't like that. That's why we wrote the skit. To piss her off . . .

Matt: She knows we don't approve of it. She's my cousin, so she knows how my family is, she knows that we're totally against . . . she knows it and then she goes and does this and goes against the family and all.
           . . .

Susan: Why use the skit to say it? Why not just say it to her face?

Jason: Because we could say it in front of everybody and not get in trouble. (Personal interview, September 24, 2002)

The skit speech, then, was directed against Jenny in particular, who by dating a black man had created a tie linking Matt and his family to African Americans. Used in the space of the classroom in this way, racist language—rather than a simple reflection of racist attitudes or beliefs—becomes a key tool in producing and policing identities and relations, their meanings inflected by at least one other system of meaning: sexuality.

Following Bobo and Hutchings, the skit can be looked at as *sexually inflected* racist discourse, as the male skit writers may be trying to enforce "assumptions of *proper or proprietary claim over certain rights,* resources, statuses and privileges" (1996, 995) being usurped by members of an "outgroup"—here, sexual control of a white woman. The males in the skit wonder if Jill's daddy "knows about" her dating a black male, and they go collect Jill's brother so he can react accordingly.

The boys' use of racialized language in the classroom—in the presence of Mrs. Taylor—may also be viewed as enacting an insider-outsider boundary. According to Matt, "As far as I'm concerned and I'll tell any of the teachers here, if they don't want to hear the word they don't need to come down to Rivertown because Rivertown is just 99.9 percent rednecks and everybody, nobody around here likes black people. That's why we got like a total of three black people in our entire school" (personal interview, September 14, 2002). What is interesting here is not whether "nobody around here likes black people"—some of the students, like Jenny, clearly do—but that Matt links the language restrictions not just to black-white relations in the town, but also in terms of the community's relations to teachers and administrators. Matt's characterization of school personnel as people who "come down" to Rivertown (which is situated in a river valley)—the dominant towns in the district are both "burgs" higher up in the mountains—defines them as outsiders. The tensions generated by the community's unequal/subordinate relations with the more affluent towns, and the resistances to transformations introduced from the outside, may or may not be fundamentally organized around race, but the boys contextualize their use of racist terms within those tensions.

Conclusion

As we noted at the outset, the connections of rural communities and schools to regional, national, and international processes are changing. Transnational migrations bring new groups and languages into rural communities. The popular media introduce new cultural categories and linguistic resources for constructing place and difference. Educational reforms and policies spread from urban systems to rural schools. Shifting economic relations change the forms and meanings of work.

These and other processes are transforming the local worlds of rural young people, stripping away many of the identity-building resources that were traditionally available to them. But as Kraack and Kenway (2002) suggest, rural youth will find and utilize alternative identity-constructing resources. The Rivertown students, as we've seen, responded creatively to changes in the representation and contestation of rural meanings, appropriating some elements of the new cultural landscape (categories and imagery from the popular media) while rejecting or subverting others.

Our aim in situating the boys' uses of race in such processes is not to downplay their racism but to suggest that we can only *understand* that racism by contextualizing it and looking at how its social meanings were interactively produced. Whatever the boys' reasons for using epithets loudly in the halls of the school, once their resulting suspensions were explained in terms of new school policies, the race terms also became resources for commenting on and challenging the perceived agendas of administrators and teachers to redefine local, rural practices. Jenny was already being harassed about her boyfriend, but the teacher's construction of a unit on historical persecution allowed the boys to bring that harassment into the classroom in ways that also let them distance themselves from the teacher's efforts to situate persecution in a national, historical past (through the Salem witch trials) rather than a local present. In short, the racist terms and acts were part of the boys' limited repertoire for producing and controlling difference across multiple domains, and for distancing themselves from actors and sociocultural processes seemingly associated with encroaching urban influences.

Although the research reported here cannot provide solutions to these struggles, it clarifies a key issue any solution will have to address: rural schools cannot ignore the existing relations and tensions among rural communities, bordering towns, and the global voices that vie for the identities of rural places. Rural, place-based educators (Donehower, Hogg, and Schell 2007; Haas and Nachtigal 1998; Theobald 1997) have encouraged rural school administrators and teachers to establish pedagogical conditions that would enable rural youth to critically analyze how dominant definitions and uses of rural spaces come to be "dominant"—and how such definitions influence territorial identity making (Haymes 1995). One way to do this, as Gruenewald (2003, 5) suggests, is for educators to redefine conventional notions of print-based literacy and conventional school curriculum, using as "texts" the images of rural students' and teachers' own concrete, situated experiences.

For example, amid tensions surrounding the flying of the Confederate flag atop the capitol dome in Columbia, several rural South Carolina high school teachers (Carlson, Schramm-Pate, and Lussier 2005) used over two hundred pages of photocopied articles on the controversy from local newspapers and Web sites as classroom texts, and taught standpoint theory (Collins 2000) to help the students understand how the differing views and perspectives circulating in the texts—and how identity positions and interest—influenced the differing views. Groenke (2004) suggests using as pedagogical texts in rural classrooms popular culture artifacts that caricature rural peoples—for example, "Billy-Bob" teeth (wax inserts that give the wearer the appearance of protruding, decaying buckteeth).

Finally, Thompson and Kutach (1990) suggest a canonical text, Steinbeck's *The Grapes of Wrath* (1939), can be taught in such a way as to help rural youth understand that the loss of farming communities and changing sociopolitical class transitions in rural areas are not the result of poor production choices, natural disasters, bad fortune, or the will of God, but rather neoliberal socio-economic forces at work that promote technological innovation and resource depletion (see also Brown 2000).

The skit the boys wrote for Mrs. Taylor, along with their daily negotiations with the convenience store owners, the relations of their school community to the bigger towns of the school district, and the historical treatment of African Americans in their area, could all have served as pedagogical materials for interrogating the marking and use of racial categories in identity-negotiating processes. To use them for such purposes, however, presupposes that teachers and administrators take analytical, reflective stances that bring the teachers out of the classrooms and focus their attention on the history as well as the ongoing activities of the local area.

School officials and teachers obviously cannot accept the use of racist language, but they need to attend to how their responses to such language build on or ramify into oppositional student identities, and this entails understanding what place-based and global resources students draw from in constructing those identities. Lacking this kind of awareness, schools too readily ignore or try to suppress the everyday experiences and perspectives that students bring into the classroom. As Mrs. Taylor complained, "Some days it would take me as many as 15, to 20–25 minutes to rein them in from the drama of their daily lives." It might behoove rural educators, school administrators, and researchers

to both attend to this "drama" if we are to better understand the social processes young people in rural settings engage with on a regular basis, and, perhaps
more important, acknowledge rural youth as active players in shaping future
"rurals."

References

Agyeman, J., and R. Spooner. 1997. Ethnicity and the rural environment. In P. Cloke
and J. Little, eds., *Contested countryside cultures*, 197–217. London: Routledge.

Appadurai, A. 1996. *Modernity at large: Cultural dimensions of globalization*. Minne-
apolis: University of Minnesota Press.

Ares, N., and E. Buendía. 2007. Opportunities lost: Local translations of advocacy
policy conversations. *Teachers College Record* 109 (3), 561–89.

Arnot, M. 2004. Male working-class identities and social justice: A reconsideration of
Paul Willis's *Learning to Labor* in light of contemporary research. In N. Dolby
and G. Dimitriadis, eds., *Learning to labor in new times*, 17–40. New York:
Routledge Falmer.

Asim, J. 2007. *The N word*. Boston: Houghton Mifflin.

Bauman, R., and C. Briggs. 1990. Poetics and performance as critical perspectives on
language and social life. *Annual Review of Anthropology* 19, 59–88.

Bickel, R., and C. B. Howley. 2000. The influence of scale on school performance: A
multi-level extension of the Matthew Principle. *Education Policy Analysis
Archives* 8 (22). Retrieved September 14, 2009, from http://epaa.asu.edu/epaa/
v8n22/.

Blot, R. K. 2003. *Language and social identity*. Westport, Conn.: Praeger.

Bobo, L., and V. Hutchings. 1996. Perceptions of racial group competition: Extending
Blumer's theory of group position to a multiracial social context. *American
Sociological Review* 61 (6), 951–72.

Brown, D. L., G. V. Fuguitt, T. B. Heaton, and S. Waseem. 1997. Continuities in size of
place preferences in the United States, 1972–1992. *Rural Sociology* 62 (4), 408–28.

Brown, M., M. Carnoy, E. Currie, T. Duster, D. Oppenheimer, M. Shultz, et al. 2003.
Whitewashing race: The myth of a color-blind society. Berkeley and Los Angeles:
University of California Press.

Brown, S. G. 2000. *Words in the wilderness: Critical literacy in the borderlands*. Albany:
State University of New York Press.

Carlson, D., S. L. Schramm-Pate, and R. R. Lussier. 2005. Risky business: Teaching
about the Confederate flag controversy in a South Carolina high school. In L.
Weis and M. Fine, eds., *Beyond silenced voices: Class, race, and gender in United
States schools* (rev. ed.), 217–32. Albany: State University of New York Press.

Castells, M. 1998. *End of the millennium*. London: Blackwell.

Cloke, P. 2005. Rurality and racialised others: Out of place in the countryside? In N.
Chakraborti and J. Garland, eds., *Rural racisms*, 17–35. Cullompton, Devon, UK:
Willan Publishing.

Cloke, P., and J. Little. 1997. *Contested countryside cultures: Otherness, marginalization, and rurality.* London: Routledge.

Collins, P. H. 2000. *Black feminist thought: Knowledge, consciousness, and the politics of empowerment.* New York: Routledge.

Council of State Governments. 2004. *Drug abuse in America: Rural meth.* Lexington, Ky.: Council of State Governments.

Davidson, O. G. 1996. *Broken heartland: The rise of America's rural ghetto.* Iowa City: University of Iowa Press.

Dempsey, V. 2007. Intersections on the back road: Class, culture, and education in rural and Appalachian places. In J. A. Van Galen and G. W. Noblit, eds., *Late to class: Social class and schooling in the new economy,* 287–312. Albany: State University of New York Press.

Donehower, K., C. Hogg, and E. E. Schell. 2007. *Rural literacies.* Carbondale: Southern Illinois University Press.

Emerson, R., R. Fretz, and L. Shaw. 1995. *Writing ethnographic fieldnotes.* Chicago: University of Chicago Press.

Feagin, J. R., and H. Vera. 2004. The study of racist events. In M. Bulmer and J. Solomos, eds., *Researching race and racism,* 66–77. London: Routledge.

Feagin, J. R., H. Vera, and P. Batur. 2001. *White racism* (2d ed.) New York: Routledge.

Flora, C. B., J. L. Flora, and S. Fey. 2003. *Rural communities: Legacy and change* (2d ed.). Boulder: Westview.

Gates, H. L. 1994. War of words: Critical race theory and the first amendment. In H. L. Gates, A. Griffin, D. Lively, R. Post, W. Rubenstein, and N. Strossen, eds., *Speaking of race, speaking of sex: Hate speech, civil rights, and civil liberties,* 17–58. New York: New York University Press.

Gaventa, J., B. E. Smith, and A. Willingham. 1990. Toward a new debate: Development, democracy, and dignity. In J. Gaventa, B. E. Smith, and A. Willingham, eds., *Communities in economic crisis,* 279–91. Philadelphia: Temple University Press.

Gorelick, S. 2002. Facing the farm crisis: How globalization hurts farmers and destroys farm communities. In B. Bigelow and B. Peterson, eds., *Rethinking globalization: Teaching for justice in an unjust world.* Milwaukee: Rethinking Schools Press.

Groenke, S. L. 2003. Troubling literacy in the contact zone of a rural high school English class. Ph.D. diss., Virginia Tech.

———. 2004. Stories we haven't heard yet: Imagining critical literacy in a rural high school. *Talking Points* 16 (1), 26–31.

Gruenewald, D. 2003. The best of both worlds: A critical pedagogy of place. *Educational Researcher* 32 (4), 3–12.

Gusfield, J. R. 1986. *The symbolic crusade* (2d ed.). Urbana: University of Illinois Press.

Haas, T. 1990. Leaving home: Circumstances afflicting rural America during the last decade and their impact on public education. *Peabody Journal of Education* 67 (4), 7–28.

Haas, T., and P. Nachtigal. 1998. *Place value.* Charleston, W.Va.: ERIC Press.

Hall, S. 1997. The work of representation. In S. Hall, ed., *Representation: Cultural representations and signifying practices,* 13–74. London: Sage.

Hammersley, M., and P. Atkinson. 1995. *Ethnography: Principles in practice* (2d ed.). New York: Routledge.

Haymes, S. 1995. *Race, culture, and the city: A pedagogy for black urban struggle.* Albany: State University of New York Press.

Heminway, M. T. 2002. *Maine's disappearing youth: Implications of a declining youth population.* Augusta: University of Maine, Maine Educational Leadership Consortium.

Hoffman, J. 2001 (January 26). Students' fight has "racial overtones." *The* [Town] *Times,* A1–A2.

Johnson, J., and C. B. Howley. 2000. [Review of the book *The city and the country*]. *Journal of Research in Rural Education* 16 (2), 146–51.

Johnson, K. 2006. *Demographic trends in rural and small-town America.* Durham, N.H.: Carsey Institute.

Kalb, D. 2006. Uses of local knowledge. In R. Goodin and C. Tilly, eds., *The Oxford handbook of contextual political analysis,* 579–94. Oxford: Oxford University Press.

Kannapel, P. F., and A. J. DeYoung. 1999. The rural school problem in 1999: A review and critique of the literature. *Journal of Research in Rural Education* 15 (2), 67–79.

Kennedy, R. 2002. *Nigger: The strange career of a troublesome word.* New York: Pantheon Books.

Kiesling, S. 2001. Stances of whiteness and hegemony in fraternity men's discourse. *Journal of Linguistic Anthropology* 11 (1), 101–15.

Kimmel, M., and A. L. Ferber. 2006. "White men are this nation": Right-wing militias and the restoration of rural American masculinity. In H. Campbell, M. M. Bell, and M. Finney, eds., *Country boys: Masculinity and rural life,* 121–37. University Park: Penn State Press.

Kraack, A., and J. Kenway. 2002. Place, time, and stigmatized youthful identities: Bad boys in paradise. *Journal of Rural Studies* 18 (2), 145–55.

Kroskrity, P. 2004. Language ideologies. In A. Duranti, ed., *A companion to linguistic anthropology,* 496–517. Malden, Mass.: Blackwell.

Kurtz, M. 2006. Ruptures and recuperations of a language of racism in Alaska's rural/urban divide. *Annals of the Association of American Geographers* 96 (3), 601–21.

LeCouteur, A., and M. Augoustinos. 2001. The language of prejudice and racism. In M. Augoustinos and K. Reynolds, eds., *Understanding prejudice, racism, and social conflict,* 215–30. London: Sage.

Lefebvre, H. 1991. *The production of space* (D. Nicholson-Smith, trans.). Oxford: Blackwell.

Lipman, P. 2002. Making the global city, making inequality: The political economy and cultural politics of Chicago school policy. *American Educational Research Journal* 39 (2), 379–419.

Mayo, C. 2004. The tolerance that dare not speak its name. In M. Boler, ed., *Democratic dialogue in education: Troubling speech, disturbing silence.* New York: Peter Lang.

McCarthy, C. 1995. Multicultural policy discourses on racial inequality in American education. In R. Ng, P. Staton, and J. Scane, eds., *Anti-racism, feminism, and critical approaches to education,* 21–44. New York: Bergin and Garvey.

Miller, A. [1953] 1976. *The crucible: A play in four parts.* New York: Penguin.

Moore, R. M., III. 2001. Introduction. In R. M. Moore, III, ed., *The hidden America: Social problems in rural America for the twenty-first century,* 13–21. London: Associated University Presses.

Ozga, J. 2000. *Policy research in educational settings.* Buckingham: Open University Press.

Panelli, R. 2002. Young rural lives: Strategies beyond diversity. *Journal of Rural Studies* 18 (2), 113–22.

Peshkin, A. 1978. *Growing up American: Schooling and the survival of community.* Chicago: University of Chicago Press.

Pollock, M. 2004. Race bending: "Mixed" youth practicing strategic racialization in California. *Anthropology and Education Quarterly* 35 (1), 30–52.

Reeves, C. 2003. *Implementing the No Child Left Behind Act: Implications for rural schools and districts.* Naperville, Ill.: North Central Regional Educational Lab. (ERIC Document Reproduction Service No. ED475037.)

Riehl, C. J. 2000. The principal's role in creating inclusive schools for diverse students: A review of normative, empirical, and critical literature on the practice of educational administration. *Review of Educational Research* 70 (1), 55–81.

Ronkin, M., and H. E. Karn. 1999. Mock Ebonics: Linguistic racism in parodies of Ebonics on the Internet. *Journal of Sociolinguistics* 3 (3), 360–80.

Rosaldo, R. 1989. *Culture and truth.* Boston: Beacon.

Rural School and Community Trust. 2004 (January). *The devil is in the details: Rural-sensitive best practices for accountability under No Child Left Behind.* Washington, D.C.: Rural School and Community Trust.

Sassen, S. 1998. *Globalization and its discontents.* New York: The New Press.

Scollon, R., W. Tsang, D. Li, V. Yung, and R. Jones. 1998. Voice, appropriation, and discourse representation in a student writing task. *Linguistics and Education* 9 (3), 227–50.

Seidman, I. 1998. *Interviewing as qualitative research* (2d ed.). New York: Teachers College Press.

Silverstein, M. 2003. The whens and wheres—as well as hows—of ethnolinguistic recognition. *Public Culture* 15 (1), 531–57.

Smith, M. L., W. Heinecke, and A. J. Noble. 1999. Assessment policy and political spectacle. *Teachers College Record* 101 (2), 157–91.

Steinbeck, J. [1939] 1979. *The grapes of wrath.* New York: Penguin.

Tarca, K. 2005. Colorblind in control: The risks of resisting difference amid demographic change. *Educational Studies* 38 (2), 99–120.

Theobald, P. 1997. *Teaching the commons: Place, pride, and the renewal of community.* Boulder: Westview.

Thomas, M. 2005. "I think it's just natural": The spatiality of racial segregation at a U.S. high school. *Environment and Planning* A (37), 1233–48.

Thompson, P. B., and D. N. Kutach. 1990. Agricultural ethics in rural education. *Peabody Journal of Education* 67 (4), 131–53.

Tyson, A. S. 2005 (November 4). Youths in rural U.S. are drawn to military. *Washington Post,* A1.

Weis, L. 2003. Constructing the "other": Discursive renditions of white working-class males in high school. In M. Fine and L. Weis, eds., *Silenced voices and extraordinary conversations,* 68–87. New York: Teachers College Press.

4

FIELDS OF DISCOURSE:
A FOUCAULDIAN ANALYSIS OF SCHOOLING
IN A RURAL, U.S. SOUTHERN TOWN

Alecia Youngblood Jackson

Introduction

This research focuses on one particular school system in one particular rural place: Garner.[1] Garner is a small, seemingly "tight-knit" community in the southern United States. The residents of Garner have successfully constructed a "truth" about what it means to be educated in the rural South, and they take great pride in their accomplishments. Garner is a captivating place, ostensibly untouched by the globalizing world as the community holds on to traditional beliefs, values, and attitudes, which permeate the school system.

In this chapter, I am less interested in the "truth" of the romanticization and idealization of rural schooling in Garner and more drawn to how those ideals were (and continue to be) constructed, deployed, and circulated in discourse in a specific place. In particular, I am interested in how community members who are invested in Garner's school system produce their vision of schooling through their material, political, and cultural practices. Therefore, the work that I have undertaken in this chapter is a Foucauldian study of the discourse of rural schooling in Garner.

So why this framework, this approach to a study of discourse? I believe that such an analysis focuses attention on the contradictory ways in which local/community control and autonomy, which are often heralded as a "solution" to

---

1. All place and people names in this chapter are pseudonyms.

globalization (e.g., see Theobold and Wood; and Howley and Howley, in this volume), can be exclusionary and oppressive; this becomes important in my present analysis of Garner's institution of schooling. My analysis will show that globalizing trends compelled the members invested in the community into fierce resistance to structural, impositional threats to a rural identity. The point here is that community resistance to globalization can, in turn, limit the lives of the people whom that very resistance attempts to "protect." Discourses make visible the ways that values, beliefs, customs, and so on become normalized and normalizing in a community, and this chapter will show how discourses of rural schooling in Garner appear to be stable and unified—but only insofar as the community members are invested in sustaining those discourses. In Garner, the desire for perpetuation is grounded in the historical, yet it remains relevant as the community overtly organizes to resist global influences and effects through its control of schooling. A Foucauldian analysis of discourse reveals these complex intersections among power, identity, change, and community to show how they are imagined, idealized, and maintained.

Garner as a rural place is not unlike other rural places in the United States. The population is just under ten thousand, and the town is situated approximately sixty miles from a large metro area. The town of Garner lies within what is classified as a nonmetro county and is characterized by wide-open, expansive spaces that were previously agrarian; presently those spaces remain open but house isolated distribution centers rather than farms. The town has maintained its bucolic feel by curtailing development, tightening community connectedness, and limiting in- and out-migration patterns (the population growth has not changed significantly in the last thirty years)—all of which will be described later in this chapter. White people dominate the community as 75 percent of the population, with blacks and Hispanics evenly splitting the remaining 25 percent. My comparison of data from the last two government censuses shows that the Hispanic population doubled in the last ten years; Garner's town manager claims that Hispanics are drawn to Garner to work in the distribution centers and in the poultry plants in the neighboring county. The housing situation in Garner is a unique one that will be detailed later in this chapter, but it is important to understand for now that Garner's residential growth has been severely curtailed in recent decades. As a result, 70 percent of residents own their homes, while 30 percent rent. What is named the Watson Hills area of Garner houses almost the entire black population of about 1,200 people in dwellings ranging from mortgaged homes to neglected rental houses to public housing units. Alma Plantation, consisting of 245 apartments, is home to five hundred Hispanics—almost half the population living in Garner. The remaining Hispanic population is spread throughout other rental properties and in the single mobile home community. Ten percent of Garner residents live below the poverty level, which is about average for the state, and Garner boasts a 75 percent graduation rate from its schools, which is higher than the state average.[2] The K–12 school population is about two thousand, with 30 percent on free or reduced lunch. Of the students, 65 percent are white, 21 percent are Hispanic, and 14 percent are black (the largest number of Hispanic students are in the elementary grades). Elementary teachers whom I interviewed told me that in the 1999–2000 school year black students, for the first time in Garner history, became the smallest population of minorities in the school system.[3] The social characteristics of Garner provide a particular grounding for this analysis, especially in the intimate relationship between the desire for autonomy within/ against change and the preservation of an idealized image of Garner via its institution of school, including how this plays out with regard to identity categories (i.e., race, class, gender) and community responses to globalization.

With this demographic "picture" of Garner in mind, I now turn to the theoretical lens through which I analyze the emergence and maintenance of discourse. The questions that I address in this chapter are: "How does discourse function? Where is it to be found? How does it get produced and regulated? What are its social effects?" (Bové 1990, 55). I describe how a discourse of rural schooling functions in a particular place such as Garner; where this discourse is found (or where it becomes visible); and how a discourse of rural schooling in Garner affects the lives of people in the school system. To engage in these questions and this analysis, I use Michel Foucault's theories of discourse, strategies, and practices, which I explain in the next section.

Discourse, Strategies, and Practices

Michel Foucault (1980; 1972; 1978; 1979; 2000) believed that by reflecting certain values, discourses organize knowledges, practices, bodies, and emotions that produce certain conditions for living. In this way, discourses are regulated and regulating. Discourses are regulating in that they produce "acceptable" and "normal" rules that make possible certain activities, beliefs, and desires. In

2. All demographic data taken from the 2000 U.S. census. The graduation rate data is taken from local school source material that is provided to the state.

3. This interview data is supported by school records kept by the central office.

turn, discourses and their ensuing rules and regulations are regulated—or made visible—by the practices of people within discourse. Further, discourse enables certain knowledge about places and institutions. Discourse creates specific ways of being and acting in the world, and it shapes institutions (such as schools) "in which we largely make ourselves" (Bové 1990, 58).

In volume 1 of *The History of Sexuality,* Michel Foucault described the domain of nineteenth-century bourgeois sexuality as historically constructed and as an assemblage of a dispersed system of values, techniques of power, and specific discourses. To investigate the domain of sexuality, Foucault was not interested in whether people engage in sex, if prohibitions on sex are effective, or if there is one truth about sexuality. Instead, Foucault (1978) studied how sexuality was "put into discourse" by locating "the forms of power, the channels it takes, and the discourses it permeates in order to reach the most tenuous and individual modes of behavior" (11). In sum, Foucault studied how sexuality became situated as a problem of truth—how it has become something spoken about, who speaks about it and what they say, and the institutions that prompt and sustain such knowledge about sexuality. Similarly, my analysis is focused on how rural schooling became something to be protected, sustained, and controlled—and how people invested in schooling produced knowledge about rural schooling in Garner.

Foucault believed that discourses themselves could not be objects of investigation. That is, the object of investigation consists of the practices and strategies that *form* discourses. Strategies make certain discourses visible; they produce the rules and regulations of discourse, and the practices of people sustain or disrupt discourse and its strategies. This analytic approach therefore inquires into how discourses function, where they may be found, how they are produced and regulated, and what their social effects may be. For example, in volume 1 of *The History of Sexuality*, Foucault isolated four strategies that produced sexuality as an object of knowledge: (1) a hysterization of women's bodies (as sexualized, then pathologized, then socialized as a hysterical or nervous); (2) a pedagogization of children's sex (fight against early sexual activities, including masturbation); (3) a socialization of procreative behavior (duties of the conjugal couple to create future citizens for the state); and (4) a psychiatrization of perverse pleasures (anomalies, such as sodomy and pedophilia, from "normal" sexual behavior). Foucault argued that these four strategies produce sexuality as a historical construct and that these four strategies form a set of rules, knowledge, behaviors, beliefs—all of which provide the structural conditions that enable a discourse of sexuality.

I follow Foucault's analytic construct to focus on the history of strategies of Garner's residents that produce what can be called a discourse of rural school-ing. Just as Foucault identified four strategies that produced a discourse of sexuality, I name four strategies that emerged in my analysis of rural schooling: (1) a maintenance of tradition; (2) a privilege of access; (3) a unity in commu-nity; and (4) a control of public image. I elaborate on these strategies below; for now, I remain focused on the analytical processes of identification and definition.

Power/Knowledge Practices

In his own work, Foucault (1978) located strategies by examining historical documents and the practices of people. Strategies are animated by the practices of people within power/knowledge relationships. Foucault explained that it was in the institution of the "normal" family (i.e., the heterosexual family) that the four strategies listed above formed to deploy a discourse of sexuality. The fam-ily engaged in certain *practices* that anchored sexuality, closely monitoring and controlling it, thereby providing it with support. If sexual abnormalities appeared within "normal" families, then families enlisted doctors, priests, teachers, and psychiatrists for help. These abnormal sexualities within families incited the practice of seeking help in healing these abnormalities, yet these very practices further contributed to the deployment of sexuality. Rather than being censored or prohibited, sexuality was talked about, analyzed, and chan-neled into a network that governed certain social *practices*.

These practices were functions of power/knowledge. Again, I turn to Fou-cault to integrate his explanations of power, knowledge, and discourse to show how Garner residents' relations and practices were invested in producing a particular version of rural schooling. Foucault (1978) formulated a notion of power that is productive, forming a chain that relies on relations to advance, multiply, and branch out deeply into social networks. He was very clear in his assertion that power relations exist only when the field of possibilities is open and people may react to one another in various ways; that is, power becomes possible through the "moving substrate" of unequal, yet unstable, *local relations* (1994, 292). Power relations are specific and local to subjects who are in mutual relations with one another. Power, then, "is everywhere; not because it embraces everything, but because it comes from everywhere"; it is not a consol-idating and invincible unity or structure but a repetitious and self-producing effect of mobile, strategic practices and relations within particular social networks (1978, 93).

Knowledge becomes an effect of these strategic relations. Knowledge is an *activity* that produces subjects and the ways in which they interact within and against their social and material worlds. A knowing subject, then, is an acting subject; Garner residents' actions (ways of knowing and becoming in the world) are *local* reactions and responses, even struggles and resistances, and are embedded within specific relations of power. Therefore, power and knowledge constantly articulate each other in the practices of people.

When writing about the individual, Foucault thought that there was not a rational subject presiding over practices; the rationality of practices is found *in the relations in which they are inscribed* (Foucault 1978). That is, practices take on significance not for their truth value but for the ways in which they disrupt or sustain relations of power and advance knowledge. Therefore, Garner residents' practices become significant only when they preserve, perpetuate, or disrupt what it means to claim an identity of rural schooling. A power/knowledge practice, then, is a *responsive interpretation* of the situation at hand. One of my methodological moves in this present analysis involved identifying and isolating certain practices of the people of Garner, how they were exercised, *and* the historical conditions (many of them recent) that shaped their possibility and acceptance at a given time. Asking certain questions of identified power/knowledge practices helps to determine their significance. These questions do not assess whether practices are rational but, inversely, how rationality inscribes itself in practices (Foucault 2000, 230): What rationalities and needs are satisfied by certain practices? Why are such practices needed *now*? I explain this method in the following section.

Methods and Data

To conduct an analysis of a discourse of rural schooling, I examine the social, cultural, and material practices of the people who are invested in the community. That is, as Foucault looked to the institution of the *family* as the site of strategies and practices that anchored and supported *sexuality*, I look primarily to the institution of the *community* to see how strategies formed to deploy a discourse of rural schooling. Strategies combine power and knowledge within discourse to produce certain domains (e.g., sexuality or rural schooling) as objects of knowledge. For example, as Foucault analyzed, the strategy of a hysterization of women's bodies produced particular knowledge about women within a discourse of sexuality. For my analysis, I use the term strategies as Foucault did, and I differentiate strategies from practices. I refer to *strategies* as formations that organize and deploy discourse, and I use *practices* to signify the daily activities and behaviors of people.

How rural schooling was put into discourse relies on the practices of people; it does not emerge out of nowhere. To identify discourse and its rules and regulations of rural schooling in Garner, I used an ascending analysis by first focusing on the significance of the community members' practices. During the course of a yearlong ethnography, I collected interview data, observational data, and document data. I interviewed (formally and informally) community members, parents, students, teachers, and school officials about the school system in Garner. I observed and took field notes (Wolcott 1995) on the following: (1) how parents, teachers, community members, and local businesses supported the high school (and what activities they most supported); (2) how the high school represented itself to the community; (3) the rhetoric of all sorts of "texts" in the high school such as the morning announcements, bulletin boards, the school Web site, and the current yearbook and monthly newsletters; and (4) my observations of and interviews with students in the senior class at Garner High (focusing on students who had attended Garner Town Schools since kindergarten). Additionally, to understand how a discourse of rural schooling was historically produced and regulated, I conducted an analysis of these extant public documents that were housed in Garner Town Schools' Central Office: Board of Education meeting minutes (1968–present), high school yearbooks (1949–present), and scrapbooks containing county newspaper articles about Garner Town Schools (1975–present). These interviews, field notes, and document data revealed not only how discourses enable practices but also how practices advance and condition discourse.

These data allowed me to construct the analytic categories that I am also calling the strategic conditions that enabled a discourse of rural schooling in Garner. These four strategies are the following: (1) *a maintenance of traditions* (doing things the way they have always been done for the sake of tradition); (2) *a privilege of access* (access to certain aspects of education for some students and not others by virtue of race, class, gender, sexuality, and ability); (3) *a unity in community* (the ostensibly seamless connections among school, family, and community); and (4) *a control of public image* (presenting a certain, unified image to the public). A discourse of rural schooling in Garner combines normalization, entitlement, control, self-identity, and surveillance in specific ways that organize knowledges, practices, bodies, and emotions into certain conditions that produce and regulate an identity unique to its place.

Because space is limited for this chapter, I focus on only one part of my data and analysis, pointing out historical key events (i.e., conditions), in genealogical fashion, that enabled a discourse of rural schooling in Garner. I rely primarily on historical and contemporary documents (named above) and observational data to present my interpretation, though I do include some interview data where relevant.[4] And though I use the strategic conditions as analytic categories, the descriptions are not contained. Instead, the descriptions are meant to show how these conditions intersect, combine, and fracture to produce discourse. The formation and maintenance of discourse is a spiraling process that allows conditions to overlap, gain momentum, and sometimes fall apart. My documenting this process will hopefully reveal this cyclical character.

1874–1974: The Formation of Discourse

The first one hundred years of Garner's school system involved many community practices that served to shape an emerging discourse of rural schooling. I will condense them here and then discuss their significant formation to describe a discourse of rural schooling in Garner. These social and cultural practices were: (1) a local vote to sever the relationship with other schools in the large county system, thereby making Garner an independent school; (2) the selection of school officials by the mayor rather than by democratic vote; (3) the strict segregation and then subsequent integration of schools, much resisted by community members; and (4) the funding of four new school buildings on land donated by the owner of the local tannery.

What was constructed as *maintaining tradition* in the early years of Garner schools was establishing and preserving independence from Olivett County. Community members voted to break from Olivett County in 1912, and the voters continued to refuse consolidation through the years. Although referendums came up in 1956 and 1974 on the issue of consolidating the Garner school system with that of Olivett County, Garner voters rejected consolidation each time, and the town remained committed to maintaining and operating its independent school system. While the members of the board of education were

4. For interview and other ethnographic data that is used for the latter half of this present genealogy and is beyond the scope of this chapter, see Jackson (2008).

appointed by the mayor and the town commissioners from 1912 until 1970, after
1970 community voters elected four BOE members and three town commissioners whose platform was to sustain the tradition of independence from Olivett
County. Further, the town commission chair automatically serves as the chair
of the school board, rounding out the five-member board and keeping tightly
woven the relationship between the town and the school system.

A *privilege of access* formed as a discursive strategy of rural schooling in
Garner in these early years. The citizens of Garner wanted to keep local control
over education, thereby monitoring who had access to their schools. Establishing independence from Olivett County ensured Garner's ability to provide a
school system solely for its own residents. In later years, when the Thornton
School was built (as the "colored" school), the strategy of a privilege of access
circulated to deploy further a discourse of rural schooling in Garner. The
Thornton School was located within the Watson Hills area of Garner, an area
that, at the time, was described as the poor, "colored" side of town. Once the
schools were integrated in the early 1970s and the Thornton School became
Garner Middle School (GMS), a road was built on the west side of Watson Hills
that circumvented the area and gave whites easy access from "their" side of
town. This decision and action by the BOE and Garner residents further accen-
tuated a strategy of access: whites could get to the integrated Garner Middle/
Thornton Building via the familiar white-trodden area of town, rather than
accessing GMS through the "colored" neighborhoods of Watson Hills.

The strategy of a *unity of community* became visible through the schools'
being deeply embedded in the cultural practices of the community and functioning to perpetuate the values of that community. Establishing and maintaining independence from Olivett County seemingly built unity among
community members and a sense of ownership of the school system. That one
of the town commissioners automatically holds the seat as the chair of the
board of education is a practice (and a tradition) of unifying the town, the
community, and the schools.

A *control of public image* is an additional strategy formed to deploy a discourse of rural schooling in Garner, which I discuss below. This control of
public image was formed by Garner school officials' desire to control physicalities, appearances, and public images through BOE policies and the construction
of state-of-the art school facilities. This control of public image did not emerge
from nowhere; it was born from and is intersected by the strategies of tradition,
community, and access.

A Control of Public Image: Further Incitement to Discourse

In the thirty years after integration in Garner, policies and practices of community members continued to produce a particular discourse of rural schooling. The year of 1969 marked a certain girl's disappearance from Garner High School's yearbook. The spring 1968 yearbook showed this white adolescent girl in her ninth-grade year as a trumpet player in the marching band, a point guard on the basketball team, a member of the Beta Club, a class officer, and first runner-up in the Miss Garner beauty pageant. This girl gave birth in December of her sophomore year, and she was not pictured in the spring 1969 yearbook. She completed her high school diploma at an adult education program a one-hour drive away. She would rather have remained at Garner High with her two older sisters and lifelong friends, but in those years before Title IX, Garner's policy on the education of pregnant girls was as follows: "Any pregnant student must withdraw from school immediately. Any pregnant student not reporting such pregnancy will be dropped and will not be eligible for readmission."[5] Because she had given birth, she was forced out of her school community, and her talents were deemed irrelevant and unimportant. This policy affected five girls between 1968 and 1971.

This policy would be amended three years later in 1972, following a resolution of the state board of education. The Garner BOE changed the wording of its policy, but not its effect, which was to remove the abject teen girl from her educational environment, on which she was apparently a bad influence. The revised policy involved "*asking* the girl to drop out of school as soon as it is known that she is pregnant" and "*encouraging* the girl to enroll in the Adult Education Program" in a neighboring county.[6] A new addition to the policy provided an option for the pregnant girl to continue her education in the system through a home study plan organized by her teachers, the counselor, and the principal. She would complete the same assignments and take the same final exam as other students in the class, but she would be out of sight. These policies were to be enforced with "compassion."[7]

In 1975, the Garner BOE "decided to allow pregnant students to go to school as long as possible"[8] and created a more formal statement the following year, one that was to be aligned with the federal Title IX nondiscrimination policy.

5. *Handbook for School Administration,* Garner Public Schools, 1968.
6. Garner Public Schools, board of education meeting minutes, February 1972.
7. Ibid.
8. Garner Public Schools, board of education meeting minutes, August 1975.

The BOE policy on pregnant girls would be revised again in 1987 (the one that currently holds). The current policy states that pregnant girls are *eligible for* (not *entitled to*) "enrollment in the general educational and occupational programs."[9] This statement is followed by the provision that the superintendent has the authority to remove pregnant girls from their regular classes and to assign them, within the regular daytime educational program, to "special programs" such as "prenatal care" and "child care."[10] These regulations sadly perpetuated the pervasive idea that pregnant girls should not have been (or should not be) visible in mainstream education at Garner High School.

I detail this historical condition because it is illustrative of the importance of physicalities, appearances, and public image to Garner schools in the 1970s, 1980s, and 1990s. In those three decades, Garner school officials proposed and community members approved various bond referendums to construct state-of-the art, multimillion-dollar facilities. Garner school officials, who were also town council members, formed an industrial development board (IDB) to attract new business to the area (while at the same time curtailing residential growth). Yet the IDB denied access to "big-box business" (e.g., Wal-Mart) and other chain stores; the IDB, keeping the funding of the school system in mind, recruited only particular types of business: ones that would increase the tax base for funding the school system and that would provide employment for Garner's residents, yet businesses that would not threaten the local goods economy. As a result of the IDB's efforts, six large companies built manufacturing plants and distribution centers on the outskirts of Garner's rural area. The town remained a hub of industry (as it had in the early twentieth century as a center for textile production), and local tax revenue from these prosperous businesses helped to finance the school system.[11]

Another significant practice involving community members occurred throughout the 1970s, when a flux of new teachers were hired, teachers who would remain in the system for their entire careers, including a few teachers who had graduated from Garner High in the late 1960s (the current superintendent graduated from Garner High in 1969 and began teaching at Garner Middle School in 1974). This tradition would continue as graduates of Garner schools

9. *Garner Public Schools Board Policies,* December 1987.
10. Ibid.
11. All of Garner's property tax collections are used to operate the school system. The town itself operates from monies derived from its profitable utilities sold to contiguous counties, beer and wine tax, business licenses, and sanitary fees (personal interview with the Garner town manager, March 18, 2002).

returned to teach (or work as staff) alongside their former teachers. Further, as teachers remained in the school system for twenty years or more, they began teaching multiple generations of families.

These decades also saw the construction of four new school buildings, with a state program (based on demographics) funding more than half the cost. The current Garner High School was designed for 650 students and cost eight million dollars. The school sits on thirty-five acres, and the circular drive that leads to Garner High's front entrance is paved with cobblestone. Those who pass through the front glass doors and into the tiled lobby are greeted by a forty-foot wall lined with glass trophy cases, packed with literary and athletic awards won by Garner students since the 1930s. One of the most impressive classrooms is the pre-engineering lab, where (mostly male) students learn about solid modeling computer design, digital circuitry, radio communication, and principles of robotics. Three other school buildings—middle, elementary, and the academy—were built across the street from Garner High, with each housing no more than four hundred students. It is important to note that the back of the new Garner Middle School's property line meets up with the front yards of black families who live in Watson Hills, one of the most racially segregated areas of Garner. City officials closed Poplar Street, which runs between the black residents' homes and the site of the new Garner Middle School, purportedly to decrease traffic in the residential area (and to redirect and restrict traffic away from the black community to the front entrance on Ashburn Avenue).

Through the construction of these new facilities, the community was able to maintain the tradition of the intimacy of a "small neighborhood school" that had characterized the rural system since its inception. The roomy, modern school facilities have enabled the Garner BOE to implement a policy of selectively admitting nonresident students to Garner Public Schools under certain conditions. The school's superintendent described those conditions as follows: (1) the student has (and maintains) good grades; (2) the student not be (or become) a discipline problem; and (3) the student's family can afford the two-thousand-dollar-per-year tuition to attend Garner Public Schools.[12] These three conditions are made public on the school's Web page for the application process. The superintendent further explained that the demand of outsiders "wanting in" results in the BOE having to turn down more than half of the applications it receives, admitting no more than ten students (K–12) per academic year. Because the BOE does not want the Garner School System to be

12. Per-pupil expenditure was $9,069 for the 2005–6 school year.

viewed as an "alternative school," the BOE (including the superintendent) reviews each student's application very carefully and admits only the "cream of the crop": students who can positively and successfully contribute to the academic and extracurricular programs offered by Garner and whose parents intend to be involved in the school community.[13]

The allure of this place is constructed by the members of the community who value certain aspects of it and who participate in the perpetuation of these values: a unity of community and school; a family-like atmosphere; and pride and excellence in its facilities. These are the values that identify the town of Garner, that permeate the halls of its schools, that presumably represent the community's needs, and that are claimed to make Garner schools "work." A winning tradition in sports and the fine arts also gives the community pride in its school system. The money that the town council and taxpayers contribute to the facilities and programs makes visible their pride in the school system and gives Garner a certain status in Olivett County and in the northeastern part of the state.

Discursive Practices, Power/Knowledge, and Schooling

Over the course of 130 years, a discourse of rural schooling in Garner was enabled through the strategies of a maintenance of tradition, a privilege of access, a unity in community, and a control of public image. Above, I have described the cultural and material practices of the community members who have made possible, sustained, and elaborated the discourse. Here, I turn to consider how this discourse produces certain conditions for the lives of people who are invested in the schools, including those students who attend Garner Public Schools.

For more than a century, community voters continued the tradition of reelecting BOE members and town commissioners multiple times, and these government representatives were always prominent citizens whose families had been in Garner for generations (no "nonnative" has been elected to town government positions in Garner, and commissioners typically leave their service through retirement or death). More often than not, candidates for reelection run unopposed, and there has been only one major upset in the reelection of a town commissioner: a former Garner schoolteacher and native of Garner, the

13. Personal interview with the superintendent of Garner Public Schools, June 19, 2002.

first woman elected to the town commission, ousted the incumbent male who had served on the commission for the previous ten years. Illustrating the intense protection of tradition in Garner is the fact that the current chair of the BOE has served on the town commission (and, off and on, as the BOE chair) since 1975. Two of the current BOE members are former K–12 students of Garner Town Schools. The significance of the length, stability, and identity of certain commissioners' tenure is that it enables the commission to keep consistent the vision of Garner. And that a town commissioner is also the chair of the BOE keeps the town government in complete command of the school system. No decision about the school system can be made without approval from a member of the town commission.

The town commission keeps Garner small and contributes to the maintenance of the town's rural traditions. While Garner town officials worked to draw industry to the town, thereby broadening the tax base but not requiring an increase in public services, they maintained the traditional vision of keeping what Garner commissioners call its "rural feel"[14] by curtailing the amount of land zoned for housing development. Further, the building permits issued in the last twenty-five years have been for single-family housing only; no new apartment complexes have been constructed since two (the only two in Garner) were built in the late 1970s. Currently, new housing development is altogether prohibited within Garner's town limits. The town has restricted all residential development in Garner so that the schools' population remains small (as tradition would have it), yet the town officials continue to work to attract industry to the area so that the tax base can fortify the school system. This *intentionality* of exclusion-based residential restrictions is grounded in the desires of Garner officials. I interviewed Hilary Brock, the adult daughter of Pete Brock, who has served on the town commission and the board of education since 1975; she had this to say about her father's tenure as a public official:

> Daddy could see the future. He knew in the '70s and '80s that if we [Garner] built a bunch of subdivisions, or even apartment buildings, then our schools would get too big. He didn't want that. So he and the other commissioners turned down requests to build anything but distribution centers. He knew that if our schools got too big, we would lose what is special about Garner. You know, the way we can compete with the bigger

14. This identity is repeatedly used by Garner elected officials in public documents, such as board of education minutes, newspapers, community speeches, and political platforms dating from 1972 to 2002.

schools because we have the best facilities. And how the students never change. They are always kids of people who live right here in Garner, who have lived here all their lives. Daddy wanted Garner to always have a family feel. He didn't want outsiders to come in and change everything.[15]

Therefore, the "face" of Garner—its demographic identity—is tightly controlled and surveilled by the town commissioners and BOE members, who are interested in maintaining a certain demographic (i.e., white, middle-class, high-achieving students, high parental involvement) for the schools. While this control has been effective historically, recent years have seen an increase in the Hispanic population in Garner—particularly in the elementary grades. Despite this trend, Garner officials were not, at the time of this study, responding to these changing demographics in any of their structural decisions regarding zoning needs for a population that is causing residential rental spaces to burst at the seams. And though the school population is growing slightly, the BOE had not reacted with ESL programs or community support for this new need. This dynamic illustrates Foucault's notion of power as not simply a force of domination that is stable and outside of social relations. Power, within this rural discourse, functioned as a relation that constantly threatened the meaning and identity of rural schooling and its traditions; however, even if a changing demographic challenged the coherence of rural schooling, there is no guarantee that people's practices, which sustain the discourse, will immediately change. In fact, it seemed as if "change" simply caused Garner residents to hold more tightly to their values.

Teachers and students sustained a version of rural tradition as well. Many teachers (and support staff) were students of Garner Public Schools, and they return to work there because it is a "special place" and because they support the district's vision. Their return helps to maintain the traditions of a rural schooling, and their return gives the community a sense of continuity, unity, safety, and care. Community members and parents of students in the schools believe the strength of the school lies in the teachers' knowledge of the students' families and backgrounds. Teachers who were also students at Garner serve as a sort of continuous surveillance system, where teachers are bound by the values of the community to keep a close watch on students—in not only physical ways but also cultural. A mother of a Garner teenager (who was also a Garner student herself) told me, "I like that my son's teachers were my teachers. I

15. Personal interview with Hilary Brock, December 1, 2001.

know that they would call me at home if Brad were getting off-track. And I know that they share my Christian values, so if he's not acting Christian at school, I'll know about it. I always knew not to act up at school, because I knew my teachers would call my mama. And that hasn't changed."

Most of these teachers are highly visible in the community, so their surveillance extends beyond the walls of the classroom: they also shop, attend church, and raise their own families in Garner. The spaces of teachers' surveillance seem to be extensive in Garner. And while it would be difficult to argue that close, caring relationships can be beneficial to students, I contend that this surveillance had specific purposes in a Foucauldian sense: to use surveillance as a form of panoptical, social control (Foucault 1979). Garner students learn to internalize—and normalize—that they are always being watched, so they learn to discipline themselves in anticipation of being disciplined. In this process, Garner students also learn to conform to the rules of discourse, so that they take them as "common sense." In turn, if the rules and regulations of a discourse are internalized and normalized by its subjects (i.e., Garner students), then Garner students may be less willing to contest what they come to believe as normal and true (thus using their own social and material practices to sustain the discourse).

A privilege of access is another strategy that deployed a discourse of a rural schooling in Garner, a strategy that formed through the decisions and practices of people in the community. Town officials controlled the residential development in Garner by zoning residential areas for particular types of housing development (e.g., zoning for subdivisions rather than apartment buildings), thereby also controlling who those residents would be. The town's prohibition of any new residential development in Garner is also a means of controlling access to the schools (no new development means no new students). The BOE does admit nonresident, tuition-paying students to Garner schools, but access is granted only to particular types of students who are smart, successful, middle-class, and well-behaved. It is worth noting that every one of the fifty-three nonresident students formally admitted by the BOE in the years from 1992 (the advent of the policy) through 2002 (the year of this study) were white and middle-class.[16] This significant fact further points to the value-laden aspect of access and its strategy to control and normalize who "gets in" and who "stays out."

The political decisions and practices surrounding the construction of Garner

16. Garner Public Schools, board of education meeting minutes, 1992–2002.

schools also contribute to the strategy of access that conditions the discourse. The Garner community invested much of its money and enthusiasm into building state-of-the art schools that instilled a sense of pride, independence, ownership, and excellence in students, teachers, and community. Despite these stately facilities, access remains an *uneven* privilege. The strategy of a privilege of access as it intersects with gender is made visible through the privileging of male athletics in the Garner School System. Boys have access to more opportunities for participation in sports programs (seven teams for boys versus four teams for girls). In the spring of 2002, the traditional celebration of the football team's state championship permeated the school and intruded on nonathletic events, including the spring variety show in the Fine Arts Center. The Field House was constructed to privilege boys' athletics; the building has no amenities for girls' exclusive use (e.g., separate showers), and girls on sports teams at Garner do not use the facility for working out or preparing for a competition. While these are obvious Title IX violations, Garner's principal justifies these infringements by saying, "The boys' football team is our bread and butter around here. Everyone comes out to the games on Friday nights. They paid for our stadium. They paid for that fieldhouse."[17] The strategy of a privilege of access enables girls to construct a certain knowledge of themselves as valued (or not) by the school system in a particular way and sends a distinct message about girls' entitlements in Garner.

A privilege of access also intersects with gender through Garner's BOE policy on pregnant girls. Though the policy was revised to be in accordance with the law, it is still an unfair, if not dangerous, response to Title IX. The current policy states that the superintendent can remove a pregnant girl from her regular classes and assign her to attend courses in prenatal and child care. What is not considered in this BOE policy is that pregnant girls do not have access to these specific courses at Garner High because they are not currently (nor have they ever been) offered. Further, these courses, as part of a mandated "special program" that is traditionally vocational in nature, could potentially *replace* courses that pregnant girls need for advanced placement, honors, or college-prep graduation requirements, thereby potentially restricting pregnant and parenting teen girls' access to higher education. The BOE's and school officials' traditional practice of limiting a pregnant and parenting teen girls' education shows that the schools support a particular type of access to education for these girls; these policies do not apply to parenting teen boys. Nowhere in the policy

17. Personal interview with Garner High School principal, May 2002.

does it state that boys may also be forced into special programs. In addition, at the time of this study, one boy athlete, who was also the father of a baby born to a Garner teen girl, continued to play on the spring baseball team and was not required to change his class schedule. The teen mother was excluded from cheerleading, an extracurricular activity that she had participated in for the previous three years. She was also required to drop honors English for what she was told were "attendance reasons": she missed six weeks of class while she was home after her baby was born, even though she kept up with her assignments with the help of a homeschool tutor.

Unfair access is evident in the city of Garner's decision to reroute traffic to the new Garner Middle School from Garner Highway by closing off Poplar Street, which winds through the black community of Watson Hills, thus denying blacks easy access to GMS and Garner Highway—not to mention forcing drivers away from a black community, rendering it invisible to outsiders. The closing of Poplar Street forces a specific access, and it inconveniences Watson Hills residents who need quick access to Garner Highway, the central thoroughfare of Garner City. Even more significant than this material access is a highly *symbolic* access as it is bound to race and Garner's obsession with public image.

The strategy of controlling Garner's public image through its school system is enabled by the practices of people who want to project a certain image of rural schooling to the public (to Garner's residents as well as to outsiders). As an independent school system, Garner schools are burdened with the responsibility of showing that "bigger isn't always better." Garner residents have traditionally prided themselves on financing modern, state-of-the art facilities and consistently hosting regional and state tournaments to "show off" their schools. The zoning restrictions on multifamily housing in the town of Garner is a practice that controls the type of affordable housing—and therefore class of people—who publicly represent Garner. And finally, the BOE's policy on pregnant and parenting teens (which could have the effect of limiting a girls' education) and its policy on admitting certain nonresident students are practices focused on removing, or keeping out, those students who do not conform to the desired image of students in Garner.

The strategy of *a unity in community* continued to form throughout the decades to advance a discourse of rural schooling in Garner. Community members voted to build modern facilities, and many turn out in droves to support the schools' athletic teams (primarily the football team). The "place to be" on fall Friday nights is the Garner Panthers football game, regardless of where they play. Residential development restrictions keep the community and schools small, contributing to the "rural feel" of Garner. Multiple generations of families live in Garner, attend Garner schools, and work in the school system itself—traditions that contribute to a sense of unity in community. Many teachers work for Garner Town Schools for decades, former students return to teach and work, and many teachers not native to Garner choose to live there as community members. Therefore, teachers have a connection—oftentimes a multigenerational connection—to Garner. They may know their students' parents (they either taught them or went to school with them or another family member), and parents want their children to attend Garner because of this close-knit feeling. In sum, town and school officials, teachers, parents, students, and residents unite within relations of power to produce a particular knowledge about quality rural schooling in Garner—what they describe as safe, caring, and family-like.

Conclusion: Exclusion

The analysis of power and discourse in Garner is meant to reveal how the institution of schooling, which may be a site of powerful local control and autonomy, can also exist as a structure of exclusion. My main thesis here is that rural schools cannot always escape the power effects of their own resistance to globalizing trends. While rural places may yearn to hang onto their traditional identities, doing so can be dangerous to people in the community and schools. The desire for control can lead to power effects that can be damaging to the ways in which students learn to value themselves and their communities.

Garner is a conservative community that privileges white middle-class athletic boys over others. The pervasive celebration of the all-male football team, the admission of (only) white middle-class nonresident students, the discriminatory policies on pregnant and parenting teens—all these practices point to the unity of a *certain type* of community, limited to connecting only with those of the same gender, race, and class. There is no completely unified community in Garner, but rather small groups of diverse others that are segregated into the haves and have-nots. The unity in community that seems to exist in Garner is more of a mystique that silences and erases difference, a community that is exclusionary and imperial rather than unifying of all people (Brown 1995). The larger community in Garner is not *equally accessed* by all people. This is not to say that community is impossible, but that a *certain type* of community that erases difference may not be desirable to those who get subsumed in such an exclusionary community, one that assumes unity among certain types of people by essentializing identity and denying or even distorting difference. Therefore, this discursive analysis of Garner's rural schooling reveals that the idea of unity in community is a fiction—a constructed condition of discourse.

The preceding description and interpretation of the formation and deployment of a discourse of rural schooling in Garner illustrates that people's practices are always conditioned by certain rules and codes within a specific "social, economical, geographical, or linguistic area" (Foucault 1980, 177). Garner's community members' practices constructed particular knowledge and contributed to the conditions that enabled a discourse of rural schooling. As Chris Weedon (1997, 40) wrote, "Discourses represent political interests and in consequence are constantly vying for status and power." Garner's constructed discursive identity is indeed a powerful one; it provides specific conditions for the possibilities of living as well as for who or what is welcomed, and who or what is not, in Garner Public Schools. Town and school officials, teachers, parents, students, and residents united within relations of power to produce knowledge about rural schooling in Garner.

This chapter offers a brief, rather than comprehensive, glimpse into how power and knowledge combine, within discourse, to produce place identity. What is important about this type of discursive analysis is its emphasis not only on knowledge about rural schooling itself, but also on how that knowledge was formed, and how that knowledge functions within discourse to open up or limit the lives of people. In this way, meanings of "community" can be critiqued and reimagined. Such an analysis also moves the focus from individuals (such as students who "fail" within certain places) to a rigorous tracing of how problems become possible within discourse. For example, within a discourse of rural schooling in Garner, certain expectations emerged as a result of values, beliefs, practices, politics, and so on. Those who do not "fit" into those discourses run the risk of being cast aside. Yet if those structural conditions are exposed as oppressive, overly regulatory, and panoptical, then perhaps new meanings of rural schooling can be rearticulated.

References

Bové, P. A. 1990 Discourse. In F. Lentricchia, ed., *Critical terms for literary study*, 55–58. Chicago: University of Chicago Press.

Brown, R. M. 1995. The Furies Collective. In P. A. Weiss and M. Freeman, eds., *Feminism and community*. Philadelphia: Temple University Press.

Foucault, M. 1972. *The archeology of knowledge and the discourse on language* (A. M. Sheridan Smith, trans.). New York: Pantheon Books.

———. 1978. *The history of sexuality.* Vol. 1, *An introduction* (R. Hurley, trans.). New York: Vintage Books.

———. 1979. *Discipline and punish: The birth of the prison* (A. Sheridan, trans.). New York: Vintage Books.

———. 1980. *Power/knowledge: Selected interviews and other writings: 1972–1977* (L. Marshall, C. Gordon, J. Mepham, and K. Soper, trans.; C. Gordon, ed.). New York: Pantheon Books.

———. 1994. *Ethics: Subjectivity and truth* (R. Hurley, trans.; P. Rabinow, ed.). New York: The New Press.

———. 2000. *Essential works of Foucault, 1954–1984.* Vol. 3, *Power* (R. Hurley et al., trans.; P. Rabinow, ed.). New York: The New Press.

Jackson, A. Y. 2008. Power and pleasure in ethnographic homework: Producing a recognizable ethics. *Qualitative Research* 8 (1), 37–51.

Weedon, C. 1997. *Feminist practice and poststructural theory* (2d ed). Oxford: Blackwell.

Wolcott, H. F. 1995. *The art of fieldwork.* Walnut Creek, Calif.: AltaMira Press.

2

PLACING EDUCATION

5

THE CHALLENGES OF STUDENT TRANSIENCY FOR RURAL SCHOOLS AND COMMUNITIES IN THE ERA OF NO CHILD LEFT BEHIND

Kai A. Schafft, Kieran M. Killeen, and John Morrissey

> We just enrolled a girl within the last two weeks and she sat
> in that chair and, you know, she was teary-eyed and she
> said, "I have been to four other school districts this year."
> Why all the moves? What is the story? Sometimes they tell
> you and sometimes they don't. . . . She is saying to me,
> "I just cannot do this anymore. I just do not want to do
> this anymore." She is flat out telling me, "We will not be
> here another month. I think we are moving."
>
> —MIDDLE SCHOOL GUIDANCE COUNSELOR

Introduction: Social and Economic Change in the Rural United States

Local school teachers and district administrators call them the "Route 51 kids," after the state road that runs east–west through this part of rural upstate New York.[1] Described as "bouncing" or "ping-ponging" back and forth across area districts, transient school children tend to be disproportionately low-income, low-achieving, and high-need students who may over the course of several years repeatedly enroll, withdraw, and enroll again in the same district. While veteran educators joke about advising new teachers to enter student names in their rosters in pencil, there is a deeper and more disconcerting awareness that these students represent the youngest members of an increasingly dislocated

---

1. All place names have been changed to protect respondent anonymity.

population—and a window into the pronounced social and economic change affecting much of the rural United States.

This chapter uses a case study of poverty and student transiency to discuss the convergence of three trends affecting rural schools and the children, families, and communities they serve: (1) macro-level changes in the structure of labor markets and economies in rural areas, especially those areas historically dependent on manufacturing as an economic base; (2) the growing and entrenched degree of poverty in many rural communities, of which student transiency and the chronic residential mobility of low-income families is a particular symptom; and (3) the push for school accountability with standardized testing used as the primary metric to assess school performance. We argue in this chapter that these three trends are related and, to some extent, mutually reinforcing. Together they place many rural children, families, schools, and communities at disproportionate social and economic disadvantage. We discuss each of these trends, tracing the linkages among them, then explore how they are manifested locally through a case study of poverty and student transiency in a set of economically declining, postindustrial communities in rural upstate New York.

Globalization, Neoliberalism, and Economic Change in U.S. Rural Communities

The story of the rural United States in the last several decades has been one of transitioning economies, particularly as driven by neoliberal policies that have lifted international barriers to trade and production, yet often have undermined local economies and created new uncertainties for rural communities (Lyson and Falk 1993; Struthers and Bokemeier 2003). Neoliberalism generally refers to a set of political and economic assumptions regarding the role of markets and the creation of wealth (Bourdieu 1998; Finlayson et al. 2005; Gill 1994; Harvey 2005). The neoliberal position asserts that the most efficient and socially optimal mode of resource allocation is through the free market, largely unfettered by governmental regulation. Under neoliberal thought, governmental oversight is ideally confined to guaranteeing property rights and legal contracts and, when appropriate, instituting measures to increase economic efficiencies, such as policies encouraging privatization. All these conditions help reduce the economic frictions of space to promote a global system of production, distribution, consumption, and wealth generation (Harvey 2005; Hursh

2007; Patel 2007; Robbins 2004). Neoliberal assumptions are further embodied and enacted by supranational governance bodies such as the World Trade Organization and the International Monetary Fund, and by global trade agreements such as the North American Free Trade Agreement that attempt to increase international trade and economic growth through disciplinary structures intended to prevent the violation of trade agreements (McMichael 2003; Patel and McMichael 2004).

While proponents argue that neoliberalism on balance creates greater economic growth and prosperity (Sachs 2005), for rural areas the outcomes have been mixed at best, and in many cases have meant job loss and manufacturing shutdowns in response to lower costs of global outsourcing or offshore production. Agriculturally based communities have experienced the disappearance of the family farm as forces of consolidation, increasing debt, and falling commodity prices have knocked smaller farmers out of operation, and production has become increasingly dictated by multinational agribusinesses (Patel 2007).

For many rural places this economic restructuring has resulted in out-migration, labor market contraction, the prevalence of low-paid service-sector employment contributing to rising inequality, increased levels of household-level poverty, and economic insecurity (Collins and Quark 2006; Glasmeier and Salant 2006; Lobao, Brown, and Moore 2003; Massey, Sanchez, and Behrman 2006; McGranahan 2003; O'Hare and Savage 2006; Shulman 2005). These changes have additional secondary effects including reductions in housing values and revenues available to local governments in the form of property tax, decreased disposable income for local residents, and closure of locally owned businesses (Eberts and Hart 1999).

Rural areas are particularly vulnerable in part because their local economies generally are less diversified, and residents tend to have lower levels of education and other human capital assets (Falk and Lobao 2003; Hobbs 1992; Lichter, McLaughlin, and Cornwell 1995). Between 1997 and 2003 more than 1.5 million rural workers employed in industries that had been the mainstay of rural economies lost their jobs (Glasmeier and Salant 2006). Demographic trends in upstate New York reflect these broader changes. Between 1990 and 2002 over 1.7 million people left the region, while only 1.3 million people moved in. But nearly 30 percent of these new residents were in fact incarcerated within the state and federal penitentiary system (Pendall 2003)—long noted as one of the few "growth industries" for the rural United States (Fitchen 1991).

These economic policies have been simultaneously coupled with the dismantling of social safety nets for vulnerable populations. Arguably the most visible sign of this was the 1996 welfare reform legislation known as the Personal Responsibility and Work Opportunities Reconciliation Act. Embedded within its very name is the assumption that poverty and economic disadvantage are largely, if not wholly, within the power of the individual to address through greater personal accountability, increased labor market attachment, nuclear family formation, and the reduction or elimination of children born out of wedlock. This bill did not recognize the significant structural barriers that prevent upward mobility for the poorest Americans (Hays 2003; Rank 2005; Shipler 2005). As Zimmerman and Hirschl note, "Welfare reform represents yet another escalation of market reliance, demonstrating an unparalleled experiment in self-reliance to provide for the needy" (2003, 364). As such, it also represents a new level of vulnerability for poor children and their families living in areas with declining economies and, therefore, fewer employment prospects.

No Child Left Behind in the Context of Rural Restructuring

No Child Left Behind is just boiled down to one thing about education—you had better have those test scores or else your district is going to suffer. I mean that is clear . . . the basic [gist] of No Child Left Behind is that everybody comes out of a Xerox machine, [that] we are all the same. Well, we are not.

—SPECIAL EDUCATION TEACHER

These changes in social and economic policies have taken place concurrent with sweeping educational reforms that have had profound effects on the substance and organization of public education in the United States. The No Child Left Behind Act (NCLB), signed into law in early 2002, represents the most comprehensive educational reform since the Elementary and Secondary Education Act of 1965,[2] particularly in terms of its provisions for assessments, accountability, and teacher-qualification requirements (Anderson 2007; McGuinn 2006). NCLB thus represents a shift away from the historical and somewhat constrained governmental involvement in schools, to a federal mandate requiring that states adopt comprehensive systems of high-stakes accountability and assessment to be implemented in all public schools.

Based on a system of carrot-and-stick incentives designed to increase school

2. NCLB is, in fact, the latest reauthorization of the Elementary and Secondary Education Act.

accountability, educational administrators and teachers face unprecedented pressure to produce standardized test scores demonstrating that students and their schools are making "Adequate Yearly Progress" (AYP) toward 100 percent student proficiency by 2014. For schools, failure to make AYP can mean underwriting the cost of students to attend other "non-failing" schools, providing tutoring, replacing staff and curricula, or complete reorganization, including charter school reformation (McGuinn 2006).

Akin to the neoliberal economic policies described earlier, NCLB emerges out of an economic logic that privileges growth, international economic competitiveness, and the assumption that market principles will lead to better schools and improved educational achievement (Apple 2001, 2007; Brantlinger 2003; Howley 1991; Kohn 2004; Paige 2006). Consistent with neoliberal ideology, accountability-based school reform stresses individual achievement, competitiveness, choice, and economic growth in an increasingly globalized economy (Edmondson 2003; Edmondson and Shannon 1998; Hursh 2007). The National Education Summit on High Schools, for instance, describes secondary education as "the front line in the battle for our economic future" (Achieve Incorporated and National Governors Association 2005), and Michael Engel similarly argues that the sanctions-based educational reforms pushing accountability and standardization have accomplished "the institutionalization of market ideology as the unchallenged point of view on the purpose and direction of education" (2000, 30).

In rural communities experiencing prolonged economic decline, however, large proportions of the students for whom schools are accountable often experience lives of profound social disorganization. In addition to multiple social and economic stressors affecting academic achievement, families in poverty are often highly mobile due to unexpected household economic shocks coupled with the relative unaffordability of adequate housing (Colton 2004; Fitchen 1994, 1995; Foulkes and Newbold 2008; Schafft 2006). That is, this residential change is largely not a premeditated movement toward economic opportunities or improved living circumstances, but rather is frequently a "push" out of unsafe, overcrowded, unaffordable, or otherwise unacceptable living conditions, necessitating sudden and often unplanned, disruptive residential change (Schafft 2006). This residential movement inevitably leads to the movement of children in and out of schools and school districts, resulting in social and academic dislocation for students, and turnover rates[3] for schools that can approach or exceed 30 percent annually (Schafft 2005).

3. The turnover rate is the number of unscheduled student entrances plus the unscheduled

Student mobility is often associated with migrant student populations. But transient students are typically not migrant students. While both groups tend to be economically disadvantaged and academically underperforming, migrant students generally follow predictable patterns of movement in and out of a school district in accordance with seasonal agricultural work. Nor are transient students generally identified by local educational administrators as *homeless* in the sense of clearly lacking a regular or adequate nighttime residence.[4] Rather, chronic residential movement of poor families—and the student transiency that results—is both a symptom of and a contributing factor to community distress (Foulkes and Newbold 2008; Schafft 2006; Killeen and Schafft 2008). For transient students and the schools in which they are enrolled (however briefly), NCLB seems less a guarantee of equal educational opportunity than an additional penalization on top of the already significant consequences of poverty, insecurity, and chronic mobility.

The Effects of Poverty and Student Transiency Within Upstate New York Communities

> In talking with this student and his mother and setting up his schedule, I said to him, "Are you guys staying in this district now?" I mean, I'm just compelled to ask these questions now, and he said, "Oh I doubt it." His mom said, "Oh no, we have a house and we're staying this time." He said, "Yeah, that's what you said last time, and we had a house before."
>
> —MIDDLE SCHOOL PRINCIPAL

To illustrate the local effects of these three interrelated trends—rural economic restructuring, rising poverty, and increased school accountability—we turn to a case study of community change in upstate New York. The data used in this chapter come from interviews conducted with thirty school personnel, including teachers, administrators, guidance staff, and others, across three contiguous

---

exits over the course of an academic year as a ratio of the total enrollment. Hence, a turnover rate of 30 percent means that in a given year three out of ten students enrolled in a district will make a non-promotional entrance or exit.

4. The criteria for determining whether a student is homeless, as defined by the federal McKinney-Vento Act of 2002, is purposefully broad, leaving much room for interpretation. In practice, however, parents of homeless students are often unaware of the educational rights of their children, and similarly, schools may be in noncompliance with federal regulations because local administrators may lack sufficient knowledge about the specifics of a child's living circumstances—or of the federal regulations themselves. See Killeen and Schafft (2008) for a more complete discussion of these issues.

rural upstate New York districts, as part of a larger study of the causes and consequences of poverty-related student mobility.

We selected respondents representing a range of educational and administrative roles within each district and, when possible, with at least four years of experience within their positions. The interviews, which were conducted to better understand school district personnel perspectives on the causes, consequences, and most appropriate responses to student transiency, lasted approximately an hour, were taped, and were later transcribed. Using qualitative data analysis software, the transcriptions were then coded for key themes, including causes of mobility; student, classroom, and district level consequences of mobility; the effect of mobility on NCLB accountability procedures; and community contexts of student movement. The following discussion is based on the analysis of these data.

The districts in this study have total K–12 enrollments of between 1,000 and 1,600, although district records show enrollment figures have been slowly but steadily dropping. Enrollment levels now are about two-thirds of what they were fifteen to twenty years earlier, a consequence of the economic and demographic changes discussed earlier. While many families live in the small towns within the districts, others live in the outlying areas in farm houses, trailer parks, rentals, and converted migrant-worker housing. Across the three districts, eligibility rates for participation in the free and reduced-price lunch program are between 30 and 40 percent.[5] Student turnover rates vary from 18 to over 26 percent.

Initially made wealthy by agriculture and the commercial and industrial development associated with the Erie Canal, and later with the network of freight rail lines crisscrossing this part of the state, much of that wealth has dissipated. As employment opportunities have decreased, many residents have left the area in search of opportunities elsewhere. This has left many communities with populations that not only are shrinking but are older and poorer because of the disproportionate out-migration of young, working-age adults.

This has resulted in a devaluing of residential real estate and a conversion of owner-occupied homes into rental units, often owned by landlords who no longer live in the area but have found it more economical to rent rather than

---

5. Federal income eligibility guidelines for child nutrition programs stipulate that children from families with incomes 130 percent or less of the poverty-line figure are eligible for free school lunches. Students from families with incomes greater than 130 percent but less than 185 percent of the poverty-line figure are eligible for reduced-price school lunches. Guidelines are published in the U.S. *Federal Register* 71 (50), 13336–7.

sell at a loss. The area therefore has an abundance of rental property, although it is often of poor or marginal quality. This combination of community- and household-level economic insecurity, availability of rental housing, and the gradual impoverishment of local residents thus increases the likelihood of residential churning among poor families (Fitchen 1995; Foulkes and Newbold 2008; Schafft 2006).

While some towns close to tourist amenities such as the Finger Lakes and the upstate New York wineries have managed to maintain economic vitality, other towns are checkered with vacant storefronts and decaying downtown areas. Previously these towns had thriving local economies and a solid entrepreneurial class. But the infrastructure of locally owned business has gradually been replaced by franchise restaurants and big-box retail development, often on the outskirts of towns, leaving the downtowns to crumble.

The local effects of these changes are clear when talking with local longtime residents. A school administrator who had grown up in the school district adjacent to where he now works told us:

> Oh it was beautiful. We had a store where you could go in and buy your sports jackets, your ties, and your shirts. We had a store where you could go buy your shoes, Paula's Shoe Store, wing tips, and Dominico's had the dress clothes. Next to that was Vicks. Off from that across the street was Solerno's meat market. Best meat in the county. Paula's Shoe Store is gone. Vicks Men and Boys clothes is gone. Newberry's is now a dollar-or-more store. We used to have Sachs Red and White, we had Ammo's as the corner store.
>
> They're all gone because you have the interstates, you got Wal-Mart. Wal-Mart comes in, people go crazy. They go down to Wal-Mart to the super store, they have services, it has everything in the world under one roof and it's going to hire two hundred people. What they don't tell you is that the other two hundred people who worked in [locally owned businesses] just lost their job because Dino's closed, the men and boys store closed, Newberry's is gone over there. All these people, it's all gone. Once you have a store close you've lost tax revenue. You've lost jobs. So have we really come a long ways? No. I don't think so. It's too bad. But that's what you pay for progress.

For those within the school system, one of the most significant trends over the past ten to twenty years has been the increase in students who come from impoverished family backgrounds, are academically underperforming, and are highly mobile. Though mobile students are largely invisible outside the school walls, inside the institution they are recognized as one of its biggest challenges. A high school teacher noted, "Overall the economic status in this community is not very high. It just seems the economic status and family breakdown is kind of like a combined picture. I think that what ends up happening is families are not together anymore. The whole environment has changed. They go back and forth from one parent to another and the parent moves from one community to another."

While most people typically associate residential change with premeditated movement toward opportunity or improvement in living arrangements such as a new job, a bigger house, or a better school district, for families of transient students residential change far more often is reactive rather than proactive. Many moves are sudden and stopgap; they are frequently the consequence of unaffordable, inadequate or unsafe housing, or domestic conflict or household economic crisis (Fitchen 1994; Schafft 2005, 2006). Because of these factors, residential moves also tend to be highly localized as families rely on family and other social networks, and local knowledge of housing and employment possibilities in securing new places to live.

A district administrator told us, "We have the same families that move [across our local districts]. If I run into them [in the neighboring district] I've either had their brother, their sister, their cousin, their father, their mother . . . so if it's not that particular person, it's someone in their family."

Describing this population of students, a principal related:

> We get families that move out of the district because their homes were condemned. They could not live in them any more. They moved into our district and they seem to move in this general area. I had a family last year with about five different children. Their house was not livable. They found a place [about eight miles north of here]. They were driving the kids in, in the back of a pickup, and dropping them off out in front. We were aware that they were doing this, but they were also in the process of trying to find another place to live in the community. So I mean you see some of that. Some [movement is because] the house is condemned. We have had them where they had to move out because they could not afford the heat anymore or they had used up all of their fuel oil or whatever and could not replenish it. So they take up a temporary residence outside of the district in order just to keep going. We had four in the building this year, but for that very reason they were living outside the district. Their intent was to get back and they have since been able to

get oil back into the house and now they can heat it. So they are back in the district. Some of it is job-related, but not a lot.

Unlike homeless students or students from migrant families, highly mobile students are institutionally unrecognized and not typically targeted as children in need, yet schools in the area increasingly recognize transient students as a significant factor in school demographics. It is not uncommon to witness a student attend three or more school districts during grades 7–12, and often far more than that. Among the lowest achieving, these students invariably have overarching educational, familial, economic, and emotional needs that have a significant impact on their functioning both inside and outside school settings.

Highly mobile students transferring across districts find themselves thrust into classes that in all likelihood have a different syllabus taught in a different sequence than their previous school. Even in a state such as New York, which has highly prescribed courses and curricula, differences among districts are significant, particularly in the order that topics are covered. The increasing emphasis on standards does not, in practice, necessarily lead to the standardization of curricula. Further, students from rural areas are particularly vulnerable to learning new curricula when changing schools because school changes are nearly synonymous with district changes. In urban settings where movement is more likely to be intra-district (Kerbow 1996) such disruption is less likely to be the case.

The academic and social discontinuity experienced by mobile students not surprisingly results in their overrepresentation within compensatory educational services. These services range from short-term academic assistance, called Academic Intervention Services, to comprehensive program and instruction modifications given to students with educationally handicapping conditions as determined by a district's Committee on Special Education. Thus knowledge gaps that develop over time are magnified by poor skill development and the fragmented connections to school and community. This already difficult combination becomes even more daunting when it is accompanied by frequent moves from district to district.

NCLB and Accountability in Districts with High Student Mobility

I think [policy makers] need to realize that these children are people,
that their needs are greater than how we can get them to be a
"four" on the ELA.

—ELEMENTARY SCHOOL TEACHER

While the academic and social needs of mobile students represent significant challenges in small, often resource-poor rural districts, these challenges are made vastly more complex in the face of NCLB requirements. Educators in all districts expressed frustration and anxiety about accountability standards for students who not only may have experienced entirely different curricular and testing sequences elsewhere, but who also may be learning-disabled or experiencing multiple social and economic stressors at home. A school social worker told us, "I have heard teachers say, 'I think this kid is moving. God, I hope they move before the state tests.' They are very aware of it. The teachers are very aware of who is coming and going."

Newly entering students often have missing or incomplete records, may have moved numerous times, and often represent a large unknown as far as their needs, abilities, and how they will perform both academically within the classroom and on standardized assessments. An acting superintendent explained that when a student arrives in the district, questions are automatically raised about how the student will perform on state assessments:

> Oh boy, is this kid [going to score] a one or two or three or four? This is not our fault—this kid just got here. We do not know this kid's needs. The level of accountability for teachers and the level of accountability for districts really have a lot of people almost running scared as to how they are going to be compared to other places. There is a lot of worry about how in a district of this size, where we have 102 kids taking a test, that three or four kids that score poorly can really skew our results. That is out there. Not publicly, but privately. People kind of wring their hands and say, "Oh gee, I hope this kid is bright."

Over the course of our interviews it became clear that many teachers, and even some administrators, were misinformed as to how school accountability actually works. Federal law stipulates that all enrolled students must be given the state assessment tests, regardless of how long they have been enrolled within the district. But in New York State only those students continuously enrolled in the district from the first Wednesday in October until the date of test administration are counted for the purposes of determining AYP. Nonetheless, we often heard comments like those of a twelfth-grade English teacher who bluntly stated, "Why should the English scores, for example, on that school report card reflect that student when that student has not been in our district except for maybe a cup of coffee?" Teachers expressed both concern and fear in how transient students may negatively affect school scores, and therefore negatively affect them.

Irrespective of state assessments, a guidance counselor described a frequent reluctance among teachers and administrative staff to make emotional and professional investments in new students. "We have had a number of kids move in and out quickly and so there is a [question] of how much do you get invested in this kid before they are gone again," he explained. But the misperception that newly arrived students will "bring down" a school's scores and reflect poorly on individual teachers only increases the risk that mobile students will experience social and academic exclusion in new school settings. This reluctance to make personal and professional commitments to new, mobile students is reflected in the very language used by teaching staff (see also Schafft 2005). A middle school teacher told us that the arrival of new students at testing time triggered a feeling of "Well, there goes my results because I know what kids of *mine* are not going to perform well" (italics added). She continued, "I do not know if these [new] kids can perform or not. If I am going to have bad results, let it be because I know this kid cannot do this. This kid never caught on. You know what I mean? Holy cow, there goes my numbers again. That is the first thing that comes to mind. I said to the eighth-grade teacher, 'I just got four new kids that are going to take my test.' She said, 'Better yours than mine.'"

Linked in this manner, the institutional mandates of NCLB coupled with the needs of transient students directly affect how these students are perceived and treated within school settings. While teachers and administrators have built careers around working with and educating children, as Nichols and Berliner point out, "the public ratings of public schools mean that all school personnel receive public accolades or a public scolding as a consequence of school and district test scores" (2007, 8). In smaller rural schools this may take on a magnitude not found in larger, urban schools, and teachers find that they may be cast suddenly in the spotlight because of low-scoring students. As an elementary school teacher told us, "When you are talking about the fourth grade ELA and math scores, it is four teachers. Everybody knows it is those four teachers. Yes, teachers' names are not in the paper, but if you live in [this community] and you have kids who go here, you know that John Morgan is the global studies teacher. So when it says that the global score in the paper, you know who that is. It won't say his name in the paper, but it is as good as saying his name."

Under these conditions, the education of students becomes subverted by the exigencies of exams and the pressures to avoid the formal and informal sanctions associated with low-scoring students. "Sometimes it is like . . . you know, we really want to work with [our students] so they are passing the test and our scores look really good," a middle school teacher explained. "It really is not about how comfortable this child is or how much they have learned. [Rather], is it going to make us look good?"

Another teacher, an instructor of secondary-level science, explained:

> It shows up in the newspapers. You hate to think in those terms because it [shouldn't] matter if it is in a newspaper or not. It matters what [is happening with] the kids, but certainly if you see these results of a certain school and they are good, people in the community feel proud and if their school is consistently like that you know people do not mind moving into that community. If the school is consistently doing poorly, in part because of transient students or students with handicaps and things that we cannot get to pass these exams, then that affects the community at large in terms of people not wanting to live there. The tax base shrinks and all of those kinds of things are affected in some way.

Student transiency creates a very real dilemma for the professional, raising many difficult questions. How much time, effort, and district resources can or should one devote to a student who, in all likelihood, will change schools before a lasting difference can be made in his or her life? How does one calculate the energy, time, and resources mobile students need relative to the needs of the rest of the population, particularly when substantial needs exist for nonmobile students as well? How can professionals balance the realities of the daily lives of the students they work with against the multiple social and institutional pressures to produce adequate standardized test scores? Caring, supportive professionals must grapple with these dilemmas on a daily basis. Most of the professionals we are familiar with practice a type of educational triage, patching the gaping holes as well as possible, in the hope that a program of ongoing, critical care will occur somewhere down the line. But this "critical care" is rarely provided in schools, which do not have the needed personnel and resources to adequately address these students' needs. And it does not address the broader problem of deepening community economic stress and dislocation.

Discussion

While thirty years ago student mobility was not an issue in the districts at the center of this chapter's discussion, it has over time come to the forefront.

Changes in the social and economic structure of these rural communities have left in their wake fragmented families who are economically insecure, socially dislocated, and highly mobile. The children from these families have an entire spectrum of needs that schools and educators must scramble to address, often in the context of limited and shrinking resources and institutional mandates that, under the threat of disciplinary action, necessitate a primary focus of school energies and resources on achieving a largely arbitrary standard of AYP. As David Berliner (2006) writes, "Many scholars and teachers understand, although many politicians choose not to, that school reform is heavily constrained by factors that are outside of America's classrooms and schools. Although the power of schools and educators to influence individual students is never to be underestimated, the out-of-school factors associated with poverty play both a powerful and limiting role in what can actually be achieved" (250).

Stephen Gill argues that "economic liberalism promotes the survival of the fittest in the marketplace. Those fittest to survive are generally the holders of wealth and power" (1994, 85). In the era of economic restructuring and NCLB, this holds as true for schools and communities as it does for families and individuals. But rural communities have always been peripheral to the centers of power and privilege in the United States (Howley 2004; Theobald 1997). Consequently, public policies have rarely been kind to the social, cultural, and economic "inefficiencies" of rural life. With sink-or-swim economic policies and educational reforms, too often rural people and institutions have been left to sink.

NCLB is driven in large part by concerns about the need to raise academic achievement to maintain global economic competitiveness (Hess and Rotherham 2007; Hursh 2007), but it also represents a far more fundamental public policy push toward privatization and the economic logic of the marketplace (Apple 2001, 2007). It comes as little surprise then that NCLB in many ways *replicates* the global logic of neoliberalism at a more micro level. We can see this, for example, in parallels drawn between NCLB and structural adjustment policies.

Structural adjustment refers to measures imposed on debtor nations by global lending institutions such as the World Bank and the International Monetary Fund to increase economic growth and improve debt servicing. Used as a condition for obtaining loans or for rescheduling existing loans, since the 1970s structural adjustment policies have been used to discipline and place conditions on developing nations dependent on international aid. Taking the form of regulative and normative conditions, structural adjustments include political and economic reforms and the restructuring of national-level economic policies to promote trade, productivity, and export-led growth (McMichael 2003; Patel and McMichael 2004).

More specifically, these reforms have typically involved the elimination or reduction of barriers to trade, privatization of state-held industries and utilities, and the removal of supports for firms producing for domestic markets. This has been done to encourage exports and eliminate inefficient and noncompetitive firms. These measures are coupled with fiscal belt-tightening, often in the form of reductions in spending on public goods such as health care and education, regardless of local social or cultural logics that may militate against the wisdom of particular reforms. Structural adjustment policies have, for example, destroyed the conditions necessary for the growth of domestic firms, generated significant import growth without concomitant export growth, and increased unemployment while reducing wages. Privatization of public utilities and extractive industries have similarly resulted in environmental degradation, price leaps, and, coupled with the removal of social safety nets, disproportionate hardship on the most vulnerable (SAPRIN 2002). Regardless, failure to comply with structural adjustment policies may result in further "adjustments" (such as increased interest rates) and sanctions (including decreased access to international credit and state aid).

NCLB, by extension, may be thought of as a kind of "structural adjustment" for underperforming schools.[6] Similar to structural adjustment policies imposed on developing countries by global lending institutions, NCLB imposes market logic and disciplinary measures to reduce or eliminate "inefficiencies" that threaten academic achievement. With achievement as the "bottom line," the operating assumption is that educational improvement can be attained through regulative and normative measures designed to increase accountability and, by extension, improve institutional and academic performance. Schools failing to make AYP receive technical assistance and must provide school choice for those students who opt to attend other "non-failing" schools. Continued failure to reach AYP results in increased sanctions and threat of further "structural adjustment," which may ultimately involve school closure and privatization through the reconstitution of public schools as charter schools (Kohn 2004; McGuinn 2006).

And like structural readjustment at the global level, NCLB has the strongest effects on the most resource-poor schools and, as we have seen from our case

6. We are thankful to Emelie Peine for this insight.

study, the most vulnerable students. Advocates of NCLB and accountability measures point to examples of "high-flying" low-resource schools with high-need populations that nonetheless demonstrate consistently high academic achievement. Yet research recently completed on over sixty thousand schools shows that low-poverty, low-minority schools are *eighty-nine times* more likely to be consistently high-performing as compared with high-poverty, high-minority schools. This alone is clear evidence that NCLB not only does not reward schools for what they can control, but actually punishes them through accountability and disciplinary sanctions for what they *cannot* control (Harris 2007). Although the rhetoric of NCLB is equity-based with its language of accountability and achievement across subgroups, a growing body of research suggests that the dynamics of NCLB in fact work to reproduce class- and race-based hierarchies and ultimately school-, community-, and student-based disadvantage (Hursh 2007).

Conclusion

We argue that student transiency and its associated academic outcomes are largely beyond the control of local schools and school districts. Because of this, we also maintain that it is not only unfair to hold schools accountable for the social and academic effects of rural poverty, but that doing this serves to shift the locus of the problem of student transiency from a broader set of societal insecurities to an issue largely bounded by school policy and practice. Nonetheless, there are still ways that schools and communities may act strategically to address student transiency and the needs of mobile students.

One of the consistent findings from our research (Schafft 2005, 2006) and the work of others (Fitchen 1995; Foulkes and Newbold 2008) is that transiency is localized. Poor families making residential changes don't tend to move far, often within the school district or to a neighboring school district. Because of this, we believe it is important for schools to track student mobility to better understand when during the school year it occurs, which students are most likely to be mobile, what their needs are, and where students tend to come from and go to. In the short term, this information gathering can help shape coordination of record keeping and programming across neighboring school districts. In the longer term such documentation may also be used to help leverage external resources from state and local agencies in the form of grants and other supports. It can also help demonstrate the magnitude and impacts of transiency to state departments of education and to the policy-making communities more broadly, including state- and national-level legislators.

Record keeping on student mobility can similarly provide the basis for developing strategic and collaborative relations not only with neighboring school districts, but with other local social service agencies, including departments of social service, community action agencies, and public housing organizations. Housing agencies may be particularly important partners given that much of the movement of low-income families is related to the limited availability of adequate and affordable housing (Schafft 2006; Killeen and Schafft 2008). In short, because of the nature of student transiency, its roots in local disadvantage, and its occurrence over space, we argue that interagency coordination and communication should be a crucial component of district practice.

At the school level, relatively simple procedures can be put in place to ease the social and academic transitions of mobile students and increase school attachment (Killeen and Schafft 2008). These include new student orientations, "buddy" programs, and the active and targeted recruitment of new students into school clubs and extracurricular activities. Information packets can be compiled for both students and parents about the school and the community, with information about various local organizations that offer social support and promote community integration.

School administrators also need to provide staff with appropriate training and information to help them work effectively with mobile and at-risk students. In particular we are concerned that NCLB and the emphasis on high-stakes testing may lead to the social and academic exclusion of mobile students because of the potential threats to accountability that mobile students rightly or wrongly represent. Administrators must ensure that teachers understand how school accountability procedures work and that mobile students are not further disadvantaged socially or academically because of their transient status.

Unfortunately, for the children, families, schools, and communities of distressed rural communities in upstate New York and elsewhere, student transiency—and the social and economic conditions that give rise to it—defy simple policy prescriptions. This is particularly true of policy prescriptions singularly leveled at schools. While NCLB may significantly compound the disadvantage already experienced by low-resource schools with large transient student populations, its elimination or alteration will not change the basic circumstances facing poor children and their families. Rather, these conditions are the necessary result of the deep structural roots of U.S. poverty, which are shaped by an economic ideology that concentrates political and economic power and, in so doing, makes social inequality inevitable.

References

Achieve Incorporated and National Governors Association. 2005. *National Education Summit on High Schools 2005 Briefing Book*. Washington, D.C.: Achieve Incorporated and National Governors Association. Retrieved January 15, 2010, from http://www.achieve/org/files/Achievebriefingbook2005.pdf.

Anderson, L. W. 2007. *Congress and the classroom: From the cold war to "No Child Left Behind."* University Park: Penn State Press.

Apple, M. W. 2001. Markets, standards, teaching, and teacher education. *Journal of Teacher Education* 52 (3), 182–96.

———. 2007. Ideological success, educational failure? On the politics of No Child Left Behind. *Journal of Teacher Education* 58 (2), 108–16.

Berliner, D. C. 2006. Our impoverished view of educational research. *Teachers College Record* 108 (6), 949–95.

Bourdieu, P. 1998. *Acts of resistance: Against the tyranny of the market*. New York: The New Press.

Brantlinger, E. 2003. *Dividing classes: How the middle class negotiates and rationalizes school advantage*. New York: Routledge Falmer.

Collins, J., and A. Quark. 2006. Globalizing firms and small communities: The apparel industry's changing connection to rural labor markets. *Rural Sociology* 71 (2), 281–310.

Colton, R. D. 2004. *Paid but unaffordable: The consequences of energy poverty in Missouri*. Washington, D.C.: National Low Energy Housing Consortium.

Eberts, P., and A. Hart. 1999. New York's industrial structure: How viable? In T. A. Hirschl and T. B. Heaton, eds., *New York State in the 21st Century*, 141–53. Westport, Conn.: Praeger.

Edmondson, J. 2003. *Prairie town: Redefining rural life in the age of globalization*. Lanham, Md.: Rowman and Littlefield.

Edmondson, J., and P. Shannon. 1998. Reading education and poverty: Questioning the reading success equation. *Peabody Journal of Education* 73 (3–4), 104–26.

Engel, M. 2000. *The struggle for the control of public education*. Philadelphia: Temple University Press.

Falk, W. W., and L. M. Lobao. 2003. Who benefits from economic restructuring? Lessons from the past, challenges for the future. In D. L. Brown and L. E. Swanson, eds., *Challenges for rural America in the twenty-first century*, 152–65. University Park: Penn State Press.

Finlayson, A. C., T. A. Lyson, A. Pleasant, K. A. Schafft, and R. J. Torres. 2005. The "invisible hand": Neoclassical economics and the ordering of society. *Critical Sociology* 31 (4), 515–36.

Fitchen, J. M. 1991. *Endangered spaces, enduring places*. Boulder: Westview.

———. 1994. Residential mobility among the rural poor. *Rural Sociology* 59 (3), 416–36.

———. 1995. Spatial redistribution of poverty through migration of poor people to depressed rural communities. *Rural Sociology* 60 (2), 181–201.

Foulkes, M., and K. B. Newbold. 2008. Poverty catchments: Migration, residential mobility, and population turnover in impoverished rural Illinois communities. *Rural Sociology* 73 (3), 440–62.

Gill, S. 1994. Knowledge, politics, and neo-liberal political economy. In R. Stubbs and G. R. D. Underhill, eds., *Political economy and the changing global order*, 75–88. New York: St. Martin's Press.

Glasmeier, A, and P. Salant. 2006. *Low-skill workers in rural America face permanent job loss* (Carsey Institute Policy Brief No. 2, Spring). Durham, N.H.: Carsey Institute.

Harris, D. N. 2007. High-flying schools, student disadvantage, and the logic of NCLB. *American Journal of Education* 113 (3), 367–94.

Harvey, D. 2005. *A brief history of neoliberalism*. New York: Oxford University Press.

Hays, S. 2003. *Flat broke with children: Women in the age of welfare reform*. New York: Oxford University Press.

Hess, F. M., and A. J. Rotherham. 2007. NCLB and the competitiveness agenda: Happy collaboration or a collision course? *Phi Delta Kappan* 88 (5), 345–53.

Hobbs, D. 1992. The rural context for education: Adjusting the images. In M. W. Galbraith, ed., *Education in the rural American community*, 21–44. Malabar, Fla.: Krieger.

Howley, C. 1991. The rural education dilemma as part of the rural dilemma: Rural education and economics. In A. J. DeYoung, ed., *Rural education: Issues and practices*, 73–145. New York: Garland.

———. 2004. A critical introduction to useful works about rural life and education. *Journal of Education Finance* 29 (3), 257–72.

Hursh, D. 2007. Assessing No Child Left Behind and the rise of neoliberal education policies. *American Educational Research Journal* 44 (3), 493–518.

Kerbow, D. 1996. Pattern of urban student mobility and local school reform. *Journal of Education for Students Placed at Risk* 1 (2), 147–69.

Killeen, K., and K. A. Schafft. 2008. The organizational and fiscal implications of transient student populations. In H. F. Ladd and E. B. Fiske, eds., *American Education Finance Association handbook of research in education finance and policy*, 631–50. New York: Routledge.

Kohn, A. 2004. NCLB and the effort to privatize public education. In D. Meier and G. Wood, eds., *Many children left behind*, 79–97. Boston: Beacon Press.

Lichter, D. T., D. K. McLaughlin, and G. Cornwell. 1995. Migration and the loss of human resources in rural America. In L. J. Beaulieu and D. Mulkey, eds., *Investing in people: The human capital needs of rural America*, 235–56. Boulder: Westview.

Lobao, L., A. Brown, and J. Moore. 2003. Old industrial regions and the political economy of development: The Ohio River Valley. In W. W. Falk, M. D. Schulman, and A. R. Tickamyer, eds., *Communities of work: Rural restructuring in local and global contexts*, 3–30. Athens: Ohio University Press.

Lyson, T., and W. Falk, eds. 1993. *Forgotten places: Uneven development in rural America*. Lawrence: University Press of Kansas.

Massey, D. S., M. Sanchez, and J. R. Behrman. 2006. Of myths and markets. *Annals of the American Academy of Political and Social Science* 606 (1), 8–31.

McGranahan, D. A. 2003. How people make a living in rural America. In D. L. Brown and L. E. Swanson, eds., *Challenges for rural America in the twenty-first century*, 135–51. University Park: Penn State Press.

McGuinn, P. J. 2006. *No Child Left Behind and the transformation of federal education policy, 1965–2005*. Lawrence: University of Kansas Press.

McMichael, P. M. 2003. *Development and social change*. Thousand Oaks, Calif.: Pine Forge Press.

Nichols, S. L., and D. C. Berliner. 2007. *Collateral damage: How high-stakes testing corrupts America's schools*. Cambridge: Harvard Education Press.

O'Hare, W. P., and S. Savage. 2006. *Child poverty in rural America: New data shows increases in 41 states* (Carsey Institute Fact Sheet No. 1). Durham, N.H.: Carsey Institute.

Paige, R. 2006. No Child Left Behind: The ongoing movement for public education reform. *Harvard Educational Review* 76 (4), 461–73.

Patel, R. 2007. *Stuffed and starved: Markets, power, and the hidden battle for the world's food system*. London: Portobello.

Patel, R., and P. McMichael. 2004. Third worldism and the lineages of global fascism: The regrouping of the global South in the neoliberal era. *Third World Quarterly* 25 (1), 231–54.

Pendall, R. 2003. *Upstate New York's population plateau: The third-slowest growing "state."* New York: Brookings Institution.

Rank, M. R. 2005 *One nation, underprivileged: Why American poverty affects us all*. New York: Oxford University Press.

Robbins, R. H. 2004. *Global problems and the culture of capitalism*. Boston: Allyn and Bacon.

Sachs, J. 2005. *The end of poverty*. New York: Penguin.

Schafft, K. A. 2005. The incidence and impacts of student transiency in upstate New York's rural school districts. *Journal of Research in Rural Education* 20 (15), 1–13.

———. 2006. Poverty, residential mobility, and student transiency within a rural New York school district. *Rural Sociology* 71 (2), 212–31.

Shipler, D. K. 2005. *The working poor: Invisible in America*. New York: Vintage Books.

Shulman, B. 2005. *The betrayal of work: How low-wage jobs fail 30 million Americans*. New York: The New Press.

Structural Adjustment Participatory Review International Network (SAPRIN). 2002. *The policy roots of economic crisis and poverty: A multi-country participatory assessment of structural adjustment*. Washington, D.C.: SAPRIN Secretariat.

Struthers, C., and J. Bokemeier. 2003. Stretched to their limits: Rural nonfarm mothers and the "new" rural economy. In W. W. Falk, M. D. Schulman, and A. R. Tickamyer, eds., *Communities of work: Rural restructuring in local and global contexts*, 291–315. Athens: Ohio University Press.

Theobald, P. 1997. *Teaching the commons*. Boulder: Westview.

Zimmerman, J. M., and T. A. Hirschl. 2003. Welfare reform in rural areas: A voyage through uncharted waters. In D. L. Brown and L. E. Swanson, eds., *Challenges for rural America in the twenty-first century*, 363–74. University Park: Penn State Press.

6

WHARF TALK, HOME TALK, AND SCHOOL TALK:
THE POLITICS OF LANGUAGE IN A COASTAL COMMUNITY

Michael Corbett

At One Point in Time and Space

In the small rural elementary school in Nova Scotia where I worked through the 1990s there were several seasonal rituals. One of these was, and continues to be, the traditional Christmas Concert. Another is the annual "leaving ceremony" held at the end of June to mark the transition from the village elementary school to the regional secondary school "in town" over twenty miles away. Other rituals include readings, songs, and a community meal on the Friday before the Canadian Thanksgiving Day in October. These rituals have a long history. A more recently invented ritual is a weekly assembly featuring almost exclusively child-generated content. These events draw many people from the Digby Neck community and they serve a kind of traditional accountability function because they open the doors of the "schoolhouse" (as it is still called by many people) to interested parties who get to see what the children are capable of doing. Both the concert and the leaving ceremony involve rehearsed presentations by children.

I came to this school as a support teacher in 1990 when the staff consisted of several women who were very close to retirement age, and who (with one exception) had worked in the school for decades. These veteran teachers understood the community, pedagogy, and child development not so much through textbooks and abstractions as through lived experience in place and in classrooms. They illustrated and shared this knowledge through lunchtime stories and after-school conversations and in staff meetings that seemed to me to go on forever. They were interested in learning about progressive pedagogies and particularly in how they might support literacy education within the frame of the whole language movement. They were also critical of what they considered to be its excesses and blind spots. I worked with these women for several years and went through my own socialization process, which included those meetings that often seemed to me to be more about historical community narratives and genealogy than about running a school. The process of enculturation, though, was a process of learning about *where* I was and understanding the dense networks of family and kinship that both made the place work as a community and at the same time made schooling a particular kind of challenge within the community.

When I came to the school in 1990, the principal was relatively new. While she was not "from" the community, she was "from" the same generation and "from" a long career in a similar kind of Nova Scotian rural community school. She had been influenced by the ideas of the whole language movement and the even more challenging ideas contained in critical pedagogy (Giroux 1988), narrative inquiry (Ashton-Warner 1963), constructivism (Dewey 1938), and, to a lesser extent, sociological theories of schooling that problematized many of our routine practices as teachers (Bourdieu 1984a; Bernstein 1977). I remember this as a time of change in the school when the staff began to open doors to the community in ways that were new, exciting, and even a bit frightening. One of these openings was to begin to accept and find a place in the institution for vernacular language. Whole language gave us a strong pedagogical and pragmatic starting point for doing this, and critical pedagogy provided a set of political reasons why we ought to problematize our work and investigate the context and larger implications of our practice as teachers.

By the mid-1990s when I took over a fifth- and sixth-grade classroom position, this work was well under way in a project called "Community into Curriculum" designed principally by reading specialist Tony Kelly. The project emerged from a study of early school leaving that I did for the district school board on a brief secondment in 1990. In this work I found a very high dropout rate in the community as well as what I interpreted at the time to be a strong desire on the part of many of those who "dropped out" to stay "around" in the local area (Corbett 1991). In fact, for many of my informants to stay the educational course meant to drop out of their community. Postsecondary and even secondary education was fundamentally about leaving (Corbett 2007a) and the whole process was shot through with tension, conflicting emotions, and ambivalence. As a result of this work the school staff began to look at how the community was represented in our practices and in the textual materials the students used in school. Not surprisingly we found that there was little actual local content or recognizable local representation, and that if we were to look at the school as a large text, it was fundamentally a story about somewhere else.

Community into Curriculum then was an attempt to develop curriculum from community sources. With a small grant from the provincial teachers' union we purchased video equipment and still cameras and began to fill the walls of the school with images from the community.[1] We also began to collect common artifacts from the community, and with children started to "unpack" their meaning through dramatic presentations, visual art and music, and video. As we did this work, the colloquial language of the community generally seemed appropriate and even necessary to tell the kinds of stories that emerged to be told, and thus the kind of linguistic censorship and control that were common school practices came into question. How should children be expected to talk about their home places and the lives they see around them if not in the language used in the community?

The Principal's Gaze

But what happens when home language becomes an accepted medium for communication in school? What happens when "ain't" and "we was over to his place" are not only accepted in school (as they always were at some level from the time when children were permitted to speak in rural schools), but where these utterances are encoded, recorded, written, spoken in public on a stage, and generally given the status normally only accorded to Standard English? This, of course, is the thorny question of the place of colloquial language in formal education (Delpit 1995; Dowdy and Delpit 2003). There are no easy answers to this kind of question, but the traditional answer had always been that students were to use Standard English and that the role of the teacher is to correct nonstandard usage. The fact that after several generations this approach seemed to have had little impact on those who remained in the community did little to dull the zeal of most teachers for teaching Standard English.

I had been puzzling over this problem since the early 1980s when I taught

---

1. In subsequent years we would tap other funding sources to establish a computer lab for the school and community and to extend artistic, photographic, and video work in the school.

on a First Nations reserve in northern Manitoba, but during the leaving ceremony in June 2000 the issue was problematized powerfully for me. A student was giving a presentation to the community assembled in the school gym. He was, at twelve years of age, a big lad, already as strong as I was, and (as things turned out) destined for the fishing boat and probably a life in the local community supported by an extensive extended family. He was talking about his time in elementary school and treating the audience to an animated discourse about his friends' antics on a school trip, and doing it in his home language, the language of the wharf, the language spoken fluently by most of the adults in the community, a language considered to be ungrammatical and a marker of a lack of formal education. To me, this was and is a rich language, but to the former principal, a woman who presided over the school from the 1940s through the early 1980s, this language had no place in public discourse around the school. From my place on the stage I turned from this young man and met the gaze of this former principal. There was a mixture of shock and disgust in her eyes. Hers were powerful eyes even though the woman was in her late seventies. Her lips were pulled tight, and she seemed about to rise in her seat and lecture the boy about grammar and me about pedagogy and responsibility.

From that moment, the problems we were dealing with in the Community into Curriculum project came to take on a new meaning. At one level, the former principal was right. By letting students operate in a colloquial register I was not preparing them for other language communities, and particularly for a smooth trip through to higher education. This would limit their chances outside a rural home community. Yet, on the other hand, years of browbeating, grammar work sheets, and incessant correction had done little to either change the language patterns of those who spoke the local dialect, or to help those who spoke in these patterns feel competent about who they were as language users. The ultimate result was a very high dropout rate among young people, and particularly among men whose language was most intimately connected to life in the community.

The very idea of a person as a "language user" was enshrined in the elementary school grammar textbook in common use in Nova Scotia schools until the 1980s; the title of the text was *Learning Our Language*. The implication was clear for those whose language diverged from the allegedly standard patterns: people like *us* do not speak and use *our language* as it should be used. The construction "our language" is something that sits outside the everyday discourse of people like *us,* and as such, it is something that must be explicitly *taught to us* by those who speak properly and are trained to correct and fix deviations. Language, real language, was langue, the abstract and foreign set of rules of speech and written representations of that speech contained in texts. Language was not something anyone *around here* did in ordinary speech acts. These utterances were abominations that made allegedly committed teachers cringe.

I have thought a lot about this since. When we say or even imply to an individual that the way they use language is wrong, we say a great deal about the worth of that person. To say that a person's language is incorrect or a corruption of a superior linguistic form is to say that the way they form concepts and the way they think is flawed. The basic human tool that we use as a species to navigate and negotiate the world is, in your case, broken, truncated, restricted (Bernstein 1977), uncultured, and just plain wrong. The concepts you use are incorrect and your very way of understanding and structuring the world is substandard. This is a powerful indictment. Since language is embedded in a lifeworld that uses it as a tool to make things happen, there is no getting around the inevitability that language will be used as it is used, as parole. The men on the wharf will not, suddenly, through instruction, change the nature of their discourse, because this discourse is intimately tied up in the processes and local knowledge that go into fishing the Bay of Fundy. This language will be spoken in families, in love, and in anger, with authority and importance, with shame and humility, day after day after day. Its persistence, its utility, its poetry, the pleasure it invokes, its ubiquity, and its omnipresence in spaces outside school will insure that its life will go on. Language is tied up in who people are; it is not something that most children can really be taught to use much differently than they do at the time without removing them from their parents. This language "works" and the work it does is giving shape and nuance to a particular kind of life in a particular place. To speak formal Standard English in most ordinary life spaces would be to mark oneself out as other and as a person who is ignorant of, or arrogantly contemptuous about, how things are done in the community (Ching and Creed 1997; Dews and Law 1995; hooks 1994; Kincheloe and Pinar 1991).

To speak formal English is to stand outside the discourse space of the community and to mark oneself as a sophisticate and, indeed, an outsider. Another space, outside the community (and implicitly "above" it) is the space occupied by the rural school teacher in a modern school. The school curriculum, particularly the language curriculum, is a technology of standardization and translation. The child comes to school with thoughts, images, dispositions, a sense of the body and how to present and use it, a way of appearing and speaking, a particular knowledge of tools and artifacts, an array of literate experience, in short, the package that we call by the name identity. It is the business of school to teach the child of a family, of a place, of a neighborhood, of a peer network, how to fit into a matrix of relationships we call by names such as community, society, region, nation, and even globe.

Schooling and Placelessness

Increasingly, schooling has been invoked as a space for both risk assessment and management (Beck 1992) as well as for the establishment of early trajectory lines for the individual project of the self (Bauman 2001, 2004; Giddens 1991). To accomplish the former task, an array of standardized assessment instruments now map and document the character, deportment, cognitive functioning, interests, and proclivities of individual children. This documentary record serves the traditional purpose of sorting and selection but also creates the detailed personal risk profile that will establish educability, employability, security risk, credit limits, mental stability, targeting for marketing and increasingly personalized advertising, and a variety of other contemporary identity parameters. Indeed, being included in the surveillance system database is no longer something to be feared, but rather, something to be desired, because "the records confirm the 'credibility' of the people on record—their reliability as clients and *choosers*" (Bauman 1998, 51).

As most contemporary sociology has shown, to function in these larger spaces, many of which are now virtual spaces, is increasingly important. We no longer inhabit physical places in the same way that we did a generation ago; as Anthony Giddens puts it with his bizarre turn of phrase, place is "phantasmagorical." In one sense this is true, but it does beg the question, "Who are we?" At the same time, each of us still lives somewhere concrete. Yet, for the time being, we still have bodies. We sleep in a bed somewhere if we are lucky enough to have a home. We get up and negotiate a room, a house, an apartment. We dwell in some kind of physical place, typically a city. According to one estimate, for the first time in history, in 2004 or 2005 more people were living in cities than in rural places (Davis 2004).[2] In other words, we continue to live locally

2. Davis writes, "Sometime in the next year, a woman will give birth in the Lagos slum of Ajegunle, a young man will flee his village in west Java for the bright lights of Jakarta, or a farmer will move his impoverished family into one of Lima's innumerable *pueblos jovenes*. The exact event is unimportant and it will pass entirely unnoticed. Nonetheless it will constitute a water-

unless we are part of the global jet set endlessly traveling between here and there (Urry 2000; Castells 2004).

The point I want to make is that most of us—and not just a localized impoverished underclass, as Bauman (1998, 2004) suggests—continue to live in communities that are geographically bounded but not necessarily stable. We may change location regularly and move from one place to another more than at any previous point in history, but we continue to move in and out of established human dwelling places where face-to-face interaction and patterned colloquial language practices are the foundation of life. Global capitalism and radical mobility have not altered this fundamental reality and it is perhaps most visible in rural communities where localized language patterns continue to predominate. Place still matters.

Down to Earth

When we move from a lofty consideration of globalization, risk society, mobility, modernity and postmodernity, discourse, and other abstractions to consider the role of place in the education of students in a particular school like the one where I was left standing on the stage, getting the eye from the ex-principal, these large problems assume a real shape. One arguably noble purpose of school has been to mobilize people, to pluck them out of particular places and specific language communities and give them credentials that certify that they possess a generic intellectual capital that is negotiable anywhere. The ex-principal fixed me in her gaze, I think, because as principal of a small rural school, she believed it was first and foremost my business to elevate my students out of this place. It was my job to create in the school a space apart and above the community and enact this idealized space with my teacher's body (Popkewitz 1998). It was my job to prepare these children for leaving and assuming a place in the secondary school where they would receive the "high" schooling that would provide them with a more subtle and deeper form of placeless knowledge. As one man I interviewed put it, secondary school was just an elaboration of elementary school; it was still people sitting around talking about things.

But what kinds of things? And in what kind of language? Chet Bowers argues

shed in human history. For the first time the urban population of the earth will outnumber the rural. Indeed, given the imprecisions of Third World censuses, this epochal transition may already have occurred" (2004, 5).

that languages are not neutral, abstract frameworks for passing around ideas; they are also means by which deep cultural patterns are encoded and shared (2001, 176–78; 2006). Bowers identifies how indigenous knowledge and indigenous cultures and even dialects contain within them space and place markers that locate individuals within communities and that encode pragmatic knowledge about how things are done. Members of fishing families do not talk about fishing in Standard English, but rather in a nuanced language specific to fishing but also to the particular bioregion in which the practice of fishing is carried out. To speak this dialect is to be a member of the community and to be party to the knowledge and practice that community contains (Dowdy and Delpit 2003). To speak Standard English is to stand outside that community and its discourse. In other words, when we attempt in school to unify and standardize discourse patterns we lose the opportunity to help preserve regional dialects and the particular place-based knowledge they contain. Many (if not most) teachers have been doing this for so long and so relentlessly in our everyday practices in school that it will be very difficult to imagine how we might do things differently.

Good students learn to sit. They learn to speak and write. They meet the prescribed outcomes.[3] They are quiet. They learn structural knowledge from the sciences, which abstract and atomize the everyday into principles, elements, and formula. Good students are taught to translate their thoughts out of their dialect and into standard speech and writing. Of course, as Bourdieu (1984a) demonstrated, in this act of translation much important knowledge is lost. Language must be "natural" to be authentic; it cannot be "schooled" and have the same value. The minuscule distinctions that separate the fluent native speaker from the person who has acquired "language" later in life serves as a good analogy for this process. An accent, however slight, can be easily distinguished by a native speaker. Even good students from rural places and working-class homes never quite "get it"; their knowledge is "schooled" rather than

---

3. One reviewer pointed out that there is a distinction between the standardization of curriculum and the standardization of outcomes. Different students will make different things of what is presented to them in school even under conditions of highly controlled "delivery" systems. So standardization in this sense is a modernist dream that is never achieved, as Foucault (1997) and others have demonstrated. I accept this. A more productive way to look at the problem of educational outcomes and curriculum, for me, is to understand the tensions and inevitable incongruence between the official curriculum, the taught curriculum, the received curriculum, the null curriculum, and the many other layers of curriculum identified by contemporary curriculum theorists. This of course moves us beyond simple input-output, information-processing models that have tended to dominate contemporary educational reform movements.

"natural," and so they always appear to be stilted and never hit quite the right register.

There is always the sense that those who acquired what Bourdieu calls their cultural capital through family channels in the deep, "natural" processes of a lifetime of socialization have a higher form of knowledge and what is constructed in schools as intelligence. Bourdieu has gone so far as to say that common formulations of allegedly natural scholastic "gifts" like intelligence, as well as the supposedly acquired achievements of scholastic achievement, are effectively forms of racism (1984b). In other words, schools take ascribed characteristics like the language use patterns of a particular social group and set these up as grammatical or correct English. Those raised in homes where these forms of discourse are mundane already "know" how to use language without having to be taught by teachers; thus their talents are constructed as natural "gifts" (a sign of an innate intelligence) and ascribed as dispositional, cementing the socially privileged child's advantage in the neutral realm of biology, chemistry, and particularly in the powerful synthesis discipline of neuropsychology. Such socially "gifted" children float easily in disembedded and abstracted institutional spaces (Corbett 2007b) of Giddens's (1990) "expert systems," where crucial "symbolic tokens"[4] like educational credentials are dispensed and transformed into various forms of capital.

The gaze of the ex-principal contained for me all this ambivalence. I did not know whether I was right. It also assumed the form of a tough teacher calling an incorrigible boy to account. When we met briefly after the ceremony, all she said was that things had changed a great deal. Yes they had, I agreed. We now inhabit a different space, one in which we never know, one that is thoroughly permeated by ambivalence and manufactured risk (Giddens 1990; Beck 1992) generated by the very processes that are supposed to bring things under control. I stood in the postwar/postmodern world described by Zygmunt Bauman (1991), who argued that since the Holocaust it is no longer possible to imagine an unproblematic, unified, and coherent framework within which to think about anything anymore, because the big dream contains within it the seeds of oppression and horror. The certainties that informed the principal's practice reproduced patterns of objective social inequality and formed the basis of my night terrors. So what is the alternative? Recently, Deborah Hicks, an educational researcher and teacher who works in white working-class North America,

---

4. Bourdieu is much more critical about this same process, calling it by the name of "symbolic violence" (1984a).

wrote that she entered into the community in which she worked intending to help integrate young women and help them "become leaders who could reclaim their streets as they forged productive economic futures for themselves and their families" (2005, 39). In the end, Hicks came to understand that the girls themselves simply wanted to "get out."

I did not reach this conclusion after my encounter with the ex-principal. I continued, for better or worse, to promote and support the language of the community, teaching children a bit (probably much too little) about the useful-ness and power of Standard English for navigating what Hugh Kenner (1998) calls "elsewhere communities," spaces I'm not sure my students could see very well at all. I also wanted them to understand that the differentials in value connected with each form of discourse had everything to do with the differen-tial power of speakers and nothing in particular to do with correctness. I wanted them to be bilingual, code switchers using context-bridging knowledge (Garfinkel 1967). But we must begin at the beginning, and the beginning is where the children live.

When Life Comes to School It Brings Politics: Fish Stories

I expect that a big part of the change the ex-principal noted is the sense that things have spun out of control and that the predominant social mission of the school, that of drawing a line between the place children are and the space school creates, has been lost. I think I experienced a kind of lingering postmod-ern moment that clarified the fundamental ambivalence of the educational project represented in part by my practice. What I did understand and continue to believe is that orderly, linear, and standardized educational practice is deeply problematic. Expecting everyone to think and speak the same way and to follow the same pedagogical script is probably no better than making explicit the dif-ferences in the way different groups speak and designing pedagogies that attempt to compensate for these differences. As French social theorist and his-torian Jacques Ranciere (1995) has argued—drawing on the example of the French school system that was influenced by the work of Bourdieu and Pass-eron (1979)—progressive, socially differentiated, and compensatory pedagogies have simply made social-class differences more rigid by identifying and mea-suring them. The same is arguably the case with the movement toward a heavily tested national curriculum in the United Kingdom, the No Child Left Behind program in the United States, or similarly focused programs throughout the industrialized world. For the most part institutional education continues to produce vastly unequal educational outcomes, notwithstanding the current round of hand-wringing about "raising the bar and closing the gap." Yet on the other hand, liberal, progressive pedagogies that have implicit standards and that rely on what Bernstein (1977, 80) called "invisible pedagogies" also tend to reinforce preexisting social advantages by their very failure to problematize power and language (Delpitt 1995). There are no easy answers here, and the complex set of problems around language and pedagogy are thorny ones indeed.

One interesting suggestion for thinking about the seeming intractability of problems of social reproduction in schools comes from Ranciere (1995). Ranciere argues that democratic practice remains messy and involves a collision of the interests of different groups (which themselves contain multiple and even contradictory understandings of the very nature of education) in struggle. In other words, democracy is much better served by attending to the ways that school systems actually fail to reproduce inequality, where they come apart momentarily around a racial or a social-class issue, where normally silent voices are for a moment heard. This idea recalls Foucault's (1997) and de Certeau's (1984) way of thinking both about resistance as an ever-present chafing against power and about the persistent failure of every social control scheme. Schools do not reproduce anything in a linear and predictable way; they are ambiguous and ambivalent sites of strategy, tactics, negotiation, and resistance:

> The ambiguity of the school's form opens it up to a multiplicity of choices and meanings: for some it is the realization of equal citizenship, for others a means to social mobility and for yet others a right, independent of its actual use, be it successful or otherwise—a right which democracy owes to itself and to the wishes of its members, however indeterminate these may be. Most of the time all these meanings mingle, making education neither the mask of inequality nor the instrument of inequality's reduction, but the site of a permanent negotiation. (Ranciere 1995, 54)

When the "ambiguous form" of the school is opened up to embrace not just community dialect, but also the difficult problems the community faces in an unstable globalizing economy, school then becomes both a mobilities-focused dream space and a site in which a community might do the hard intellectual work around how it moves forward. I will present a concrete example from my own classroom practice.

Part of my own practice in the elementary school was to create a new ritual, which has continued under the direction of other teachers to this day. This ritual was a yearly dinner theater/fund-raiser for a class trip. I took the central idea of the community Christmas Concert and generated a series of musical theater pieces between 1995 and 2002. Any performance that includes children is a surefire way to bring people into the school. By including a dinner with the performance, we were able to charge admission substantial enough to fund school trips. We wrote the scripts, built sets, wrote music, choreographed, rewrote, practiced, did special effects, found or made costumes, and practiced some more—all the things that go into a theatrical performance. The whole business was cross-curricular and generally took about a month of half-day sessions.

The musicals combined Standard English with vernacular language in some-times odd juxtapositions, but through this kind of intensive engagement a new hybrid kind of language was made possible. These pieces also became increas-ingly political as we experimented with themes that pushed at the edge of con-tested issues in the community. The first of these overtly political pieces was staged in 1997 during a federal election campaign. It was called *Fish Stories* and the idea came out of an invited presentation given to my class of eleven- and twelve-year-olds by a local fisherman.[5] Our guest presented a picture of the small-boat inshore fishery that, as it turned out, is very well-known to my students. It is the story of the decline of stocks, the gradual industrialization

5. *Fish Stories* was the first of a series of musical theater pieces that attempted to challenge and engage the community around key issues of development and sociopolitical questions. The most notable of these productions were *Copper Sunrise* in 2001 and *Magic Fog* in 2002. In 2001, in the wake of a key Supreme Court decision (the Marshall Decision) on Aboriginal fishing rights, the class mounted a play based loosely on Brian Buchan's 1972 novel about the genocide of the Beothuk people. *Copper Sunrise* investigated the process of colonization and racism through the eyes of two eighteenth-century children in Newfoundland, and challenged the local reaction to the Marshall Decision. In 2002 the class transformed *Magic Fog*, a classic children's story set in the community (Sauer 1943), and used its structure to problematize a mega-quarry project proposed by a New Jersey–based stone company. The play helped galvanize community opposition to the construction. After a five-year federal and provincial review process the quarry project was finally rejected in late 2007 by both levels of government on the grounds that the action was too environmentally risky, that the proponent had not established a sound strategy for mitigation of the effects of the operation, and that the entire project ran contrary to commu-nity values and traditional knowledge and uses of the land. For an engaging discussion of the entire process and some of the politics involved, see Richler (2007).

and corporatization of the fishery. In the 1960s, when our guest started fishing, the industry was pretty much unregulated and open to "any young fuller who had a bit of ambition" (in his words). As he saw it, this opportunity to work hard and to make a living was manipulated out of the hands of men in the community by the twin forces of state policy and commodification/corporate concentration.

So into the space of my classroom, with its language arts, math, science, social studies, music, physical education, and health time slots and curriculum outcome expectations, this visitor from life introduced a problem. For him and for many other fishing families, it is *the problem* facing the community. Since most of my students came from families with direct connection to the fishery, they wanted to "do something" about this problem, a problem that they grew up hearing articulated in fish sheds, on boat decks, and around kitchen tables. Given that our yearly dinner theater was on the horizon, we followed up the presentation with a discussion of how we might do something about this problem.

We decided to write our dinner theater in the form of a question to the politicians vying for the federal seat and to combine our performance with a political, all-candidates debate. In the end we performed the piece three times: once for the dinner theater, once at the all-candidates meeting that we successfully organized in the school gym, and once in another Nova Scotia community the class visited on a field trip. The question was simple: "What, Mr. and Ms. Politician, can we expect in our community when we become adults?" The musical itself took the form suggested by our local guest, who encouraged us to take a fifty-year look at the fishery in the community: First, interview community elders about what the fishery was like twenty-five years ago before regulation and corporate involvement. Then, interview parents about what the fishery is like today. Finally, extrapolate in an imaginative way some possible futures that could emerge twenty-five years from now.

The students became very involved in the process of researching, creating, and presenting this musical. So did I—so much so that I think I became so caught up in the process of building the piece that I failed to notice exactly what kind of message our work actually contained. There was a great deal of interest in the community, and our first performance (which was a dinner theater) went very well and was warmly received by the community. I detected a bit of unease, but parents and grandparents are always well pleased to see their children perform and amazed when they learn that the children themselves conceived and wrote the entire production. Summer residents[6] in the village were also highly complementary and expressed amazement that this small rural school was doing the same work with children as that paid for by the urban middle classes to private schools.

The second performance launched what became a very lively, even raucous, all-candidates debate about the fishery, the state, and the community. One of my students even participated in the debate after the performance, asking a very tough question. I felt pretty good about actually helping my students enter the difficult waters of the complex politics of the Atlantic fishery and subsequently into the politics of their family's livelihoods. I saw this as the beginning of political engagement, enfranchisement, and a source of personal empowerment and hope for these children. They had engaged in important political questions, people had taken them seriously, and their work has made a difference in the adult world.

One indicator of the importance of our work was the way the media began to take an interest in what we were up to. I should not have been, but I was a bit surprised to see the regional media present at this performance. After the performance several journalists asked to interview the children. In one of these interviews a national (Canadian Broadcasting Corporation) radio reporter sat five or six children in a circle. He placed his tape recorder on a chair in the middle of the circle and turned it on. Then he asked a number of questions. The first were simple questions obviously designed to put the children at ease. It worked, and they spoke freely. Then he asked a question that has haunted me since. He asked what they learned about the future of the fishery in their community. All five children around the circle answered the question, and using different images, each of them said that they learned that there was no future for them in the fishery and in the community. I was astounded. I couldn't believe it.

Then the reporter turned to me and asked me to respond to the same question. I didn't know what to say. I think I mumbled something about how when children can't see a future, then we adults had better pay attention and think about the kind of world we are building for young people.

6. The phenomenon of summer residents, or "summer people" as they are called locally, is one that could take up another entire chapter. Digby Neck has been a tourist destination for several generations. Additionally, several villages on Digby Neck have been for many years a part-time home for middle-class New Englanders and other Americans as well as for people from central Canada. Coastal properties have been bought up over the years by residents who, for the most part, live on Digby Neck for only a few months of the year.

The Trouble with Outcomes

I now think that by opening up the doors of the school to the complexity of real community issues, we enter a space that is out of control, where we really cannot predict the outcomes. These children reached what I now see as a rather obvious conclusion. A sober investigation of the development of the fishery in a coastal community in Atlantic Canada from the early 1970s to the present day from the point of view of small boat fishing family members is not likely to support anything other than the conclusion that things have gone steadily downhill and will likely continue to do so. This is the history and this is the discourse that swirls around the community and has done so for some time. This interview was a test, a powerful assessment of my teaching methods and the educational outcomes of the whole exercise, which ran essentially counter to the kinds of outcomes I anticipated and hoped for. I thought for a long time that the whole project was a massive failure because children came away from it convinced that their community was crumbling.

The truth is that the community is indeed transforming in ways that place the small boat fishery in jeopardy and that probably mean that most of these children will dream of leaving for a more stable and arguably better life. To leave they will require the "wings" of a formal education, the credentials that show them to possess transferable educational capital in other places. Part of this learning to leave is that they will have to speak the language of larger spaces. In the end, it is very possible that my own naïve sense of how outcomes could be predicted and how the children I taught could live inside a linguistic, social, and economic universe provided by their community was, as the principal's gaze might have suggested, misplaced. Any curriculum, standardized or place-based, will have outcomes, consequences, and nuances that can never be predicted.

In later pieces, I moved with my students between the vernacular language and political concerns of their families, and the poetic language of literature and a more subtle take on the difficult relationship between community issues and the practices of schooling. The politics of language and of language teaching have continued to generate a productive and powerful tension in my pedagogy, a tension that is partially resolved by a kind of bilingual approach that tries to help students see that languages can speak to one another in the heteroglossia of a contemporary classroom. This multiplicity of subcodes mirrors the multiple linguistic representations contained within the same language outside school (Shields 2007). Rather than serving as sites for the inculcation of a unified, "correct" language, schools might alternatively operate as places in which different forms of language usage that reflect diverse histories, social class, ethnicities, and cultures could come together in a linguistically democratic space.

Support for the development of what Ulrich Beck has recently called a "cosmopolitan vision" (2006) does not mean to forget the local and to orient social research away from the specificity of place. On the contrary, Beck suggests that qualitative research now has a particularly poignant relevance at this juncture because "cosmopolitan sensibility and competence arise from the clash of cultures within one's own life," where it is no longer possible to ignore the "copresence and coexistence of rival lifestyles, contradictory certainties in the experiential space of individuals and societies" (2006, 89). Likewise, it seems to me that desirable rural teaching practice ought to build similar bridges between the local and the global by helping young people investigate systematically the ways that globalization transforms, complicates, and infuses necessarily local lives.

References

Ashton-Warner, S. 1963. *Teacher*. New York: Simon and Schuster.

Bauman, Z. 1991. *Modernity and ambivalence*. Ithaca: Cornell University Press.

———. 1998. *Globalization: The human consequences*. London: Polity.

———. 2001. *The individualized society*. London: Polity.

———. 2004. *Identity: Conversations with Benedetto Vecchi*. London: Polity.

Beck U. 1992. *Risk society: Towards a new modernity*. London: Sage.

———. 2006. *The cosmopolitan vision*. Cambridge: Polity.

Bernstein, B. 1977. *Class, codes, and control*. Vol. 3, *Towards a theory of educational transmissions*. London: Routledge and Kegan Paul.

Bourdieu, P. 1984a. *Distinction: A social critique of the judgement of taste* (Richard Nice, trans.). Cambridge: Harvard University Press.

———. 1984b. Le racism de l'intelligence. In *Questions de sociologie*, 264–68. Paris: Editions de Minuit.

Bourdieu, P., and J. C. Passeron. 1979. *The inheritors: French students and their relation to culture* (Richard Nice, trans.). Chicago: University of Chicago Press.

Bowers, C. 2001. *Educating for eco-justice and community*. Athens: University of Georgia Press.

———. 2006. *Revitalizing the commons: Cultural and educational sites of resistance and affirmation*. Lanham, Md.: Rowman and Littlefield.

Buchan, B. 1972. *Copper sunrise*. Toronto: Scholastic.

Castells, M. 2004. *The power of identity: Economy, society, and culture*. Vol. 2, *The information age: Economy, society, and culture* (2d ed.). Oxford: Blackwell.

Ching, B., and G. W. Creed, eds. 1997. *Knowing your place: Rural identity and cultural hierarchy*. New York: Routledge.

Corbett, M. 1991. *Dropping out in Digby: Early school leaving in a coastal community*. Digby, NS: Digby Regional School Board.

———. 2007a. *Learning to leave: The irony of schooling in a coastal community*. Halifax: Fernwood Publishing.

———. 2007b. Learning and dreaming in space and place: Identity and rural schooling. *Canadian Journal of Education* 30 (3), 771–92.

Davis, M. 2004 (March–April). Planet of slums: Urban involution and the informal proletariat. *New Left Review* 26, 5–34.

de Certeau, M. 1984. *The practice of everyday life* (Steven Rendell, trans.). Berkeley and Los Angeles: University of California Press.

Delpit, L. 1995. The silenced dialogue: Power and pedagogy in educating other people's children. In L. Delpit, *Other people's children: Cultural conflict in the classroom*, 119–39. New York: The New Press.

Dewey, J. 1938. *Experience and education*. New York: Collier.

Dews, B., and C. Law, eds. 1995. *This fine place so far from home: The voice of academics from the working class*. Philadelphia: Temple University Press.

Dowdy, J., and L. Delpit, eds. 2003. *The skin that we speak: Thoughts on language and culture in the classroom*. New York: The New Press.

Foucault, M. 1997. *Essential works of Foucault, 1954–1984*. Vol. 1, *Ethics, subjectivity, and truth* (R. Hurley, trans; P. Rabinow, ed.). New York: The New Press.

Garfinkel, H. 1967. *Studies in ethnomethodology*. Cambridge: Polity.

Giddens, A. 1990. *The consequences of modernity*. Stanford: Stanford University Press.

———. 1991. *Modernity and self-identity: Self and society in the late modern age*. Stanford: Stanford University Press.

Giroux, H. 1988. *Teachers as intellectuals: Toward a critical pedagogy of learning*. South Hadley, Mass.: Bergin and Garvey.

Hicks, D. 2005. Labor histories. *Educational Researcher* 34 (3), 34–39.

hooks, b. 1994. *Teaching to transgress*. New York: Routledge.

Kenner, H. 1998. *The elsewhere community*. Toronto: Anansi.

Kincheloe, J., and W. Pinar, eds. 1991. *Curriculum as social psychoanalysis: The significance of place*. Albany: State University of New York Press.

Popkewitz, T. 1998. *Struggling for the soul: The politics of schooling and the construction of the teacher*. New York: Teachers College Press.

Ranciere, J. 1995. *On the shores of politics* (Liz Heron. trans.). London: Verso.

Richler, N. 2007 (December). Rock bottom: With the seas nearly barren, should Digby Neck, Nova Scotia, settle for selling the earth? *The Walrus*. Retrieved November 21, 2007, from http://www.walrusmagazine.com/print/2007.12-business-nova -scotia-mining.

Sauer, J. [1943] 1986. *Fog magic*. New York: Puffin Newbury Library.

Shields, C. 2007. *Bakhtin*. New York: Peter Lang.

Urry, J. 2000. *Sociology beyond societies: Mobilities for the twenty-first century*. New York: Routledge.

7

GLOBALIZATION, ASYMMETRIC URBANIZATION, AND RURAL DISADVANTAGE IN SUB-SAHARAN AFRICA

Sarah Giroux, Fatou Jah, and Parfait Eloundou-Enyegue

Introduction

In the flattening world envisioned by Friedman (2005), globalization is viewed as the ultimate equalizer. By facilitating cross-national flow of ideas, capital, technology, and labor, this process is expected to compress geographic and socioeconomic distance between nations, and indeed, global inequality *among countries* appears to have declined steadily in recent decades (Firebaugh and Goesling 2004). At the same time, however, inequality within regions and within countries may be rising. In sub-Saharan Africa particularly, Kandiwa (2006) notes growing economic differentiation among countries since the 1960s, and there is further concern about widening inequality within countries. One dimension of this growing inequality is between rural and urban communities. Because rural communities in Africa remain at the periphery of global development, their ability to "plug and play" onto the global scene is of special interest. Urban bias in postcolonial Africa meant that urban centers controlled the provision of public services and exercised this control to their advantage. Even as globalization processes may foster geographic mobility, the socioeconomic mobility of rural populations remains an issue. The question is whether globalization processes will reverse or instead reinforce urban bias. Theoretical expectations are mixed. On the one hand, some of the transformations associated with globalization could curtail urban bias: circular migration, expansion of primary education, and a wave of political democratization in the 1990s could all foster the economic convergence of rural and urban populations

(UNFPA 2007). On the other hand, globalization can be "selective, reaching the urban middle class more than the rural poor" (Eloundou-Enyegue, McHugh, and Orcutt 2004, 196). Furthermore, slow economic growth in sub-Saharan Africa may intensify competition for off-farm employment. As global forces increasingly pit cities against rural communities, rural-urban ties may break down, resulting in an increase in rural-urban inequality.

Given these mixed expectations, the impact of globalization on rural communities is an empirical question. Can rural children compete effectively under the increasingly global and competitive urban economy of developing countries? We argue that this question is best understood by looking at two complementary spheres: the school system and the labor market. Accordingly, this chapter examines recent trends in educational attainment (and subsequent labor market outcomes) for rural children. Additionally, if rural children face discrimination, does this reflect differences in human capital versus some intrinsic effect of rural identity per se?

After a brief overview of the trends in globalization and urbanization in sub-Saharan Africa, we examine theoretical predictions from consensus and conflict perspectives. We then provide a panoramic view of regional trends in rural-urban differentials in education, using data from Demographic and Health Surveys (DHS 2007). Lastly, for a more in-depth look at the dynamics of the formation of rural-urban inequality, we turn to detailed data from Cameroon, a country where competition for off-farm employment has greatly increased in the years after 1990.

Education as an Equalizer Under Globalization

Educational access for rural children is a central concern in the globalizing and urbanizing economies of the developing world. By roughly 2008, and for the first time in human history, the majority of the world's population will be urban, a watershed event that culminates nearly five decades of steady urbanization (United Nations 2004; United Nations Population Fund 2007). The urbanization of developing countries is particularly noted for its pace[1] and asymmetry. Unlike transitions in western Europe and the United States (Pres-

---

1. Population growth in these countries is projected to average 2.3 percent per year between 2000 and 2030 (United Nations 2004). Despite higher rural than urban fertility, these countries have steadily urbanized as a result of both annexation and conversion of rural areas into urban centers, as well as continued rural-to-urban migration (Todaro 1997; United Nations 2004).

ton 1979; Williamson 1988), this urbanization occurs without commensurate growth in the economy.[2] This asymmetric growth is well captured in comparative studies of growth in employment versus urbanization (Giroux 2008). While a few countries have experienced faster growth in off-farm employment than in urban population, the vast majority of African countries have experienced the reverse scenario, where growth in urban population has far outstripped growth in off-farm employment (Giroux 2008; United Nations 2004). Not only have sub-Saharan African nations registered rapid annual rates of urbanization (ca. 2.5 percent) over the last four decades, they have also faced weak and stagnant economies during this period (Opal and Fay 2000; United Nations 2004). From 1970 to 1995, the region experienced a 0.66 percent annual decline in GDP per capita, thus intensifying competition for urban employment (Opal and Fay 2000).

Such asymmetric transitions have raised concern about urban congestion, the economic adaptation of rural migrants (Beauchemin and Bocquier 2004; Todaro 1997), and the schooling and economic opportunities of their children. Given the classic rural disadvantage in education and employment (Mehrotra, Vandemoortele, and Delamonica 2000; Moots 1976; Pattaravanich et al. 2005; UNCTAD 1997), analysts question whether current urbanization will selectively benefit urban areas (Todaro 1997).

Theoretical Perspectives

Processes of occupational attainment can be understood from the contrasted perspectives of merit versus ascription (Brint 1998; Grusky 1994). Consensus theories tend to be rooted in functional sociological theory and economic human capital theory, and thus attribute variation in outcomes to differences in individuals' cognitive abilities (Jencks et. al., 1994; Squires 1977). Researchers working within this perspective emphasize the importance of individual-level characteristics—mostly human capital factors such as IQ, ability, educational attainment, and personal aspirations—in shaping schooling outcomes. Further, differences in levels of education are cited as the source of much of the variation in occupational status attainment (Grusky 1994; Mincer 1974). Thus, poli-

2. Todaro (1997) has explained the seemingly paradoxical continuation of rural-urban migration even in the face of high levels of unemployment. In this perspective, migration is not driven solely by current wage or employment differentials, but also by rural migrants' expectation of lifetime earnings.

cies emerging from this perspective tend to contain programs that focus on job training and education, the assumption being that "human capital, and the capacity to work, [are] among the most important assets the poor [ought to gain]" (IFAD 2001, v; see also Jencks et al. 1994). Thus, for researchers working within this perspective, rural disadvantage in the labor market stems mostly from differences in educational attainment.

Conversely, conflict theorists underscore the importance of privilege and bias. Within this theoretical framework, individuals with certain ascribed characteristics are subject to discriminatory practices (Gugler 1982; Lipton 1977). Powerful groups construct and maintain a social structure that systematically discriminates against less powerful groups. This discrimination typically "involves the differential treatment of persons 'based on' race, religion, gender or some other social category, rather than criteria that are really relevant to the choices being made" (Blalock 1991, 7). While much of the literature views ascription in individual terms, community-level factors are also key. In this particular case, the question is whether rural communities, regardless of individual characteristics, bestow special disadvantage on their residents. In explaining rural-urban inequality, conflict theorists tend to stress domination and exploitation of the rural poor by urban elites. Gugler (1982) thus moves the locus of privilege or bias from individuals to communities. He explains the persistence of rural-urban inequality as being the result of urban elites' capacity to transfer the majority of national resources to urban centers, which become "the centers of power and privilege" (188). By channeling resources to cities, the elite work to preserve power and privilege. Lipton, likewise, views the rural urban divide as the largest class conflict in the third world because "the rural sector contains most of the poverty and most of the low cost sources of potential advance; but the urban sector contains most of the articulateness, organization and power" (1977, 13).

Policy initiatives that flow from conflict perspectives will thus follow a different logic. Conflict theorists see the notion of meritocracy as concealing a social order in which those already advantaged by existing social structures are also more likely to perform well (Brint 1998). Conflict theorists, therefore, support programs that provide more opportunities to those with disadvantageous ascriptive characteristics. These programs include affirmative action programs for racial and ethnic minorities. In several developing contexts, *equalizing* strategies can include but are not limited to providing greater educational access, financial assistance in forms of scholarships, and instruction relevant to the groups in question, including rural children, girls, and children from low-income families.

More Plausible Scenarios

"Consensus" and "conflict" are, of course, two extremes in a continuum. More realistic theories would include a mix of merit and privilege. The extent to which merit and privilege factors influence outcomes will vary depending on an individual's place in the occupation attainment process. It is also likely to depend on the broader national stage of development. Some theorists have thus suggested that industrialization, urbanization, and the development of mass communications should foster a more open society and a shift from achievement based on ascribed characteristics to achievement based on merit (Lipset and Bendix 1959; Treiman 1970). With this shift, the relative importance of family background (conflict factors) on occupational attainment should decline, while the importance of educational attainment (consensus factors) rises (Buchmann and Hannum 2001). Though there remains little agreement on the relationship between status attainment and level of urbanization,[3] this previous research suggests the need to examine processes of status attainment in historical perspective.

Not only can the relative influence of conflict and consensus factors change over time, but it can also shift across an individual's life course. Inequities can be confined to the school system, they can occur predominantly in the labor market, or they can occur in both spheres. Further, within the labor market, inequality can occur predominantly within in the formal sector, the informal sector, or both spheres. Portes, Castells, and Benton (1989) and Todaro (1997) recommend distinguishing between these two spheres. Despite its relative lack of regulation, the informal sector is demographically and economically important in many developing countries. This sector—conceptualized here as "a process of income-generation . . . unregulated by the institutions of society, in

3. Kelley and Perlman (1971) found that residents of Toro, Uganda, experienced higher levels of occupational mobility prior to industrialization, while Bills and Haller (1984) noted that the status attainment of Brazilian citizens was not dependent on the level of industrialization. In 1989, Treiman and Yip, using cross-national data for twenty-one countries, found that "the impact of social origins on educational and occupational attainment declines with industrialization." But they "concluded that this is primarily due to a decline in the level of status inequality in industrialized societies and is not a result of industrialization per se" (393; for a fuller review of these studies, see Buchmann and Hannum 2001).

a legal and social environment in which similar activities are regulated" (Portes, Castells, and Benton 1989, 12)—comprises "a large number of small-scale production and service activities that are individually or family owned and use labor-intensive and simple technology" (Todaro 1997, 13). Today it occupies a large share of the urban labor force in many developing countries (DHS 2007) and has been shown to support the formal sector by providing cheap basic services. While some argue that the informal sector provides economic opportunities to marginalized constituencies and fuels economic growth, research suggests that wage inequality has increased in nearly all developing countries that have undergone rapid trade liberalization, typically in the context of declining industrial employment of unskilled workers (UNCTAD 1997).

Depending on the locus and historical trends in discrimination, one can thus distinguish five main scenarios that could characterize the formation of rural disadvantage in schooling and employment:

(1) *Marginalization*: Rural children face a disadvantage in both schooling and in the labor market. Educational and economic marginalization is primarily due to their rural identity. They have increasing difficulty in securing off-farm employment and, if they migrate to urban areas, they predominantly join the ranks of the urban poor or street children. In this situation, conflict factors dominate as the determinants of an individual's socioeconomic attainment.

(2) *Structural convergence:* A second possibility occurs when, adjusting for schooling levels, rural children are not disadvantaged in accessing off-farm employment. Under this scenario, rural children may still be disadvantaged in schooling, but this disadvantage is more likely to be associated with family- rather than community-level factors. This is the situation implied in Goldscheider's (1987, 683) statement that there is "no structural feature that inhibits migrants from participation into the urban economy." In other words, much of the rural-urban inequality in employment outcomes is tied to family-based inequality in the resource endowments of children. Thus, family factors may play a role in educational attainment, but "consensus" dominates in occupational attainment.

(3) *Segregation*: Under the third scenario, rural children are disproportionately funneled into informal employment, even after adjusting for educational attainment. This segregation may arise from differences in

school quality, social connections, occupational/salary aspirations, or
family pressure to work.

(4) *Full convergence*: A fourth scenario is one of greater equity, where even
the inequalities associated with family background wane and personal
characteristics remain the only possible source of inequality. In this
scenario, outcomes of the status attainment process increasingly depend
fully on consensus factors. Under this situation, variation in human
capital would be key to differential outcomes.

(5) *Queuing*: This is an intermediate scenario where the disadvantage of
rural children fluctuates with labor market conditions. Disadvantage is
minimal in prosperous times but resurfaces during hard economic
times. Thus, when the economy can absorb more workers, disadvantage
only stems from variation in human capital. But when jobs become
scarce, the importance of privilege and personal connections tends to
reemerge.

Previous Research

Previous empirical research has typically found a rural disadvantage in schooling. In Cameroon rural sixth graders are 2.2 times more likely to drop out of
school than their urban counterparts (Eloundou-Enyegue and Davanzo 2003).
Nearly the same odds ratio (2.0) is reported in Benin, perhaps because less than
50 percent of the national education budget supports rural schools, even as
over 60 percent of the population resides in rural areas (Mehrotra, Vandemoortele, and Delamonica 2000). But as this study shows, the disadvantage does not
entirely stem from rural residence per se. Instead, an important interaction
exists between rural background and income, with "richest groups in rural
areas achieving a gross enrollment rate of 50 per cent while the poor only
manage 36 per cent" (Mehrotra, Vandemoortele, and Delamonica 2000, 16).
Thus, when considering rural disadvantage, one must account for other corre-
lates of disadvantageous outcomes, such as income, gender, and family structure.

Beyond these (relatively) easily observable factors, other, more subtle processes at the family level must be considered. For instance, educational expectations and aspirations, cultural capital, and educational resources of the
household have been proposed as relevant influences (Bourdieu 1977; Buchmann 2001; Buchmann and Dalton 2002; Spenner and Featherman 1978; Teach-

man and Paasch 1998). Teachman and Paasch's (1998) work in the United States found only a small part of the variations in educational aspirations to be tied to standard socioeconomic and demographic variables, such as parental income and education. Disadvantage could additionally result from differences in households' educational resources (fewer books or less educated adults in the household) (Mercy and Steelman 1982; Teachman 1987) or cultural capital (Bourdieu 1977). While few studies have specifically examined these factors, advanced methods of statistical analysis can account for—although not identify—these unobserved influences (Giroux 2008; Teachman and Paasch 1998). If rural children are indeed disadvantaged in schooling, this could lead to a disadvantage in securing employment as well. A fuller understanding of the disadvantage facing rural children requires attention to both schooling and labor market spheres and to both observable and unobservable factors.

Beyond family differences, broader social forces are important. Rural schools usually receive lower levels of public investments than urban schools. For example, in Uganda, despite the fact that over 88 percent of the population lives in rural areas, rural schools received about 36 cents of each education dollar spent by the government, resulting in poorer infrastructure and teacher quality (Ablo and Reinikka 1998; World Bank 2006). These inferior conditions not only translate into worse learning environments and poorer educational achievement, but also decrease the likelihood that parents will decide to enroll their children in school in the first place (Glewwe and Jacoby 1992; Lavy 1992). Many low-income countries are increasingly granting books and tuition-free primary education. Other indirect schooling costs and differences in the number of and distance to schools, teacher quality, and instructional resources, however, are still likely to preserve the rural-urban gap in schooling access/ quality and, ultimately, occupational opportunities.

General Trends in Rural-Urban Differentials in Education

To better understand the nature of rural disadvantage in schooling in sub-Saharan Africa, we provide a panoramic overview of schooling trends in the region, using data from the Demographic and Health Surveys (DHS 2007).[4]

4. The DHS data are an excellent source of information for researchers interested in educational inequality in sub-Saharan Africa as well as other developing countries, as its nationally representative surveys cover multiple countries and time points. Therefore they are appropriate to use in order to study spatial and historical variation in educational inequality.

Table 1, found at the end of this chapter, includes information from thirty-one countries. While we only report the findings from the most recent DHS surveys, nearly three-quarters of these countries were surveyed multiple times. The sample of thirty-one nations covers 65 percent of all sub-Saharan countries and over 80 percent of the region's total population (World Bank 2007).

A quick perusal of the table shows large variation in educational attainment between rural and urban populations. Data from the past five years show that Burkina Faso in 2003 and Niger in 2006 had the largest rural populations with no schooling (88 and 86 percent, respectively). In contrast, countries with the highest percentages of rural residents with secondary diplomas include South Africa (28 percent, 1998), Zimbabwe (27 percent, 2005/06), and Ghana (20 percent, 2003). Even in these cases, however, a large gap remains between rural and urban residents with regard to secondary school attainment. Further analysis of the table shows that a greater percentage of urban residents have completed secondary school and higher across all country years. The only times rural enrollment in primary school exceeds urban enrollment is in cases where there are high levels of enrollment in secondary school among the urban population. In all these cases, the overall percentage of urbanites enrolled in school is still greater than the percentage of rural residents enrolled.

A Case Study

While the previous section underscores the regional gap in rural-urban education, it does not fully address our central research question of how rural disadvantage in schooling translates into the labor market. Thus, to complement the broader discussion of the above section, we look at more focused evidence from Cameroon to examine the formation of rural disadvantage in schooling and the labor market. Cameroon, a central African country of nearly eighteen million people, is interesting as a case study because its economic and demographic profile is broadly similar to other nations in the sub-Saharan region (USSD 2006; World Bank 2006).[5] With regard to schooling, there has been a

5. Infant and child mortality rates are lower in Cameroon, but the nation's average life expectancy of forty-six years is close to the overall sub-Saharan value. Primary-school enrollment rates in Cameroon are significantly greater than the regional, but rates of primary-school completion are nearly identical (World Bank 2006). With regard to the economy, average GNI (gross national income) per capita in Cameroon is high for the region (US$810 versus US$601), though annual GDP growth is relatively similar. While the percent of land area devoted to agriculture is much smaller in Cameroon (20 percent versus 44 percent in sub-Saharan Africa), value-added agriculture as a percentage of the GDP is higher in Cameroon than in the broader region (44 percent in Cameroon versus 16 percent in sub-Saharan Africa). In terms of population growth,

persistent rural-urban differential in enrollment rates. In 1991,[6] the percentage of urban residents in Cameroon with a secondary diploma was 23.8 percent and only 7.4 percent for rural residents. While both groups gained in enrollment levels, by 2004 only 9.7 percent of rural residents had acquired secondary schooling. Conversely, this number rose to 34.9 percent for urban residents. Thus, in this case, not only do urban residents have higher levels of secondary schooling, but the rate of growth during this period was greater for urban residents.

More important, Cameroon's urbanization has been quite asymmetric. In the last two decades, the country's urbanization rate (17 percent) has far outpaced its percent growth in off-farm employment (3.5 percent), thus resulting in urban congestion and increasing urban unemployment. Further, this urbanization was accompanied by a severe economic depression in the late 1980s and early 1990s. Prior to this period, Cameroon was one of the fastest-growing nations in Africa, mainly due to the success of its primary exports, including oil, cocoa, coffee, and cotton (USSD 2006). But a drop in export commodity prices, combined with poor fiscal management and an overvalued currency, led to a significant economic depression and a decline in the per capita GNP, from US$750 in 1981 to US$490 in 1995 (USSD 2006; World Bank 2006). Both this decline and some of the adjustment policies used in response—such as shrinking the public-sector labor force through layoffs, forced retirements, and a freeze on new appointments—led to a sharp rise in urban unemployment (Eloundou and Davanzo 2003). Recent DHS statistics show urban unemployment rates of nearly 49 percent in 2004, with unemployment affecting all educational groups (DHS 2007).

Explaining Rural Disadvantage in Cameroon

What explains the formation of rural disadvantage in schooling and the labor market in Cameroon? In a recent study we investigated this using detailed event

---

Cameroon experiences an annual growth rate nearly 15 percent lower than the regional average, and the distribution of the population is drastically different from other countries in the region: while only 37 percent of the population resides within urban areas in sub-Saharan Africa, 52 percent of Cameroon's residents are urbanites (World Bank 2006).

6. For presentation purposes, data for Cameroon for 1991 was not included in the table. Researchers interested in historical trends can find this information at the DHS Web site, http://www.measuredhs.com/.

history data from a nationally representative sample[7] to look at the roots and trends in rural disadvantage. We focused sequentially on disadvantage in schooling, then in the labor market, distinguishing between the formal and informal sectors. Consistent with previous studies (Eloundou-Enyegue and Davanzo 2003; Mehrotra, Vandemoortele, and Delamonica 2000; Pattaravanich et al. 2005), our study showed that rural children fared worse than their urban counterparts in the school system. The odds of a child with rural parental background dropping out of school were about twice those of an urban child (data not shown here). While the consensus perspective would link this to differences in ability, some of our evidence suggests otherwise. If one controls for differences in ability,[8] the odds ratio declined from about 2.2 to 1.6 (data not shown here). That the gap would persist after controlling for ability clearly indicates that the rural disadvantage in schooling is not simply due to skills. Further control for fixed but unobserved[9] characteristics of families suggested that these were influential. Once we control for the "family effect," the rural-urban difference in educational attainment disappears, with the hazard ratio dropping to a nonsignificant 1.03. In sum, some unobserved characteristics of families, rather than differences in ability or family composition, explain rural-urban inequality in schooling. Finally, analyses showed that the rural disadvantage declined historically but experienced increases during prosperous economic times, suggesting that urban children gained more during prosperous times than their rural counterparts.

Granted that a rural disadvantage exists in schooling, what are the implications for labor force participation? Findings showed no evidence of rural disadvantage in overall paid employment. But the picture becomes different if one distinguishes between the formal and the informal labor markets. In the formal sector, the annual odds of employment were significantly lower (about 30 per-

7. In all, 3,369 families were surveyed and information was collected regarding the schooling and employment histories for 11,590 biological children of the main female respondents in these households. For a more detailed discussion of the analytic and methodological approach, see Giroux (2008).

8. Ability here is measured by the number of times a student has repeated grades, as well as an index of "inordinate ability." For more information, see Giroux (2008).

9. Control for these unobserved influences is made by using fixed effects modeling, a methodological technique that uses the PHREG procedure in SAS. Essentially, this procedure indexes every family and controls for the impact of residing within each household. It thus controls for the "fixed" or stable factors that exist within each family, even though it cannot specify the exact nature of these fixed family influences. As these are factors operating at the household level, plausible explanations might include variation in educational expectations and aspirations, cultural capital, and educational resources.

cent) among children from a rural background than they were among other children.

The next step was to consider whether the gross rural-urban inequality—consistent with consensus theorists—is due to differences in human capital.[10] The findings indicated that this was indeed the case. Overall, much of the inequality experienced by rural children in accessing formal employment was associated with their lower educational attainment. Moreover, an analysis of trends showed that the magnitude of the disadvantage had increased over time. This finding is important. It suggests that while the disparity in schooling has declined historically, labor market inequality that is not dependent on variation in human capital has increased. As rural children began to achieve higher levels of schooling, the significance of schooling in shaping labor market outcomes might have declined.

Conclusion

Globalization is of particular concern to African countries, which need to develop public policy that maximizes globalization's potential social and economic benefits, and simultaneously minimizes the risks of destabilization or economic marginalization (Ouattara 1997). This chapter investigates whether rural communities may be increasingly marginalized as globalization progresses, as reflected by increased disadvantage in schooling and labor market participation; and, if so, whether this marginalization primarily reflects bias associated with rural background and identity, or whether it is the result of individual merit-based factors, including human capital.

Our findings suggest a paradox in rural education. On the one hand, national governments and international agencies are pushing for increased enrollments among rural populations. Evidence from Cameroon and DHS data suggest that many sub-Saharan countries have heeded these calls, and that while rural children still lag behind their urban counterparts in schooling, the rural-urban schooling gap is narrowing. But the tightening labor markets in many of these countries mean that increased enrollments may not be enough to equalize the overall lifecourse trajectories of rural and urban children, specifically those related to occupational attainment.

In Cameroon, rural-urban inequality in occupational attainment appears to

---

10. Measured here as maximum grade attained and its squared term.

Table 1 Rural-urban differentials in educational attainment

Country and Survey Year	Urban Level of education (%)					Rural Level of education (%)				
	None	Primary	Secondary	Higher	N	None	Primary	Secondary	Higher	N
Benin 2001	45.7	37.0	15.5	1.2	4,569	73.8	22.7	2.8	0.1	7,419
Burkina Faso 2003	42.9	34.0	21.3	1.6	4,574	87.9	10.8	1.1	0	19,513
Cameroon 2004	16.2	45.7	34.9	2.6	10,131	41.6	48.0	9.7	0.2	10,570
CAR 1994–95	37.1	47.2	14.5	0.7	4,661	68.1	29.3	2.0	0.1	6,404
Chad 2004	52.2	32.9	13.8	1.0	2,283	78.3	20.5	1.2	0	8,977
Comoros 1996	45.9	30.7	21.1	1.1	1,685	64.2	28.2	6.3	0.2	4,388
Congo (Brazzaville) 2005	9.1	37.4	49.6	3.2	6,764	22.2	53.1	24.0	0.2	5,856
Cote d'Ivoire 1998–99	42.4	37.1	17.7	2.3	2,099	66.4	29.6	3.4	0.1	3,394
Eritrea 2002	30.2	44.1	22.0	2.3	7,259	67.0	30.2	2.2	0	10,994
Ethiopia 2005	30.7	34.1	30.8	4.3	3,951	72.8	25.0	1.8	0.1	23,750
Gabon 2000	12.0	44.6	39.2	3.1	9,471	31.1	55.9	12.7	0.2	3,497
Ghana 2003	25.9	27.1	43.9	2.8	4,841	46.8	31.8	20.4	0.6	5,944
Guinea 2005	49.2	32.7	16.4	1.2	4,727	81.6	15.8	1.9	0.1	11,434
Kenya 2003	13.9	50.6	24.3	10.7	3,099	25.2	61.9	10.8	1.7	12,316

Lesotho 2004	3.9	53.4	37.4	5.0	2,913	8.5	74.9	15.7	0.6	12,034
Madagascar 2003–4	11.2	48.6	35.9	3.6	3,550	28.1	57.6	12.9	0.8	11,682
Malawi 2004	10.2	63.0	24.0	2.7	3,651	27.5	67.2	4.9	0.1	20,388
Mali 2001	55.7	27.5	14.5	1.3	7,201	85.1	13.0	0.8	0.1	18,985
Mauritania 2000–1	41.9	40.6	15.1	1.3	6,343	70.4	26.0	2.2	0	8,992
Mozambique 2003	24.2	63.0	11.9	0.4	8,128	54.9	43.7	0.7	0	15,742
Namibia 2000	11.4	36.5	47.4	3.5	4,760	25.2	50.5	22.0	0.8	9,587
Niger 2006	51.1	32.5	14.6	1.0	3,287	86.4	12.2	0.7	0	15,325
Nigeria 2003	31.9	30.9	29.5	6.8	4,839	53.4	28.3	15.2	1.7	9,521
Rwanda 2005	19.4	61.7	15.9	2.2	3,103	30.9	65.3	3.4	0	16,823
Senegal 2005	41.3	39.7	16.4	1.2	12,303	74.7	22.5	1.8	0.1	15,110
South Africa 1998	7.5	35.5	48.5	7.4	13,334	21.3	48.0	28.2	1.7	10,913
Tanzania 2004	17.7	67.5	10.8	3.9	4,758	38.5	59.5	1.6	0.3	14,259
Togo 1998	32.1	47.6	18.9	1.0	5,561	59.5	36.3	3.7	0	11,159
Uganda 2006	11.5	52.5	26.7	8.5	2,441	24.8	66.7	6.8	1.2	15,174
Zambia 2001–2	12.9	55.5	26.9	4.3	5,417	31.6	59.1	8.2	0.5	9,237
Zimbabwe 2005–6	4.8	32.3	57.6	4.6	5,746	15.2	57.0	26.5	0.8	12,154

SOURCE: ORC MACRO 2007. MEASURE DHS STAT compiler. http://www.measuredhs.com, October 31, 2007.

be created as follows: First, rural and urban children differ markedly in their educational attainment. These differences are not fully accounted for by differences in human capital or urban bias per se, but rather by unmeasured processes operating at the family level, or a more generic "family effect." In turn, human capital factors influence labor market outcomes after schooling. Not only are more educated individuals more likely to be employed in the paid sector, but one's schooling performance (as indicated by limited grade repetition) is associated with higher odds of formal-sector employment. Adjusting for human capital, inequality in formal employment disappears. Thus the roots of inequality in accessing formal-sector employment appear to reside in educational attainment, as would be suggested by a consensus perspective and "structural convergence."

But the consensus perspective does not offer a full account either. First, the inequality in educational attainment itself stems from a mix of individual merit and unmeasured family-level characteristics. While we could not pinpoint the exact nature of these characteristics, they may emerge from systematic urban bias (such as lower funding to rural schools or lower aspirations in rural families) that stems from preexisting bias, which could give support to the conflict perspective. Future research on the nature of these unobservables is needed to inform educational policy seeking to redress rural-urban inequality. Additionally, as these unobservables are likely factors that are not easily captured in surveys, qualitative work (such as focus groups or observation studies) could prove quite useful in identifying the precise nature of the factors unable to be identified through conventional quantitative analysis. Second, the importance of educational attainment in explaining rural-urban inequality in the formal labor market has declined over time. As rural children caught up in education, the non-schooling barriers to entry to formal-sector employment may have grown.

Thus, the study supports a conceptual expansion beyond the habitual focus on human capital and urban bias, and beyond classic, easily measured, factors. Evidence from our case study suggests that future work on rural disadvantage in educational and occupational attainment in the sub-Saharan region may benefit from a recognition that disadvantage can emerge from both structural and individual sources. By utilizing a framework that combines these two perspectives, researchers and policy makers alike can approach a fuller understanding of how current processes of globalization are shaping the nature of rural disadvantage in sub-Saharan Africa.

References

Ablo, E., and R. Reinikka. 1998. *Do budgets really matter? Evidence from public spending on education and health in Uganda* (Policy Research Working Paper No. 1926). Washington, D.C.: World Bank, Africa Region.

Beauchemin, C., and P. Bocquier. 2004. Migration and urbanization in francophone West Africa: An overview of the recent empirical evidence. *Urban Studies* 41 (11), 2245–72.

Bills, D., and A. Haller. 1984. Socio-economic development and social stratification: Reassessing the Brazilian case. *Journal of Developing Areas* 19 (1), 59–70.

Blalock, H. M., Jr. 1991. *Understanding social inequality: Modeling allocation processes.* Thousand Oaks, Calif.: Sage.

Bourdieu, P. 1977. Cultural reproduction and social reproduction. In J. Karabel and A. H. Halsey, eds., *Power and ideology in education,* 487–511. New York: Oxford University Press.

Brint, S. 1998. *Schools and societies.* Thousands Oaks, Calif.: Pine Forge Press.

Buchmann, C. 2001 (March). Getting ahead in Kenya: The role of shadow education and social capital in adolescents' school success. Paper presented at the annual meeting of the Population Association of America, Washington, D.C.

Buchmann, C., and B. Dalton. 2002. Interpersonal influences and educational aspirations in 12 countries: The importance of institutional context. *Sociology of Education* 75 (2), 99–123.

Buchmann, C., and E. Hannum. 2001. Education and stratification in developing countries: A review of theories and research. *Annual Review of Sociology* 27 (1), 77–101.

Demographic and Health Surveys (DHS). 2007. StatCompiler, ORC, macro. *Measure DHS+ Project.* Retrieved December 2006, from http://www.statcompiler.com/.

Eloundou-Enyegue, P. M., and J. Davanzo. 2003. Economic downturns and schooling inequality, Cameroon, 1987–1995. *Population Studies* 57 (2), 183–97.

Eloundou-Enyegue, P. M., A. McHugh, and J. Orcutt. 2004. "Show me the money": Asymmetric globalization and relative deprivation in sub-Saharan Africa. In R. Christie, ed., *Achieving sustainable communities in a global economy: Alternative private strategies and public policies,* 195–219. Singapore: World Scientific Publishing.

Firebaugh, G., and B. Goesling. 2004. Accounting for the recent decline in global income inequality. *American Journal of Sociology* 110 (2), 283–312.

Friedman, T. 2005. *The world is flat: A brief history of the twenty-first century.* New York: Farrar, Straus and Giroux.

Giroux, S. 2008. Rural parentage and labor market disadvantage in a sub-Saharan setting: Sources and trends. *Rural Sociology* 73 (3), 339–69.

Glewwe, P., and H. Jacoby. 1992. *Estimating the determinants of cognitive achievement in low-income countries: The case of Ghana* (Living Standards Measurement Study Working Paper No. 91). Washington, D.C.: World Bank.

Goldscheider, C. 1987. Migration and social structure: Analytic issues and comparative perspectives in developing nations. *Sociological Forum* 2 (4), 674–96.

Grusky, D. B., ed. 1994. *Social stratification: Class, race, and gender in sociological perspective.* Boulder: Westview.

Gugler, J. 1982. Overurbanization reconsidered. *Economic Development and Cultural Change* 31 (1), 173–89.

International Fund for Agricultural Development (IFAD). 2001. *The challenge of ending rural poverty: Rural poverty report, 2001.* Oxford: Oxford University Press.

Jencks, C., M. Smith, H. Acland, M. J. Bane, D. Cohen, H. Gintis, B. Heyns, and S. Michelson. 1994. Inequality: A reassessment of the effect of family and schooling in America. In D. Grusky, ed., *Social stratification: Class, race, and gender in sociological perspective,* 329–35. Boulder: Westview.

Kandiwa, V. 2006. Hegemony and homogeneity: The socioeconomic differentiation of African countries since the 1960s. *The Current* 10 (1), 1–16.

Kelley, J., and M. L. Perlman. 1971. Social mobility in Toro: Some preliminary results from western Uganda. *Journal of Economic Development and Cultural Change* 19 (2), 204–21.

Lavy, V. 1992. *Investment in human capital: Schooling supply constraints in rural Ghana* (LSMS Working Paper No. 93). Washington, D.C.: World Bank.

Lipset, S. M., and R. Bendix. 1959. *Social mobility in industrial society.* Berkeley and Los Angeles: University of California Press.

Lipton, M. 1977. *Why poor people stay poor: Urban bias in world development.* London: Temple Smith.

Mehrotra, S., J. Vandemoortele, and E. Delamonica. 2000. *Basic services for all? Public spending and the social dimensions of poverty.* Florence: Innocenti Publications.

Mercy, J. A., and L. Steelman. 1982. Familial influence on the intellectual attainment of children. *American Sociological Review* 47 (4), 532–42.

Mincer, J. 1974. *Schooling, experience, and earnings.* New York: National Bureau of Economic Research.

Moots, B. L. 1976. Migration, community of origin, and status attainment: A comparison of two metropolitan communities in developing societies. *Social Forces* 54 (4), 816–32.

Opal, C., and M. Fay. 2000. *Urbanization without growth: A not-so-uncommon phenomenon* (Policy Research Working Paper No. 2412). Washington, D.C.: World Bank.

Ouattara, A. 1997 (May). The challenges of globalization for Africa. Presentation given at the Southern Africa Economic Summit, Harare, Zimbabwe.

Pattaravanich, U., L. B. Williams, T. A. Lyson, and K. Archavanitkul. 2005. Inequality and educational investment in Thai children. *Rural Sociology* 70 (4), 561–84.

Portes, A., M. Castells, and L. A. Benton. 1989. *The informal economy: Studies in advanced and less developed countries.* Baltimore: Johns Hopkins University Press.

Preston, S. 1979. Urban growth in developing countries: A demographic reappraisal. *Population and Development Review* 5 (2), 195–215.

Spenner, K. I., and D. L. Featherman. 1978. Achievement ambitions. *Annual Review of Sociology* 4 (August), 373–420.

Squires, G. D. 1977. Education, jobs, and inequality: Functional and conflict models of social stratification in the United States. *Social Problems* 24 (4), 436–50.

Teachman, J. D. 1987. Family background, educational resources, and educational attainment. *American Sociological Review* 52 (4), 548–57.

Teachman, J. D., and K. Paasch. 1998. The family and educational aspirations. *Journal of Marriage and the Family* 60 (3), 704–14.

Todaro, M. P. 1997. *Urbanization, unemployment, and migration in Africa: Theory and policy* (Working Paper No. 104). New York: Population Council.

Treiman, D. J. 1970. Industrialization and social stratification. In E. O. Laumann, ed., *Social stratification: Research and theory for the 1970s*, 207–34. Indianapolis: Bobbs-Merrill.

Treiman D. J., and K. Yip. 1989. Educational and occupational attainment in 21 countries. In M. L. Kohn, ed., *Cross-national research in sociology*, 373–94. Beverly Hills: Sage Tsai SL.

United Nations. 2004. *World urbanization prospects: The 2003 revision*. New York: United Nations Population Division, Department of Economic and Social Affairs.

United Nations Conference on Trade and Development (UNCTAD). 1997. *Trade and development report*. Geneva: United Nations Conference on Trade and Development.

United Nations Population Fund. 2007. *State of the world population, 2007: Unleashing the potential of urban growth*. New York: United Nations Population Fund.

U.S. State Department (USSD). 2006. *Background note: Cameroon*. Retrieved March 2007, from http://www.state.gov/r/pa/ei/bgn/26431.htm.

Williamson, J. G. 1988. Migration selectivity, urbanization, and industrial revolutions. *Population and Development Review* 14 (2), 287–314.

World Bank. 2006. *World development indicators online*. Washington, D.C.: World Bank. Retrieved December 2006, from http://web.worldbank.org/WBSITE/EXTERNAL/DATASTATISTICS/0,,contentMDK:20398986~menuPK:64133163~pagePK:64133150~piPK:64133175~theSitePK:239419,00.html.

———. 2007. *Gender stats online*. Washington, D.C.: World Bank. Retrieved September 2007, from http://genderstats.worldbank.org/.

8

TEACHING SCHOOL IN RURAL AMERICA: TOWARD AN EDUCATED HOPE

Jacqueline Edmondson and Thomas Butler

We are both Pennsylvania residents with strong attachments to rural communities. The U.S. federal government's census standards define our state as the third most rural in the nation. Forty-eight of Pennsylvania's sixty-seven counties are rural, and just over three million people live in rural areas across the commonwealth (Alter et al. 2007). Until the 2000 census, Pennsylvania was defined as the most rural state in the nation. When the government reworked its definition of rural, using population density, geographic space, the economy, and comparisons to urban centers as some of the indicators, Pennsylvania's official status changed; however, the conditions and realities of life in rural Pennsylvania were not altered by the change in definition.

According to the Center for Rural Pennsylvania (2007), the demographics of rural Pennsylvania parallel many of the socioeconomic characteristics of urban core areas. Ten percent of rural Pennsylvania households live in poverty (defined as a family of three with less than $17,170 in annual income), while 15 percent were considered to be affluent (annual incomes more than $84,000). Forty percent of poor rural households have children. Eight percent of rural Pennsylvania residents do not have health insurance, and 3 percent who do not have health insurance are children. Eight percent of rural residents are unemployed, and 17 percent are considered to be working poor. Twenty-three percent of rural residents who are twenty-five years of age or older hold a bachelor's degree or higher, while 10 percent have no high school diploma (see Center for Rural Pennsylvania 2007).

Just as the sociodemographic data on rural communities cited above parallels that in urban communities, other trends and effects are also similar, prompting some sociologists and researchers to call for rural-urban coalitions to solve the long-standing problems facing these communities (Wilson 1999). For example, No Child Left Behind (NCLB) has brought specific challenges to rural education (see Arnold 2005 for one commentary), just as it has to urban education. Although urban educator Jonathan Kozol speaks passionately about issues faced by teachers and children in the poorest city schools, his critiques of educational issues hold true for many rural schools and teachers as well. NCLB demands that teachers in the most vulnerable schools adhere to a stripped-down curriculum of content often irrelevant to teachers and students, and it demoralizes teachers by making them feel that they must teach to the test to continue to receive federal monies (see Jan 2007). Under the legislation, which Kozol (2007) describes as racially punitive, teachers and students face the threat of school reconstitution and other measures if test scores are not improved. Such demands have influenced the nature and direction of what it means to be a teacher; in rural communities with small student populations where slight variations in test scores can devastate the quest for adequate yearly progress, and where recruitment of new teachers is an ongoing challenge, the impact is significant (see, e.g., Goetz 2005; Reeves 2003).

Yet while the statistics and problems that urban and rural communities face share many similarities, we feel it is worth considering in more depth the unique situations facing rural schools and teachers. We believe that rural teacher education should include unique experiences and learning opportunities that value rural life, for while there may be parallels with urban communities, there are many divergences as well. Of late, much has been written about the impact of teachers on student learning within the context of schools (see Darling-Hammond 2007 as one example), but little research has explored what the expectations of teachers in particular rural contexts might be. Therefore, the purpose of our contribution to this volume on rural education is to consider current and somewhat conflicting conceptualizations of what it means to be a teacher, particularly within a rural setting. To provide some context, we begin this chapter by briefly describing the Northern Tier of Pennsylvania, where Thomas has lived his entire life, working as an educator and conducting research (see Butler 2007 for more details). While the primary context for our comments is Pennsylvania's Northern Tier, we also include statements and examples from teachers in a rural community in western Minnesota, where Jacqueline lived and worked (see Edmondson 2003). This is not intended to suggest that rural communities are homogenous; indeed, they are not. Nor do we intend to suggest that there should be standard conceptualizations of what it means to be a teacher in a rural community.

Our hope is that this piece may spark a broader dialogue across rural communities that will facilitate deeper understandings of the nature and work of rural teaching, ultimately leading to deeper and more complex understandings of what it means to become a rural teacher. We feel it is important for rural teachers to understand the communities where they teach, to understand how these rural communities are linked to the world, and to appreciate the different expectations these communities might hold for their work in relation to rural contexts. While some rural researchers and educators have begun this work (see, e.g., Brooke 2003; Donehower, Hogg, and Schell 2007), we feel further attention is timely and critical, particularly in light of recent public comments by state officials about the need to standardize teacher education (Murphy 2008). To better understand the complexities of rural teaching, we consider the most common conceptualizations of rural teachers; in other words, we ask, what is it that rural residents may expect of the teachers who work in their schools? These conceptualizations are drawn from our research, which includes systematic interviews, observations, and lived experiences in rural communities and public schools. We end with recommendations for how rural teachers and communities might reclaim the language and form of what it means to be an educator, shaping this understanding to meet the unique hopes and challenges of the places where they live.

Teachers in Pennsylvania's Northern Tier

The Northern Tier of Pennsylvania consists of five rural counties spread over four thousand square miles, twice the size of the state of Delaware. These counties are connected to one another through long expanses of farmland and narrow country roads that twist through the northern part of the Appalachian Mountain range. Nearly two hundred thousand people call this region home. Sayre is the largest urban area, with approximately six thousand residents. Each county has at least one major municipality, with populations that typically vary from just under two thousand to just over three thousand residents. The remaining people are dispersed across small rural towns and areas. The region has a long-standing reputation for high unemployment and low per capita income, and the largest employers in the region tend to be education and health care industries. There is one state university, one major regional hospital, and a public school system that includes 19 of the state's 501 school districts.

Across these small communities, the beauty of the idyllic landscape fails to mask the fact that the economy has not been kind to those who live there. Like other rural communities across the United States, many of the town centers have boarded storefronts, collapsing buildings, and a quiet desperation that beckons for solutions to problems decades in the making. Downward trends in agriculture, outsourcing of local work to globalized businesses, and widespread unemployment throughout the latter part of the twentieth century have resulted in ongoing struggles to sustain a living in the region.

In spite of the challenges, teachers who work in many of these communities are able to readily explain the reasons they continue to teach in a rural school.[1] These educators, most of whom grew up in this region,[2] talk freely yet thoughtfully about their enjoyment of the natural beauty of their community, how they appreciate the isolation, the slower pace, and the time to think that rural life affords. These teachers are drawn to rural places where people know and trust one another: these are communities where farmers can leave local produce on the roadside unattended, trusting that their neighbors who purchase the food will leave the correct amount of money in the box by the stand, and that the money will be there at the end of the day when they return from work in the fields or elsewhere.

These teachers are also well aware of the challenges of their location. They understand the economic devastation facing the community and many of its families, and they work with significantly less resources per pupil than their counterparts in suburban and urban communities. Based on the most recent information available on the Pennsylvania Department of Education Web site (2005–6), the district with the lowest expenditure per pupil in Pennsylvania is a rural one, the Northwestern School District, which spends $4,505 for each student, compared with the highest expenditure per pupil in the Lower Merion School District, a wealthy Philadelphia suburb, where over $13,289 is spent per

---

1. This information is based on Thomas Butler's extensive experience working as a teacher and administrator in the Northern Tier of Pennsylvania and Jacqueline Edmondson's recent experiences leading a workshop for rural teachers in a Northern Tier school district.

2. In the school where Tom worked, nineteen of the twenty-nine teachers grew up in the immediate area. Based on Tom's experience, this is fairly typical in the region.

pupil.[3] Northern Tier schools are on the low end of the per-pupil spending range in Pennsylvania, with the average instructional expense per pupil ($6,214) below the state average ($6,609 per student). These teachers also know all too well that the struggles of contemporary rural life, the devastating effects of drug and alcohol abuse in some rural families, domestic violence, and lack of access to health care have created unimaginable conditions for some children in these schools.

Children who attend their high schools will face limited opportunities to find work that will sustain a living if they wish to remain in the area, even those who stay in school through graduation. In some districts in the Northern Tier, half the children entering kindergarten live in poverty, and some district administrators anticipate that fully 80 percent of these poor children will not finish high school (personal communication, district administrator, August 22, 2005). Pennsylvania has the second largest number of prisons in the United States, and most of these are located in rural communities (see Prisons in PA 2004). Because of this, prisons, which are sometimes the only "good job" to find in rural Pennsylvania, are part of everyday life for many of these students and their families. Common across many rural areas in the United States, many of these students see military service as the only viable option.[4]

Amid these broader social concerns, teachers express frustration with the curriculum they are often asked to teach because they find it irrelevant to the lives of their students. For example, as part of the primary grade curriculum in one school, first-grade teachers were expected to assign all homework in the mathematics textbooks, including assignments that asked children to look at their house number to determine whether it is even or odd, and then compare their number with their neighbor's house across the street to see if it is even or odd. Textbook publishers do not understand that rural children sometimes do not have numbered houses, and they often do not have neighbors across the street. This is one example of many in which the lives of rural children do not match up with curriculum or expectations imposed by outside authorities.

Yet, these children do have extensive discourses that involve a range of inter-

3. The gap between the highest and lowest expenditure per student is therefore $8,784 per pupil, which results in a $219,600 disparity between these districts for a class of twenty-five students.

4. During the second Gulf War, approximately half of military fatalities were soldiers from towns with populations smaller than twenty-five thousand residents (Associated Press 2007; see also O'Hare and Bishop 2006).

ests and activities. Many of them know and enjoy NASCAR, four-wheelers, snowmobiles, sports, and farming, among other things.[5] These children understand well the traditions and customs that involve hunting, and many girls and boys alike look forward to "Buck Day," the first day of hunting season and an officially sanctioned vacation from school each November. These topics are not typically found in the prepackaged curriculum used in rural schools, and teachers yearn for a return to thematic units and curriculum that they can develop locally to connect more distinctly with these children's lives.

In spite of the challenges and struggles, the teachers we know continue to work to bridge gaps between the community and school. They host activities to help parents get involved with the school, including open houses, book fairs, read-a-thons, and a variety of performances involving the children. Children's families are invited for Grandparents' Day events, Mother's Day Teas, and Doughnuts for Dad. At the same time, teachers work to help the children come to know and appreciate their communities. Teachers lead walking tours that point out local architecture, landmarks, and important sites. Teachers participate in community days and contribute to local newspapers. Teachers seek out ways to make connections between the school and hunter safety programs so that all children have the hunter's safety course. They look for ways to get more information to parents about proper nutrition and clothing for children, and they hold three-way parent-teacher-child conferences to help increase the attendance at parent-teacher conferences.

With these contexts, problems, and possibilities, particularly over the past decade the nature and form of rural teaching is changing. Because of this, we would like to explore further the political discourses that influence conceptualizations of teachers in the Northern Tier and other parts of the state and country. These dominant discourses take hold in rural communities and elsewhere because they carry a commonsense appeal "to our intuitions and instincts, to our values and desires, as well as to the possibilities inherent in the social world we inhabit" (Harvey 2006, 5). To begin, we consider different possibilities for *designing* rural teaching. We use the term "design" in a way that is consistent with the New London Group's (2000) discussion of multiliteracies; that is, we intend to consider visions of rural teaching that should be discussed and debated as we consider different possible social futures for rural communities.

5. These are real interests among children and youth in the Northern Tier. This is not intended as a generalization of rural youths' interests in other Pennsylvania or rural U.S. communities.

With this in mind, and again consistent with the New London Group, we consider three areas related to rural teaching: available designs, designing, and the redesigned.

Available Designs

Many groups, institutions, and ideas influence the content and form of teacher education and public schools, ultimately designing teachers' work and teaching practices within and across specific contexts. Often, these influences come from outside the realm of public education and university-based teacher education programs, and nearly always the unique contexts of teaching, like those in the Northern Tier, are not considered. Federal and state departments of education, legislators, school boards, the media, and the public all contribute to designs of teaching, including rural teaching. The ideas that shape these designs are rooted in part in understandings of the purposes and aims of public education and corresponding beliefs about the teachers' role in realizing those ideals. Because of this, we will ground our discussion of available designs in political discourses that are prominent in contemporary society.

Political discourses are fundamentally about power and ideas as people use their influence to forward particular understandings. Education, including understandings of the role of the teacher, always comes from a point of view or is a negotiation that includes a series of compromises among different points of view. While those who subscribe to different political positions might unite behind a particular policy or point of view they might not particularly agree with, they do so because the compromises involved are not too far from their ideal for how schools or teachers should be. Someone in power (teacher, politician, administrator, businessperson) uses his or her influence to realize the ideals he or she has for particular situations, schools, and communities as decisions about texts, contexts, curriculum, and other aspects of schooling are made.

Political discourses, which are somewhat overlapping and ever changing, are grounded in values and identities that people who belong to these groups hold, and such discourses reflect specific visions for society. All these categories offer some possibilities but deny others, and because of this, the values and visions for each discourse are open for discussion and debate as we consider the future of rural teaching in the twenty-first century. In what follows, we will consider the dominant political discourses that are operating to define what it means to

Figure 1   Dominant designs for rural teachers

Political discourse	Basic tenets	Implications for rural education
Conservative	Focus on property, class, tradition, courts of law based on these notions, and spiritual hierarchies associated with organized religion. Any movement that proposes innovation is to be opposed on principle (see Shannon 2000).	Focus on a past that is not possible to recreate, providing little hope for change in rural community (see Edmondson 2003).
Neoconservative	Emphasis on character and moral education aligned with Eurocentric values and a belief that individuals are responsible for the world, so all should be equal.	Focus on Judeo-Christian values may have once coincided well with rural communities, but the increasing diversity among rural residents does not guarantee that this is the case (see Wenger and Dinsmore 2005).
Neoliberal	Focus on core values: (1) a primacy placed on fostering economic growth, in this case through education that would supposedly lead to eventual success in the job market; (2) developing a shared sense of community that helps "them" to become more like "us"; and (3) efficient educational practices modeled after business principles, including standardization and increased accountability.	Contributes to the ongoing devastation of rural communities (see Schell 2007; Theobald and Rochon 2006; Edmondson, 2003). Young people are schooled to compete with one another and ultimately to leave the rural community in search of economic prosperity, thereby depleting the population, resources, and potential for many rural areas (see Nichols 2003).
Liberal	Focus on preserving individual freedom, primarily due to belief that progress is possible through rational thought.	Tend to overlook "issues of context, culture, and change in their efforts to determine best practices," thereby further perpetuating the problems they sought to resolve (Shannon 2000, 100).

be a teacher in a rural community: conservative, neoconservative, neoliberal, and liberal (see fig. 1 for a summary of dominant designs). We begin each section with a short statement from a teacher in a rural school that helps to illustrate some aspect of the design, and then we provide further explanation of the benefits and limitations. We conclude with examples of alternate designs offered from a radical perspective.

Conservative Designs

> There's this book . . . it's called *The Day No Pigs Would Die* . . . now I've been reading this since I got here ten years ago. It's my absolutely favorite book. . . . Well, Kris, one of my students, takes it home, [his] parents read the book. They were going to get the school board, they were going to write letters to the editor, they talked to [the principal] . . . I've never seen someone so angry in all my teaching. . . . We're done. The book is done. I'm not using it anymore.
>
> —FIFTH-GRADE TEACHER, RURAL MINNESOTA, FEBRUARY 2000

Those who wish to design rural teaching with conservative ideals as guiding principles are often reacting to a trend, issue, policy, or phenomenon in society (see Kirk, n.d., for an explanation of key conservative principles). Like the parents in the vignette above, there is an attempt to direct curriculum and texts, and ultimately teachers, in ways that preserve local conditions and control, working to prevent outside or alternative ideas from infiltrating local practices: "The basic tenets of conservatism are property, class, tradition, courts of law based on these notions, and spiritual hierarchies associated with organized religion. Any movement that proposes innovation is to be opposed on principle" (Shannon 2000, 95).

Most often conservative designs are evident in their control of texts (textbooks, library books, computer Web sites, etc.), and a focus on hierarchical, systematic skill instruction as a "neutral" procedure. Conservative designs of education subscribe to bell curve logic, grounded in a belief that intelligence is predetermined (see Hernnstein and Murray 1994; see Shannon 1998 for a critique); standardized tests are offered as support for this tenet, demonstrating that some children will never learn well enough to warrant the resources being spent on them. In some cases, conservative designs are considered to be an instrument to eliminate services for special-needs children and the poor, and to close schools in some of the economically neediest communities (see Goodman et al. 2004).

Within the context of a conservative design, rural teachers would be expected to maintain the status quo, teaching students about the local community in ways that help to preserve traditions, and honor what is typically presented as an uncontroversial past. Among conservatives, there is a belief that communities are voluntary, and that people can and should make choices about their community membership; in a rural community, teachers would play a role in helping students make choices based on precedent, precept, and prejudice, rather than private judgment or rationality (see Kirk, n.d.). Such teachers would help students value prudence, to understand human freedom and basic rights under the law, including the right to property, and to know the existing moral order. Within this context, the public would expect rural teachers to help students to appreciate rural life and its customs, and to accept their position in a rural community as part of a larger societal design.

For rural teachers or students who are seeking change and new possibilities, conservative designs of rural education are not a particularly hopeful project because they are rooted in a wish to return to a past that is not possible to recreate (see Edmondson 2003 for a discussion of traditional rural literacies). These designs can lead to an exclusionary condition where the aim of preservation provides a rationale for keeping certain people out of rural communities (see Schell 2007). Conservative designs conjure nostalgia for the past, and they relegate people to accept their lives as they are with little hope for change. In addition, this tends to be a punitive design that works within the confines of testing and punishment (see Goodman et al. 2004), particularly in rural communities where there may be disconnects between the expectations and values of families, on the one hand, and schools that are expected to conform to standardized curricula and tests (Woodrum 2004). By its nature, this design offers limited potential for teachers and students to address the need for change and redesign in contemporary rural life, ultimately leading to a sense of despair.

Neoconservative Designs

> There was another guy out there, we were both first-year [teachers], and
> we came back from Glasgow, we went to a movie, and we stopped up at
> a quick shop and got some chicken, and somebody called the principal
> and said two of the teachers were out past eleven.
>
> —SECOND-GRADE TEACHER, REFLECTING ON TEACHING IN
> RURAL MONTANA, FEBRUARY 2000

Neoconservatives, such as Irving Kristol, a leader of the movement,[6] former vice president Dick Cheney, and former secretary of education William Bennett, share the liberal values that no one should be restrained because of race, class,

5. See Kristol (2003) for an explanation of core aspects of neoconservatism.

or position, but they also share the conservative beliefs that order, continuity, and community are important. Among neoconservatives, there is an emphasis on character and moral education aligned with Eurocentric values and a belief that individuals are responsible for the world, so all should be equal.

Neoconservatives identify the roots of poverty among perceived moral deficiencies in the poor. Because of this, neoconservatives propose that instruction in school should consist of moral lessons that will help the poor and minorities to overcome their moral poverty (see Bennett, DiIulio, and Walters 1996). Shannon (1998) points out that neoconservatives like Bennett have specific ideas about how schooling (with reading as its foundation) should be conducted, including its explicit and implicit curricula: "The explicit curriculum is clear. Readers ought to focus their attention on accuracy in decoding and getting the author's intended message. They should look for the facts and cultural values that will enable them to understand and engage in critical thought later. Although a start, Bennett acknowledges that the explicit curriculum is not sufficient to produce good citizens" (103). Shannon continues by explaining how Bennett perceived these implicit lessons as central to the development of character and morality. For example, the teaching of phonics, which defers "the gratification of experiencing whole texts" (103), offers implicit lessons to students about the value of hard work, perseverance, and gratification. Standardized tests are used to validate that students have worked hard and achieved in school.

Neoconservative designs for rural teaching would focus on celebrating core moral principles like diligence, discipline, and Judeo-Christian values (Bennett 2008). Some of these principles may have once coincided well with rural communities, but the increasing diversity among rural residents does not guarantee that this is the case (see Wenger and Dinsmore 2005). Teachers aligned with a neoconservative design would encourage students to appreciate and understand democracy as Alexis de Tocqueville wrote of it (see Kristol 2003). They would appreciate the military strength the United States holds and its right to develop democracies in other parts of the world. This emphasis would help to support the trends whereby rural youth enlist the military preceding or following high school graduation, in part because of the heightened sense of patriotism found in many rural areas (Spark 2007). Teachers would encourage students to tolerate diversity (including ethnic, religious, and linguistic), which is increasing in rural areas, but to work toward unity under the auspices of neoconservative values.

Such designs devalue the contributions that people from different languages and backgrounds bring to rural life. Neoconservative designs function to alienate people from one another because the design is inflexible and imposing, potentially widening the gap between school and community, providing little hope for the future of rural communities. In order to thrive, rural communities will need to learn to find strength in differences, fostering interdependence and an ethic of care.

Neoliberal Designs

> Our children out here are going to be competing, and I don't like the word competing, but they are going to be working with people from large settings, and our children need as good of an education as [other children] are getting.
>
> —FIRST-GRADE TEACHER, RURAL MINNESOTA, 1999

Neoliberalism designs education as an equalizer, promising all children the opportunity to compete in a globalized economy. Within this perspective, individuals are seen as key players in the system: teachers must provide students with skills needed for the workforce, and students must learn the skills and be prepared to compete. Neoliberals, including former president Bill Clinton, journalist Thomas Friedman, and others, focus on the lack of job training among the poor (Marshall and Tucker 1993), and assume that well-paying jobs will be waiting for those who have the necessary educational qualifications. The fact that schools have unequal resources and vast disparities in conditions to foster academic learning is overlooked, as is the fact that many people in American society are underemployed or unemployed as jobs are exported to countries with lower labor costs (see Timmons 2007, which explains U.S. workers being laid off from Hershey Foods as the company expands into Asia). Instead, teachers in all schools must work to get children to meet the same standards, pass the same standardized tests to validate that they have learned, and ultimately compete with one another for the same jobs.

Neoliberalism combines liberal ideas (i.e., the "free market" will solve social and public concerns) with conservative solutions (such as local control). While neoliberalism as a philosophy is complex (see Treanor 2005 for an introduction), several values relevant to our discussion shape neoliberal designs: (1) a primacy placed on fostering economic growth, in this case through education that would supposedly lead to eventual success in the job market; (2) developing a shared sense of community that helps "them" to become more like "us"; (3) efficient educational practices modeled after business principles, including standardization and increased accountability (see Hill 2007 for a critique of neoliberalism's effects on education). One consequence in public education is a tension between centralization and decentralization of decisions about schooling. The drive for efficiency and standardization has moved decisions away from local groups to the hands of the state and corporations, yet educators are left to address these mandates by creating local solutions for implementation of curriculum.

Neoliberal designs on rural teaching recreate educators as agents for multinational corporations as they deliver prepackaged curriculum and standards aligned with high-stakes tests. Teachers function primarily as technicians, employing the best technologies available to prepare students for yet unknown jobs being created in a high-tech, globalized, "flat" world (Friedman 2005). Teachers help students to learn to work with one another using distributed leadership principles (see Gee, Hull, and Lankshear 1997). These teachers promote the message that students need to be entrepreneurial to compete in the globalized marketplace and become travelers in a world driven by free market ideals (Bauman 2000).

A neoliberal design is increasingly the expectation in rural communities as education policies are created with market-driven goals in mind, including an emphasis on providing students skills and opportunities needed to compete in a globalized world. In many ways, this design contributes to the ongoing devastation of rural communities (see Schell 2007; Theobald and Rochon 2006; Edmondson 2003). Young people are schooled to compete with one another and ultimately to leave the rural community in search of economic prosperity, which depletes the population, resources, and potential for many rural communities (see Nichols 2003). Within this design, students are not encouraged to critically read the underlying tenets of neoliberalism: the free market, competition, and globalization. Nor are they encouraged to consider the ill effects that neoliberalism has brought to rural life around the globe as environments are polluted and destroyed, people are exploited, and gaps between the rich and poor increasingly widen (see Harvey 2006).

Liberal Designs

> One of the things in a rural area, though, we do not get to have access to museums and authors and artwork, like you would if you lived in a larger city. [Administrators] do try to accommodate that with prints and different art prints.
>
> —FIFTH-GRADE TEACHER, RURAL MINNESOTA, 1999

Liberals have worked to preserve individual freedom, primarily because of their belief that progress is possible through rational thought. Individuals who identify with this ideology often believe that histories of oppression and discrimination have kept individuals and particular groups living in cycles of poverty and despair (Shannon 1998). Liberals value equality and fraternity, advocating equal access to quality education for all children, as well as affirmative action and multicultural education.

According to liberals, education is a basic right for all children. Because of this, they hope to find the best methods of instruction that can reach all children, regardless of race, class, gender, and sexual orientation, thus enabling children from all backgrounds to learn to read and be successful in school. In addition, liberals hope to increase access to texts for children living in high-poverty areas, and hope that multicultural education and bilingual programs can lead to a society where tolerance of other races, classes, and genders is possible. Standardized tests have long been part of the liberal agenda in public education, beginning with Robert F. Kennedy's endorsement of the use of tests as part of the original Elementary and Secondary Education Act in 1965, largely because he thought these tests would show that poor and minority students needed the government to intervene to improve their education (see Shannon 1998).

Within this context, rural teachers are seen as educators who understand through scientific work the academic, behavioral, and social factors that could contribute to academic difficulties students from special populations experience in schools. Teachers can use data and research to inform practice related to student need and achievement so that each student can learn to his or her full potential. Teachers would engage students in enlightenment principles of reason, science, and rationality rather than rely on divine law or a conservative/neoconservative belief in an already established moral order. Students would work to understand and appreciate the complexities of communities, including the notion of a social contract whereby people who are governed have a voice in that governance. Through this work, teachers would help students to understand their role as participatory citizens in a democratic society.

Liberal designs fall short of providing rural teachers with possibilities for educating students in ways that will sustain rural life. While liberals emphasize recognition across different groups, in the process of relying primarily on science and due to the contradictions inherent in struggles over hopes to generalize findings, they have "overlooked issues of context, culture, and change in their efforts to determine best practices," further perpetuating the problems they sought to resolve (Shannon 2000, 100).

While each of these dominant designs offers little to resolve the conflicts and problems that rural communities face, they remain prominent discourses in the media, among policy makers, and in other discussions related to rural life. Much of the sustenance of these designs is driven by fear: fear of change, fear of the unknown, and fear of difference. Yet, as former vice president Al Gore (2007) has noted, it is clear that few people have ever made good decisions because of fear. Instead, we must learn to work through our fears, relying on reason, discussion, and debate to deeply understand the conditions of our lives and the potential for change.

Alternative Designs

> Part of my philosophy and part of what I think about teaching and learning is that what you do in your small community classroom should be tied to the local community outside your classroom . . . and then just keep expanding until it becomes part of the larger global community, but in that I want the children to see that what we're doing has a purpose.
>
> —FIRST-GRADE TEACHER, RURAL MINNESOTA, MARCH 2000

Teachers do not need to accept the dominant designs for rural education, and not all have done so. Myles Horton provides an example of a rural educator who designed teaching differently in and for rural communities, in ways that opened alternatives to dominant ideologies of teaching and learning. In 1932, Horton founded the Highlander Folk School in Grundy County, Tennessee, with the explicit purpose of training rural and industrial leaders who focused on social and economic justice. He collaborated with civil rights leaders, including Rosa Parks and Martin Luther King, Jr., and radical educators, such as Paulo Freire, to realize different forms of civic engagement that respected and upheld principles of participatory democracy in rural areas. The focus of the education center, which continues to this day, emphasizes recognition of all people and redistribution of resources to provide a more just and equitable society. The center provides a space for educators and others to research and struggle for different policies and conditions that foster justice, peace, and fairness. Within this context, rural educators work through coalitions and participatory efforts to bring social change and establish conditions for participatory democracy.

Horton and those like him who subscribe to *radical democratic* views of schooling focus on the interface among people and society and government policies. Radical democrats engage a political ideology that is committed to a view of democracy as "the development of individuals' identities that are committed to the values of freedom and equality (blended with the values of their other group memberships) and to active participation in civic life" (Shannon 2000, 101). In this view, education would help people to participate in public life, including considerations of economics and culture, to recognize and appreciate different points of view, and to engage a reflexive agency that works to change society into a more just and equitable place. Rural communities that subscribe to such aims for education would see evidence of the realization of these goals as young people become engaged in the community, as they present information and needs to school boards and other local officials, and as they work to provide solutions to the inequities and injustices that are found in rural places.

   Rural teachers working within radical democratic perspectives would understand the role of education in fostering citizens who can sustain rural community for all peoples, engage ethical decisions about the land and resources in rural areas, and struggle for new and different policies and coalitions to bring economic, environmental, and social changes to rural communities. Standardized tests and standardized curricula are largely irrelevant within this perspective because teachers would instead be instrumental in designing curricula to address local communities and needs. Such teachers would help students to critically engage local issues, to conduct research that allows students to deeply understand rural problems and concerns, and to engage the public and policy makers in public forums, discussions, and debates (see Powell, Cantrell, and Adams 2001 as one example).

Designing Among New Rural Teachers: Making Meanings Locally

Our district is going through the strategic planning process. Part of that process involves various committees with administrators, teachers, and community members participating. The meeting that "my" committee had was one that gave me a lot of hope that things can change in the public schools. As we were discussing "goals" for the district one of the teachers (who also has children in the school system) raised her hand and lodged a very adamant complaint that our school should be more than PSSA scores [the state's standardized test] and that our goals should reflect this. She went on to apologize for being cynical about the school but she said she just wanted to have her concerns heard. The rest of the teachers on the committee (four others) started to talk about how they felt the same way and they felt that they were just vessels to "give students PSSA information." The conversation was more than just the normal

complaining about teaching to the test, there was a lot of pent up
frustration and anger over the fact that they were losing control over
their profession. I told the teacher that first raised her hand that she was
not being cynical, rather she was being hopeful and that she was
articulating something that all people want for their students . . . a better
chance in life. I then introduced the concept of preparing students to live
in a democratic society and what did we want to do with the students
while we had them in the schools. This created quite a discussion. The
board member that was there asked me how they could change the
culture of the school away from the PSSA. Needless to say, the
conversation was very fruitful after that question.

—THOMAS BUTLER, PERSONAL COMMUNICATION RELATED TO
COMMUNITY PLANNING IN A NORTHERN TIER SCHOOL DISTRICT, 2006

Some teachers in the Northern Tier are redesigning what it means to be educators in the context of their rural community. They are publicly rejecting the
state's efforts to define effective teachers based on how much they raise test
scores for children, as evidenced in the reference to the PSSA (the Pennsylvania
State System of Assessment) above. These teachers are beginning to imagine
different reasons and possibilities for schooling in a rural community (Butler
2007). Their discussions engage meanings intended for them from state and
federal officials, but they are negotiating those meanings within the context of
what they know about their own community and schools and what they hope
for the future.

Yet this is clearly not easy work. While teachers recognize that the current
designs are not fulfilling the needs of their students, their communities, or their
own professional lives, these designs have long dominated the discourses and
language of schools in ways that make it difficult to engage in redesign (Butler
2007). Teachers have been given strong messages that they must follow mandates and predetermined curricula rather than engage in the intellectual work
of designing relevant curriculum to educate students (Giroux 2005), and they
sometimes fear that to do otherwise will only bring harm to their students'
potential for success in the future. As educator Colin Lankshear (1997, 30) has
observed, "Discourses of dominant groups become those which dominate education, and become established as major legitimate routes to securing goods
(like wealth and status). As a result, educational success is patterned along
distinct lines of prior discursive experience associated with membership of particular social groups." It is against this domination that educators will need to
find courage to publicly address, resist, and change what it means to be a
teacher and the nature of their work.

In addition to those policy makers and community members who seek to define the rural teachers' work in relation to the dominant designs explained above, there is the added challenge of social malaise and a sense that there is no hope for communities in the Northern Tier (Butler 2007). In these communities, like other rural communities in Pennsylvania and elsewhere, there have been generations of poverty, neglect, and economic despair that have weighed on the minds and affected the lived experiences of residents. Teachers are faced with educating students who have little imagination for how their lives could be organized otherwise, and they are working within communities where there is often cynicism and civic inattention (Butler 2007). Yet, in spite of the potential for despair, it is from these conditions that change can come. Teachers in the Northern Tier who are participating in the strategic planning work outlined in the quote that opened this section recognize the painful circumstances they face with their students and neighbors, and in spite of both the dominant groups that seek to order their lives as well as the sense of community malaise they face, these conditions may very well set the stage for educational and social change.

One possibility for addressing this combined need for change that can engage public resistance and hope is through a revitalization of public spaces in rural communities where educators and community members can come together to work on the meanings, challenges, and dreams for their lives. We turn to this critical need for public space as we consider a redesigned rural teacher.

The Redesigned: Spaces and Hope
for the New Rural Teacher

There are few places to banter ideas about.

—SUPERINTENDENT IN THE NORTHERN TIER, OCTOBER 2006

We find possibility for redesigning rural teaching and rural teacher education in the discussions among these educators and others like them across the country (see Edmondson 2003). Educators in the Northern Tier recognize the need for change, and many have expressed a hope for public spaces where they can work through the challenges they face (Butler 2007). Yet we also realize that teachers in one community are not able to change the conditions of their work in isolation.

To mobilize and bring changes to the meanings and policies that work to direct their lives, rural educators will need to have democratic public spaces to engage their efforts. Such spaces can provide opportunities for participants to discuss, question, and debate as they negotiate new understandings against the past with democracy as the frame for their efforts. These spaces are physical and intellectual in nature. Physically, teachers and community members will need to have adequate space to engage purposeful, meaningful discussions about the conditions they face. Resources to facilitate discussions, including space for mapping out plans and organizing materials, are often readily available in public school buildings. Bringing the public into the physical space of the school also allows people who may not otherwise enter the school (e.g., retirees) to realize the work that is ongoing among teachers and students.

In addition to the physical spaces needed to support ongoing discussions about schools, there needs to be a cultivation of intellectual spaces as well. Those involved in these discussions will need to have adequate resources and materials for people to read and consider so that there is time to reason through the issues and possibilities. Participants in these discussions will need to learn to balance their own ideas against the opinions and research of other experts. It is not enough for rural community members involved in redesigning education in rural communities to make decisions based on their own instincts and experiences; this would serve to perpetuate dominant rather than alternate models for rural education. At the same time, rural educators must value their own voices in this struggle and not rely solely on those of outside experts alone (see Nachtigal 1982).

To prepare teachers for such engagement, rural teacher education programs could foster opportunities for preservice teachers to participate in the public sphere. This would involve deepening understandings of the various political, social, and economic pressures that influence the discourses of people participating in these spaces in particular communities. It would also require deepening understandings of the role and purposes of education in rural communities.

The struggle to redesign what it means to be a teacher in a rural community will take a great deal of effort to sustain, but it is not impossible. At one level, there needs to be a critical reconsideration of what it means to educate rural teachers for such changes. Teacher education programs tend to work with new teachers as though all are going into the same school system and, with the exception of some specialized programs that prepare urban teachers, they often operate with dominant (i.e., suburban) models of public education in mind. Teacher education programs that focus on rural educators would provide opportunities for rural community and economic study, including historical analysis of trends and issues, as well as opportunities to study community organizing, the efforts of rural educators like Myles Horton, Paulo Freire, Rebecca Powell, and others, and internships that provide teachers with experiences in the diversity of rural life and schools.

Once they begin to teach, rural educators will need sustained support from other rural educators and leaders in rural communities: administrators, superintendents, business and community leaders, and well-respected teachers. Such efforts would help to foster public spaces for rural educators to work with students in the context of community sustainability, opening possibilities for rural communities to work against the grain of national policies and trends when needed. This entails a need for civic courage, intellectualism, and an understanding that societal change takes time and perseverance. A key element in sustaining this effort for change involves fostering and sustaining an educated hope: "Hope makes the leap for us between critical education, which tells us what must be changed; political agency, which gives us the means to make change; and the concrete struggles through which change happens. Hope, in short, gives substance to the recognition that every present is incomplete" (Giroux 2004, 38).

Building on work by Ernst Bloch, Andrew Benjamin, Michael Lerner, Cornel West, and others, educator Henry Giroux explained the importance of hope as an anticipatory and mobilizing endeavor. To Giroux, it is a pedagogical and performative practice that allows people to see their potential as moral and civic agents who can realize social change. Paulo Freire (1998) wrote of the radical nature of hope by explaining how, even when things may seem that they could never get worse, we can intervene in the process to bring change. To Freire, it is natural for human beings to feel hope; on the contrary, hopelessness is something that is learned. Rather than offering a specific utopian vision or blueprint for the future, educated hope equips people with a realization that a different future is possible and allows them to plan means to reach those possibilities.

As a broader community of educators, we need to find ways to support one another through our dissent to imposed definitions and policies as well as our efforts to bring change. As writer and activist Arundhati Roy (2002, 20) has explained, "What we need to search for and find, what we need to hone and perfect into a magnificent, shining thing is a new kind of politics. Not the politics of governance, but the politics of resistance. The politics of opposition. The politics of slowing things down. The politics of joining hands across the world and preventing certain destruction. In the present circumstances, I'd say that the only thing worth globalizing is dissent."

The issues teachers face in the Northern Tier are not unique to them alone. While the conditions of their work have specific histories and contexts, there are teachers in other rural, urban, and suburban communities who likewise face a need to gain control over the meanings and policies that direct their lives. By studying the designs and potential for rural education, and considering more deeply how rural teachers might play a role in new designs for rural schools, we can begin to foster deep and critical conversations about the purposes of public education in rural communities, what it means to be a teacher in a rural school, and ultimately how lives can be sustained in rich and rewarding ways.

References

Alter, T., J. Bridger, J. Findeis, T. Kelsey, A. Luloff, D. McLaughlin, and W. Shuffstall. 2007. *Strengthening rural Pennsylvania: An integrated approach to a prosperous commonwealth.* Washington, D.C.: Brookings Institution.

Arnold, M. 2005. Rural education: A new perspective is needed at the U.S. Department of Education. *Journal of Research in Rural Education* 20 (3), 1–3. Retrieved March 1, 2008, from http://jrre.psu.edu/articles/20-3.pdf.

Associated Press. 2007 (February 20). Rural America bears scars from Iraq war: Nearly half of U.S. soldiers in Iraq came from a small town. Retrieved May 27, 2007, from http://www.msnbc.msn.com/id/17231366/.

Bauman, Z. 2000. *Globalization: The human consequences.* New York: Columbia University Press.

Bennett, W. 2008. *The moral compass: Stories for a life's journey.* New York: Simon and Schuster.

Bennett, W., J. DiIulio, and J. Walters. 1996. *Body count: Moral poverty . . . and how to win America's war against crime and drugs.* New York: Simon and Schuster.

Brooke, R. 2003. *Place-conscious education and the teaching of writing.* New York: Teachers College Press.

Butler, T. 2007. Rural schools and communities: How globalization influences rural school and community collaboration. Ph.D. diss., Pennsylvania State University.

Center for Rural Pennsylvania. 2007. *Rural by the numbers.* Harrisburg: Center for Rural Pennsylvania. Retrieved September 22, 2007, from http://www.ruralpa.org/Rural_by_numbers07.pdf.

Darling-Hammond, L. 2007. The flat earth and education: How America's commitment to equity will determine our future. *Educational Researcher* 36 (6), 318–34.

Donehower, K., C. Hogg, and E. Schell. 2007. *Rural literacies.* Carbondale: University of Southern Illinois Press.

Edmondson, J. 2003. *Prairie town: Redefining rural life in an age of globalization.* Boulder: Rowman and Littlefield.

Freire, P. 1998. *Pedagogy of freedom: Ethics, democracy, and civic courage.* Boulder: Rowman and Littlefield.

Friedman, T. 2005. *The world is flat: A brief history of the twenty-first century.* New York: Farrar, Strauss and Giroux.

Gee, J., G. Hull, and C. Lankshear. 1997. *The new work order.* Boulder: Westview.

Giroux, H. 2004. When hope is subversive. *Tikkun* 19 (6), 38–39.

———. 2005. *Schooling and the struggle for public life: Democracy's promise and education's challenge* (updated ed.). Boulder: Paradigm.

Goetz, S. J. 2005. Random variation in student performance by class size: Implications for NCLB in rural Pennsylvania. *Journal of Research in Rural Education* 20 (13), 1–8. Retrieved March 1, 2008, from http://jrre.psu.edu/articles/20-13.pdf.

Goodman, K., P. Shannon, Y. Goodman, and R. Rapoport. 2004. *Saving our schools: The case for public education saying "no" to No Child Left Behind.* Muskegon, Mich.: RDR Press.

Gore, A. 2007. *The assault on reason.* New York: Penguin.

Harvey, D. 2006. *A brief history of neoliberalism.* New York: Oxford University Press.

Hernnstein, R., and C. Murray. 1994. *The bell curve: Intelligence and class structure in American life.* New York: The Free Press.

Hill, D. 2007. *Global neoliberalism and education and its consequences.* London: Routledge.

Jan, T. 2007 (September 21). Reading, writing, and rebellion. *Boston Globe.* Retrieved September 22, 2007, from http://www.boston.com/news/local/articles/2007/09/21/reading_writing_and_rebellion.

Kirk, R. n.d. Ten conservative principles. Russell Kirk Center for Cultural Renewal. Retrieved June 22, 2007, from http://www.kirkcenter.org/kirk/ten-principles.html.

Kozol, J. 2007. NCLB and the poisonous essence of obsessive testing. *Huffington Post.* Retrieved October 9, 2007, from http://www.commondreams.org/archive/2007/09/13/3809/.

Kristol, I. 2003. The neoconservative persuasion. *Weekly Standard* 8 (47), 23–25.

Lankshear, C. 1997. *Changing literacies.* Buckingham: Open University Press.

Marshall, R., and M. Tucker. 1993. *Thinking for a living: Education and the wealth of nations.* New York: Basic Books.

Murphy, J. 2008 (November 13). Changes to teacher education could strain colleges. *Patriot-News* (Harrisburg, Pa.). Retrieved December 26, 2008, from http://www.pennlive.com/education/patriotnews/index.ssf?/base/news/1226541311301010.xml&coll=1.

Nachtigal, P. 1982. *Rural education: In search of a better way.* Boulder: Westview.

New London Group. 2000. A pedagogy of multiliteracies: Literacy learning and the design of social futures. In B. Cope and M. Kalanztis, eds., *Multiliteracies,* 9–37. New York: Routledge.

Nichols, J. 2003 (October 16). Needed: A rural strategy. *The Nation.* Retrieved September 22, 2007, from http://www.thenation.com/doc/20031103/nichols2.

O'Hare, W., and B. Bishop. 2006. *U.S. rural soldiers account for a disproportionately high share of casualties in Iraq and Afghanistan* (Carsey Institute Fact Sheet No. 3). Durham, N.H.: Carsey Institute.

Powell, R., S. Cantrell, and S. Adams. 2001. Saving Black Mountain: The promise of critical literacy in a multicultural democracy. *The Reading Teacher* 54 (8), 772–81.

Prisons in PA. 2004. Pennsylvania is a leader in prisons. Retrieved September 23, 2007, from http://www.actionpa.org/prisons/.

Reeves, C. 2003. *Implementing the No Child Left Behind Act: Implications for rural schools.* Naperville, Ill.: North Central Regional Educational Laboratory. Retrieved September 22, 2007, from http://www.ncrel.org/policy/pubs/html/implicate/index.html.

Roy, A. 2002 (February 18). Shall we leave it to the experts? *The Nation,* 16–20.

Schell, E. 2007. The rhetorics of the farm crisis: Toward alternative agrarian literacies in a globalized world. In K. Donehower, C. Hogg, and E. Schell, eds., *Rural Literacies,* 77–119. Carbondale: Southern Illinois University Press.

Shannon, P. 1998. *Reading poverty.* Portsmouth, N.H.: Heinemann.

———. 2000. "What's my name?": A politics of literacy in the latter half of the 20th century in America. *Reading Research Quarterly* 35 (1), 90–107.

Spark. 2007 (May–June). It's still a rich man's war, but a poor man or woman's army. *Class Struggle* 55. Retrieved October 7, 2007, from http://www.the-spark.net/csart551.html.

Theobald, P., and R. Rochon. 2006. Enclosure then and now: Rural schools and communities in the wake of market-driven agriculture. *Journal of Research in Rural Education* 21 (12), 1–8. Retrieved March 1, 2008 from http://jrre.psu.edu/articles/21-12.pdf.

Timmons, H. 2007 (April 3). Hershey to buy 51% stake of food company in India. *New York Times.* Retrieved June 22, 2007, from http://www.iht.com/articles/2007/04/03/business/godrej.php.

Treanor, P. 2005. Liberalism, market, ethics. Retrieved October 12, 2007, from http://web.inter.nl.net/users/Paul.Treanor/.

Wenger, K., and J. Dinsmore. 2005. Preparing rural preservice teachers for diversity. *Journal of Research in Rural Education* 20 (10), 1–15. Retrieved March 1, 2008, from http://jrre.psu.edu/articles/20-10.pdf.

Wilson, W. J. 1999. *The bridge over the racial divide.* Berkeley and Los Angeles: University of California Press.

Woodrum, A. 2004. State mandated testing and cultural resistance in Appalachian schools: Competing values and expectations. *Journal of Research in Rural Education* 19 (1), 1–10. Retrieved March 1, 2008, from http://jrre.psu.edu/articles/19-1.pdf.

3

TEACHING COMMUNITIES

9

TRIBALLY CONTROLLED COLLEGES AND UNIVERSITIES: GLOBAL INFLUENCE AND LOCAL DESIGN

Susan C. Faircloth and John W. Tippeconnic III

Introduction

In the United States and other parts of the Western hemisphere, globalization is not a new phenomenon, but one whose effects have resonated among indigenous tribes and communities for more than five hundred years. Early European contact set the stage for the onslaught of globalization, which was heralded by the introduction of small pox and other life-threatening diseases, widespread war, availability and consumption of alcohol, the concept of land for sale, and forced migration. Each of these presented challenges to the very existence of Native peoples forcing them to adapt or perish. Throughout history, Native people have continued to fight against the hegemonic forces that have both knowingly and unknowingly worked to acculturate, assimilate, and decimate their lifeways. Their ability to adapt increased their chances of survival and paved the way for many tribal people to maintain and in some cases begin to reclaim elements of their Native languages and cultures once feared lost.

In the mid-twentieth century, American Indians and Alaska Natives began to mobilize in an attempt to assert their right to self-determination—the right to determine the direction and focus of education, community development, and economics.[1] This era gave birth to the tribal college movement in the 1960s,

---

1. See, for example, Rains, Archibald, and Deyhle (2000, 338): "The Ancestors' teachings have survived attacks of colonization, disease, destruction of food sources and habitat, Manifest Destiny, forced relocations, and ruthless economic lust and greed. . . . Through it all, Elders have remained steadfast in their insistence that indigenous knowledge must be preserved and continued."

which has resulted in the establishment of more than forty tribally controlled colleges and universities in the United States and Canada. Thirty-two of these colleges are currently recipients of federal funds as part of the Tribally Controlled College or University Assistance and Equity in Education Land-Grant Status acts.

From their humble beginnings as locally controlled institutions of higher education, tribal colleges have expanded their mission and outreach to include partnerships with non–tribally controlled colleges and universities across the nation as well as colleges and universities serving the Native peoples of Canada, New Zealand, and elsewhere across the globe. Tribally controlled colleges and universities are exemplars of how indigenous communities can and do respond to the demands and pressures of an increasingly globalized world while working to sustain and nurture the cultures and languages of the Native peoples by whom they were first established and to whom they are ultimately accountable.

Growth and Development of Tribally Controlled Colleges

An Overview of the History and Early Development of Tribal Colleges and Universities

The tribal college movement emerged in part as a response to centuries of educational disenfranchisement. Historically, Indian education had been characterized by federal policies and practices that viewed Native cultures and languages as deficits to learning in schools, resulting in forced assimilation with no voice given to parents and tribal governments in the education of children and tribal members. Boarding schools in the 1870s set the tone with their attempts to civilize Natives, followed by a brief period in the 1930s that promoted the inclusion of Indians in their own affairs and the provision of more relevant education in schools located close to home. In the 1940s the federal policy of termination again advocated assimilation and a loss of local control of education and other services (e.g., Tippeconnic 1999).

The fight for educational and civil rights intensified during the 1950s and 1960s as Native people across the United States asserted their right to self-determination and local control of education (see, for example, Pavel, Inglebert, and Banks 2001). Prior to the self-determination movement of the 1960s, American Indians and Alaska Natives had endured years of federally imposed miseducation (Charleston 1994). Education at the hands of non-

Native entities served as a means of dehumanizing Native peoples, attempting to take away their languages and cultures. In spite of these threats to their languages and cultures, Native people evidenced their ability to survive. The self-determination movement marked a period in which Native peoples rose up and demanded that the control of Indian education be returned to the local level—to the places from which their students came.

In 1965, a group of Navajos including Dillon Platero, Allen Yazzie, and Guy Gorman obtained funds from the Office of Economic Opportunity (OEO) to conduct a feasibility study for the establishment of a junior or community college on the Navajo reservation. Discussions were held with representatives of the federal government, state universities, community colleges, businesses, the Navajo nation, and other groups (Stein 1992).

On July 17, 1968, Navajo Community College (NCC), today known as Diné College, was founded as the first tribally controlled community college chartered and operated by an Indian nation. The main campus of Diné College is located in the small rural community of Tsaile, Arizona, on the Navajo reservation. Funds were initially secured from OEO for a period of three years. Additional funds were provided by the Navajo nation and the Danner Foundation. Federal funds to support basic operational costs were granted in 1971 when Congress passed the Navajo Community College Act (25 *U.S. Code* 640a et seq.).[2] NCC was established to provide higher education opportunities for Navajos, many of whom, for various reasons, did not have viable options to pursue education at existing colleges or universities. In addition to providing degree-granting programs at the local level, the philosophy of the college was based on the Navajo culture and language. This enabled the development and provision of an integrated curriculum utilizing delivery systems culturally and linguistically relevant to the Navajo people.

The second tribally controlled college, Oglala Lakota College (OLC),[3] was established on the Pine Ridge Reservation in South Dakota in 1971. OLC was followed by the establishment of Sinte Gleska College on the Rosebud Reservation in South Dakota (1971); D-Q University in Davis, California (1971); and Turtle Mountain Community College (1972) on the Turtle Mountain Chippewa Reservation in North Dakota (Stein 1992). To date, there are approximately

2. Advocates of Navajo Community College saw federal funding as critical to the continued success of the college.

3. OLC was originally chartered as the Lakota Higher Education Center. The name was later changed to Oglala Sioux Community College (American Indian Higher Education Consortium 2006).

forty tribal colleges and universities (TCUS) located in the United States and Canada. More than forty years after the tribal college movement began, commitment to this movement remains strong, as evidenced by the establishment of Comanche Nation College in Oklahoma[4] in 2002, and proposals for a host of new colleges being discussed across the nation.

Meeting local needs. Tribal colleges are defined by the federal government as "institution[s] of higher education which [are] formally controlled, or [have] been formally sanctioned, or chartered, by the governing body of an Indian tribe or tribes" (25 *U.S. Code* chap. 20). According to Hampton (1989, as cited in Cajete 2006, 57), "Tribal colleges were . . . created to introduce a new circle to Indian education founded on the roots of tribal education and reflecting Indian needs, values, and socio/political issues. The new circle was designed to encompass important ancestral traditions; emphasize respect for individual uniqueness in diverse spiritual expressions; facilitate understanding of history and culture; develop a strong sense of place and service to community; and forge a commitment to educational and social transformation."

In sum, tribal colleges were established to meet an unmet need among Native peoples across the nation. Tribal communities recognized the importance of education in maintaining their cultural and linguistic capital and in gaining access to economic capital; however, many of them felt that existing mainstream institutions of higher education were inaccessible or did not work in concert with their traditions and values. Inaccessibility of mainstream higher education programs was due in large part to a lack of monetary resources, geographical isolation, and cultural/philosophical barriers, which made these institutions seem unwelcoming to many Native peoples.

What Makes Tribal College Different from Mainstream Institutions of Higher Education

Tribal colleges are fundamentally different from mainstream colleges and universities in their control, philosophy, programs, and the students they serve. As sovereign nations, each college is chartered by a tribe or group of tribes allowing them to exercise local control and develop programs to meet local educational, economic, and social needs. The foundation of each tribal college is based on the local indigenous culture, language, and values that are used and

4. For additional information, see http://www.cnc.cc.ok.us/.

viewed as strengths in preparing young people and adults to function in the local and broader worlds.

Tribal Colleges Today

Expansion from local to national to global. During the fall of 2005, tribal colleges and universities (TCUS) served approximately seventeen thousand degree-seeking students, the majority (80 percent) of whom were American Indian (American Indian Higher Education Consortium 2006).[5] In addition to full-time degree-seeking students, tribal colleges educate an almost equal number of non-degree-seeking students, increasing the total enrollment to approximately thirty thousand students per annum. Tribal college students represent more than 250 federally recognized tribes across the nation. Many of these students reside in remote rural areas including American Indian reservations and surrounding communities. TCUS are located in fourteen states—Alaska, Arizona, Kansas, Michigan, Minnesota, Montana, Nebraska, New Mexico, North Dakota, Oklahoma, South Dakota, Washington, Wisconsin, and Wyoming. Although the majority of the TCU student population is American Indian, the colleges also serve an increasing number of non-Native students, for whom they receive little, if any, state funding (American Indian Higher Education Consortium 2007, April). Tribal colleges differ from mainstream institutions of higher education in that they have a "dual mission" (Fann 2002) of sustaining the cultural and linguistic traditions of their founding tribe or tribes while also preparing students to earn undergraduate and, in some cases, graduate degrees.

Although tribal colleges were established to meet the local needs of tribal communities, they have historically been global in their approach to higher education. According to the Carnegie Foundation (Carnegie Foundation for the Advancement of Teaching 1989), tribal colleges are "truly community institutions." They view education from a broad holistic perspective that not only integrates tribal cultures and languages but also ties education to economic, social, health, and political realities of their communities. As a result, the work of the tribal colleges is critical to economic development (Fogarty 2007), community health and healing (Yellow Bird 2007), and the survival and renewal of tribal cultures (Price 2005). Tribal colleges are also becoming increasingly

---

5. Enrollment figures reflect data from thirty-two tribal colleges and universities reporting data to the American Indian Higher Education Consortium for academic year 2005–6. For additional information regarding existing tribal colleges and universities, see the Web site of the American Indian Higher Education Consortium, http://www.aihec.org/.

global in their outreach to indigenous peoples around the world through their work with colleges in Canada and New Zealand, leadership in the establishment of the World Indigenous Nations Higher Education Consortium (WINHEC) (Ambler 2005a), and international exchange programs in such places as Guatemala and Peru (Des Jarlais and Stein 2005). According to Ambler (2005b), "As tribal college faculty and students travel to other countries and welcome foreign visitors to their campuses, they share the tribal college model. However, the visits are not one-sided. The tribal colleges and universities (TCUS) both teach and learn, giving their ideas and taking home new concepts. They learn that indigenous people in many other places suffer from unbelievable poverty and oppression. At the same time, they become enriched by their exchanges, experiencing the vitality of diverse languages, spiritual ceremonies, and centuries-old traditions. They see education models that deserve emulation" (para. 4–5). In effect, the tribal college movement fosters reciprocal relationships, both locally and globally, that provide much-needed educational services for indigenous peoples and communities.

Challenges and opportunities posed by globalization. As tribal colleges adapt to meet the demands of an increasingly globalized world, they continue to assert their tribal traditions and heritages. According to Robertson (2001):

> The forces of globalization are courting tribal colleges; [therefore,] it behooves us to know both the potential benefits and possible dangers posed by these economic interests. . . . [Other land grant] institutions[6] . . . seem no more disposed to questioning globalization than Coca Cola or Texaco. By contrast, tribal colleges raise those value questions because their origin remains grounded in the local. The land and the culture of individual tribal nations give life to tribal colleges. The ability of tribal colleges and universities to help tribal governments to improve their economic environments derives from each college's direct local connection to its tribal nation. Globalization has become such an omnipresent necessity of mainstream American life that underlying questions of its value for tribal nations too often go unasked. Tribal colleges should ask those questions, and venture answers as well.

6. Thirty-two tribal colleges are currently included in the Equity in Education Land-Grant Status Act of 1994. To be designated as a land-grant institution, tribal colleges must be accredited. Funding from this act enables tribal colleges to provide community outreach services, economic development opportunities, development of natural resources, and agricultural, health, and wellness programs (American Indian Higher Education Consortium 2007, Spring).

As demonstrated by Robertson, the twenty-first century brings with it a new wave of globalization or, as many Native and non-Native scholars have termed it, colonization. With this new wave of colonization comes the increased potential for continued appropriation of indigenous intellectual, cultural, and economic property by non-Native peoples, communities, educational systems, businesses, and governments. It is within the backdrop of this new wave of globalization/colonization that tribally controlled colleges and universities continue to forge their identities. With globalization comes the continued need to transition from subsistence-based programming and developmental structures—which are highly dependent on funding from the federal government, foundations, and other tribal, state, and private entities—to truly self-sustaining institutions driven by the guiding principle of utilizing indigenous knowledges.[7] Although this drive to respond to the challenges of globalization is not unique to tribally controlled colleges and universities, the ways that these institutions respond is indeed unique. According to Smith (2006, 550), "While . . . traditional universities prepare themselves for greater opportunities to be metropolitan, to expand their efforts and income from research and teaching on a global scale, other institutions such as tribal colleges, universities and indigenous knowledge networks respond to a powerful imperative to remain connected to place, environment, history and a people. Indigenous and local institutions meet a different set of needs that are overlooked in the drive to a knowledge economy."

Tribal colleges' response to globalization. The effects of globalization are felt by individuals, communities, organizations, and educational institutions as well as businesses. The drive to keep pace with an increasingly global world economy has forced many institutions of higher education, including tribal colleges and universities, to diversify not only their core course offerings, but also the technology by which they deliver these courses and the audience by whom these courses are consumed. Given the lack of culturally specific roots found among many nonindigenous institutions of higher education, these changes may present fewer challenges for them than for indigenous-based institutions whose very identity is rooted and grounded in their early mission to strengthen and promote Native languages, cultures, and histories.

7. There are multiple definitions and conceptions of what constitutes indigenous knowledge. For the purposes of this discussion, we use the definition offered by Battiste (2005, 8), who suggests that indigenous knowledge "embodies a web of relationships within a specific ecological context; contains linguistic categories, rules, and relationships unique to each knowledge system; has localized content and meaning; has established customs with respect to acquiring and sharing of knowledge . . . and implies responsibilities for possessing various kinds of knowledge."

Within the larger higher education context, tribal colleges are small. Many of them are located in rural, remote, and geographically isolated areas; operate with limited financial and other resources; and experience a lack of respect and acceptance from mainstream colleges and universities. This can lead to an isolationist status and the feeling that they are on an island, going it alone. Awareness of and work with other indigenous colleges around the world provides connections and opportunities for unified efforts to share information, expand networks, and develop collaborative activities.

As partnerships between tribal colleges and other institutions of higher education continue to emerge, strong leadership becomes increasingly important. According to Kouzes and Posner (2002, 382–83), leaders are the "first to encounter the world outside the boundaries of the[ir] organization. The more they know about the world, the easier it is to approach it with assurance [to learn about the] political, economic, social, and moral forces that affect organizations."

Bridging the gap between local and global. Although globalization poses a number of challenges for tribal colleges and universities, many of these institutions have begun to turn these challenges to their advantage. Utilizing Stromquist's depiction of globalization as a "multidimensional process that comprises four major sectors: the economy, technology, politics, and culture" (2007, 2), it is possible to envision the ways in which globalization can be used to foster a better understanding of common factors that have affected indigenous peoples around the world (e.g., economic, political, and educational oppression; the use of indigenous knowledge in education; and the control of educational institutions). Each of these dimensions has played a role in shaping the past, present, and future of the tribal college movement. By acknowledging and working, in some cases to "knock down" and in other cases to strengthen the effects of each of these dimensions, tribal colleges are able to initiate and strengthen collaborative initiatives and partnerships with existing colleges and programs. By aligning themselves with colleges and universities that are similar in philosophy, educational approach, and governance—no matter where they are located in the world—tribal colleges have opportunities to not only share their local indigenous knowledge, but also gain cultural, economic, social, and political cachet from the larger indigenous world that is needed to effect meaningful and sustained change for indigenous peoples across the globe.

For many Native people, one's identity is inherently tied to the place from which one comes. But this place is not merely a physical space marked by geographical boundaries or borders; it is in many ways an epistemological place, a way of thinking about who one is in terms of language, culture, and place of origin, all within the context of the historical and prehistorical events that have helped to shape that place today. To know where one is going is to know where one has been. The past in turn shapes who one is in the present. Tribal colleges and universities enable many Native people to know who they are, where they come from, and where they are going, by serving as both repositories and incubators for the intellectual, cultural, and linguistic capital that Native people and their communities possess. According to Fox (2006), tribal colleges have been instrumental in promoting and sustaining tribal histories, languages, and cultures. These colleges also provide a safe place in which students, both young and old, are encouraged to question Western accounts of Native history. In Montana, for example, the state legislature recently allocated funds to the state's tribal colleges to develop tribal histories that present an alternative, indigenous perspective on such topics as the "westward expansion" (also referred to as the "eastern invasion"), terms that are central to the discussion of globalization in Native tribes and communities. Although the terms used to describe globalization may differ in Native communities across the globe, they all have a common bond in that they reflect the impact of a movement that effected and continues to effect change on their sense of place and identity as Native peoples.

Examples of tribal college global initiatives. A sampling of tribal college initiatives are outlined below to illustrate the involvement of tribal colleges and universities in the global arena:

(1) The College of Menominee Nation's Sustainable Development Institute hosts a series of conferences titled "Sharing Indigenous Wisdom: An International Dialogue on Sustainable Development Conference"[8]— More than 120 participants representing Central and South America, New Zealand, Finland, the Philippines, India, Nigeria, Nepal, Australia, Canada, Mexico, and the United States attended the 2007 conference. Sponsors included the U.S. Forest Service and the Ford Foundation.

(2) Little Priest Tribal College—Partnered with the National Museum of the American Indian, the University of Queensland (Australia), a group of Maori from New Zealand, and an aboriginal community from Australia to utilize the Indigenous Knowledge Management System (IKMS)[9]

8. See http://sharingindigenouswisdom.org/.
9. For additional information on IKMS, see Hunter (2005).

(Davis 2005). IKMS is a technology-based system used to record and preserve Native languages, ceremonies, dances, songs, stories, and other cultural artifacts (Hunter 2005).

(3) Navajo Technical College—The Internet to Hogan initiative brought Internet connectivity to the easternmost regions of the Navajo reservation. Until recently, most of the eastern section of the reservation had been without television, Internet, and phone service (Navajo Technical College 2007).

(4) Haskell Indian Nations University—partnered with Gorno-Altaisk State University, Kansas State University, and University of Kansas to study water quality in both the United States and the Russian Federation.[10]

In addition to their individual initiatives, U.S. tribal colleges and universities have partnered with indigenous-serving institutions across the world to form the World Indigenous Nations Higher Education Consortium (WINHEC).[11] Following several years of discussion and planning, WINHEC was formally established in the fall of 2002. In keeping with its vision statement, the organization "gather[s] as Indigenous Peoples of . . . respective nations recognising and reaffirming the educational rights of all Indigenous Peoples. . . . [Members of the organization] share a vision of Indigenous Peoples of the world united in the collective synergy of self determination through control of higher education. [WINHEC] . . . is committed to building partnerships that restore and retain indigenous spirituality, cultures and languages, homelands, social systems, economic systems and self-determination" (World Indigenous Nations Higher Education Consortium 2003, 3).

WINHEC's tenets are modeled after those outlined in the United Nations Draft Declaration of the Rights of Indigenous Peoples (United Nations High Commissioner for Human Rights 1994/95), which maintains the following:

Indigenous Peoples have the right to manifest, practice, develop and teach their spiritual and religious traditions, customs and ceremonies; the right to maintain, protect, and have access in privacy to their religious and cultural sites; the right to the use and control of ceremonial objects; and the right to the repatriation of human remains (Article #13).

Indigenous peoples have the right to revitalize, use, develop and trans-

10. For additional information, see http://www.engg.ksu.edu/chsr/international/altai/.
11. See http://www.win-hec.org/ for additional information.

mit to future generations their histories, languages, oral traditions, philosophies, writing systems and literatures, and to designate and retain their own names for communities, places and persons (Article #14).

Indigenous peoples have the right to all levels and forms of education of the State. All Indigenous peoples also have this right and the right to establish and control their educational systems and institutions providing education in their own languages, in a manner appropriate to their cultural methods of teaching and learning. Indigenous children living outside their communities have the right to be provided access to education in their own culture and language. States shall take effective measures to provide appropriate resources for these purposes (Article #15).

Indigenous peoples have the right to have the dignity and diversity of their cultures, traditions, histories and aspirations appropriately reflected in all forms of education and public information. States shall take effective measures, in consultation with the Indigenous peoples concerned, to eliminate prejudice and discrimination and promote tolerance, understanding and good relations among Indigenous peoples and all segments of society (Article #16).

Implications. Tribal colleges and universities provide a unique example of the ways that localized, tribal knowledge can have a global impact. Although founded on the concept of localization rather than globalization, tribal colleges have grown to recognize the need for global collaboration, partnership, and outreach, particularly as this relates to other indigenous peoples across the nation and the world. As these collaborative networks emerge and solidify, the work of the tribal colleges remains closely connected to the knowledge bases generated by generations of Native scholars in and around the places they call home. According to Warner (2006, 149–50), "Native Ways of Knowing, in contrast to Western educational practices, are acquired and represented through the context of place, revolving around the needs of a community and the best efforts to actualize a holistic understanding of the community's environment." For many tribal colleges, the ability to engage in indigenous ways of teaching, learning, and knowing is facilitated in part by their location in primarily rural and remote areas where traditional tribal cultures and languages are routinely practiced. Although the rural location of these colleges allows them to engage in more traditional educational practices, tribal colleges are faced with a similar challenge felt by colleges and universities around the world—the need to meet the demands of an increasingly globalized world whose effects are felt both inside and outside the confines of the communities within which the colleges are located. Smith (2006, 2) argues that "globalization, and in particular, free trade agreements, technology, and the knowledge economy, are about breaking down borders, crossing borders and being free from the identities and constraints of borders." For tribally controlled colleges and universities, globalization intensifies the need to maintain the unique qualities that set tribal colleges and universities apart from other mainstream colleges and universities while responding to the diversified demands of an increasingly globalized world.

Locally derived curricula, programming, and instructional practices make tribal colleges spaces within which both Native and non-Native students[12] can thrive intellectually and culturally. To lose sight of these local-tribal foci is to risk being colonized by the mainstream educational system, whose initial failure to meet the needs of Native peoples led to the establishment of the tribal college movement in the first place. Given the small numbers of Native peoples in the United States, strength is gained by mobilizing the economic, social, cultural, and intellectual capital of Native peoples nationally and internationally. Such mobilization demonstrates the ability of Native peoples to develop, sustain, and adapt as needed to both local and global demands. The future of tribally controlled colleges and universities appears to be sound, in spite of the many challenges they continue to face. Connections and relationships they have developed with indigenous colleges around the world add strength, international purpose, leadership, and intellectual knowledge that will help to sustain both local and global growth and development.

According to Champagne (2004, 38), "Education for Native students needs to start in the community and must incorporate the interests, values, and cultural orientations of the community." The need to transcend the divide between global education as provided in predominantly white institutions of higher education is seen in Native tribes and communities across the globe. For education to be of use to many Native people, it must be able to work within the confines of local space, place, and traditions.

Conclusion

On a recent flight, this chapter's first coauthor, Susan C. Faircloth, picked up a copy of the airline's magazine and saw an advertisement from the American

---

12. According to a 2005 report (Pember 2006), approximately 20 percent of tribal college enrollment is composed of non-Native students, for which the colleges receive limited state or federal funding.

Indian College Fund—an organization dedicated to providing scholarships and financial assistance for American Indian and Alaska Native students attending tribal colleges and universities. The ad included a picture of a Native student with the caption, "If I stay on the rez I'm eight times less likely to drop out of college." A few minutes later, Susan began chatting with the gentleman seated next to her. He told her that he was flying home to his reservation in Nebraska to attend a funeral. In the middle of the conversation, he asked what she was doing in Albuquerque; she told him that she was returning home from a business meeting with the Bureau of Indian Education. Throughout the flight, they continued to talk about their work—he a paint salesman and she a college professor—their families, and the communities in which they were raised. One of the things that struck her most about this conversation was the way he depicted the challenges of growing up on the reservation—challenges marked in large part by inherent racism and classism deeply embedded in the communities surrounding his home. For this young man, the return home was a physical and emotional journey back to a place where he could no longer live, yet a place where his cultural roots remained strong. He spoke of going home to attend the funeral of his sister-in-law who had recently passed away and the burial, which would occur on the fourth day following her passing. Although the pain he felt at the loss of a family member was evident, it was clear that there was an equally emotional pain attached to the experiences he had lived as a youth—experiences that he appeared to relive as he continued to talk, and even more important, experiences that led to his moving away from his community to an area where, in his words, "it was safe to be a brown man."

We tell this story in an attempt to clarify our definition of local as used in this chapter. Although we recognize that there are multiple definitions and conceptions of local, we believe that the land and community are essential to maintaining our sense of who we are as Native peoples. The struggle to maintain our land and community has resulted in Native peoples having the highest rate of military service of any minority group in the United States. Some might find this ironic given the federal government's attempts to acculturate, assimilate, decimate, and colonize Native peoples. We, in the global sense, are able to view the land as ours to protect, honor, and defend regardless of our feelings toward colonizing forces. In essence, the way in which we define local in this chapter does not negate other notions of local, but helps to illustrate the way in which our connections to land, place, and community shape much of our historical and contemporary conceptions of who we are as Native peoples.

The work of tribally controlled colleges and universities provides concrete examples of what it means to bring the local to the forefront of indigenous education. What more can we hope for than to educate our children, youth, and elders on our homelands, communities, and other sacred places in ways that are constructed and delivered according to our indigenous values and beliefs—in essence, our Native ways of knowing.

References

Ambler, M. 2005a. Embracing the world: Indigenous educators join hands to share gifts. *Tribal College Journal of American Indian Higher Education* 16 (4), 18–20.

———. 2005b. International indigenous education. *Tribal College Journal of American Indian Higher Education* 16 (4). Retrieved October 20, 2005, from https://tribal collegejournal.org/themag/backissues/summer2005/sum 05ambler.htm.

American Indian Higher Education Consortium. 2006. *American Indian measures for success in higher education:* AIHEC AIMS fact book, 2005: Tribal colleges and universities report. Norwood, Mass.: Systemic Research Inc. Retrieved October 29, 2007, from http://www.aihec.org/documents/PDFS/AIMS/AIHEC_AIMS _2005FactB ook.pdf.

———. 2007 (Spring). Statement of the American Indian Higher Education Consortium. Submitted to the U.S. Senate Committee on Appropriations, Subcommittee on Agricultural, Rural Development, Food and Drug Administration, and Related Agencies. Retrieved October 20, 2007, from http://www.aihec.org/ resources/documents/FY08AgricStmt_spring07 .pdf.

———. 2007 (April). Statement of the American Indian Higher Education Consortium. Submitted to the U.S. Senate Committee on Appropriations, Subcommittee on Interior and Related Agencies, Department of the Interior, Bureau of Indian Affairs. Retrieved December 3, 2007, from http://www.aihec.org/ resources/documents/FY08InteriorStmt_4–19–07pdf.pdf.

Battiste, M. 2005. Indigenous knowledge: Foundations for First Nations. *Indigenous Voices, Indigenous Visions: Journal of the World Indigenous Nations Higher Education Consortium*, 1–12. Retrieved October 30, 2007, from http://www.win-hec .org/docs/pdfs/Journal/Marie%20Battiste%20copy. pdf.

Cajete, G. 2006 (Winter). It is time for Indian people to define indigenous education on our own terms. *Tribal College Journal of American Indian Higher Education* 18 (2), 56–57.

Carnegie Foundation for the Advancement of Teaching. 1989. *Tribal colleges: Shaping the future of Native America.* Princeton: The Foundation.

Champagne, D. 2004 (Winter). Education for nation-building. *Cultural Survival Quarterly* 27 (4), 34–38.

Charleston, G. M. 1994. Toward true Native education: A treaty of 1992: Final report of the Indian Nations at Risk Task Force, Draft 3. *Journal of American Indian Education* 33 (2), 1–23.

Davis, T. 2005 (Summer). IKMS offers home for indigenous knowledge. *Tribal College Journal of American Indian Higher Education* 16 (4). Retrieved October 30, 2007,

from https://tribalcollegejournal.org/themag/backissues/summer2001/sumo50c
.htm.

Des Jarlais, C. W., and W. J. Stein. 2005 (Summer). Tribal college faculty revaluating
traditional ways of knowing. *Tribal College Journal of American Indian Higher
Education* 16 (4), 10–14.

Fann, A. 2002 (January). Tribal colleges: An overview. ERIC Digest, 1–6. (ERIC Document Reproduction Service No. ED467847.)

Fogarty, M. 2007 (Spring). Commitment to building prosperous nations: Tribal colleges take aim against poverty. *Tribal College Journal of American Indian Higher
Education* 18 (3), 12–17.

Fox, E. 2006. Indian education for all: A tribal college perspective. *Phi Delta Kappan*
88 (3), 208–12.

Hunter, J. 2005. The role of information technologies in indigenous knowledge management. In M. Nakata and M. Langton, eds., *Australian indigenous knowledge
and libraries,* 94–109. Sydney: UTSePress. Retrieved October 30, 2007, from
http://epress.lib.uts.edu.au/dspace/bitstream/2100/835/1/E-book.p df.

Kouzes, J. M., and B. Z. Posner. 2002. *The leadership challenge.* San Francisco: Jossey-
Bass.

Navajo Technical College. 2007 (January). Navajo Technical College begins bridging
digital divide: The beginning of the end of the digital divide. Retrieved October
29, 2007, from http://205.242.219.103/docs/releases/release.html.

Pavel, D. M., E. Inglebret, and S. R. Banks. 2001. Tribal colleges and universities in an
era of dynamic development. *Peabody Journal of Education* 76 (1), 50–72.

Pember, M. A. 2006 (November). Deal or no deal? *Diverse Issues in Higher Education*
23 (21), 34–35.

Price, M. W. 2005 (Spring). Seeds of educational sovereignty—Sisseton Wahpeton cultivating culturally-centered learning. *Tribal College Journal of American Indian
Higher Education* 16 (4), 18–20.

Rains, F. V., J. A. Archibald, and D. Deyhle (2000). Introduction: Through our eyes
and in our own words. *Qualitative Studies in Education* 13 (4), 337–42.

Robertson, J. 2001 (August). The hidden perils of globalization. *Tribal College Journal
of American Indian Higher Education* 12 (2). Retrieved October 10, 2007, from
http://www.tribalcollegejournal.org/themag/backissues/summer2001/summer
2001.html.

Smith, L. T. 2006 (September). Introduction. *International Journal of Qualitative Studies in Education* 19 (5), 549–52.

Stein, W. J. 1992. *Tribally controlled colleges: Making good medicine.* New York: Peter
Lang.

Stromquist, N. P., with the collaboration of E. Balbachevsky, C. Colatrella, M. Gil-
Anton, R. O. Mabokela, and A. Smolentseva. 2007. The academic profession in
the globalization age: Key trends, challenges, and possibilities. In P. G. Altbach
and P. M. Peterson, eds., *Higher education in the new century,* 1–33. Boston:
Center for International Education.

Tippeconnic, J. 1999. Tribal control of American Indian education: Observations since
the 1960s with implications for the future. In K. Swisher and J. Tippeconnic,
eds., *Next steps: Research and practice to advance Indian education,* 33–53. Wash-

ington, D.C.: U.S. Department of Education, ERIC Clearinghouse on Rural Education and Small Schools.

United Nations High Commissioner for Human Rights. 1994 (August 26). *1994/45 Draft United Nations declaration on the rights of indigenous peoples.* Geneva: Office of the United Nations High Commissioner for Human Rights. Retrieved October 30, 2007, from http://www.unhchr.ch/huridocda/huridoca.nsf/(Symbol)/ E.CN.4.SUB.2.RES.1994.45.En?OpenDocument.

Warner, L. S. 2006. Native ways of knowing: Let me count the ways. *Canadian Journal of Native Education* 29 (2), 149–64.

World Indigenous Nations Higher Education Consortium. 2003. WINHEC accreditation handbook (2d ed.). Retrieved October 30, 2007, from http://www.ankn.uaf.edu/ IEW/winhec/WinhecHandDec2004.pdf.

Yellow Bird, D. 2007 (Summer). Changing the face of research: Tribal colleges address community well-being. *Tribal College Journal of American Indian Higher Education* 18 (4), 12–16.

10

THE GOLDEN CAGE OF RURAL COLLEGE ACCESS:
HOW HIGHER EDUCATION CAN RESPOND TO THE RURAL LIFE

Patricia M. McDonough, R. Evely Gildersleeve, and Karen McClafferty Jarsky

Introduction

Problems of college access stubbornly remain entrenched in the lives of under-represented students (Allen 1992; McDonough 2004; Nunez and Cuccaro-Alamin 2000; Potts 1997). Rural college access largely has been ignored as a substantive policy issue, as most recent work on college access has focused on large inner-city schools as well as the needs of African American and Latino students (McDonough and Gildersleeve 2005). Rural students remain significantly underrepresented in U.S. higher education, however, and this often includes migrant Latinos, Native Americans, and, in the South, African Americans (Gildersleeve 2006; Lawrence 1996; Potts 1997; Valadez 1996).

We argue that "the rural life," being qualitatively different than urban and suburban cultures, is unattended to by higher education. Systems, institutions, and individual organizations are not congruent with rural students' specific concerns about money, lifestyle, or academic preparation. Further, the presumed seamlessness of rural life, in which schools and community are interdependent, problematically ends at the community college for educational-opportunity concerns (Budge 2006; Collins, Flaxman, and Schartman 2001; Herzog and Pittman 2003). These broader issues culminate in the underrepresentation of rural students. In this chapter, we tease out these broader issues, illustrating their micro-level manifestations as discovered in a qualitative study conducted by McDonough and McClafferty (2001), as represented in their technical report to the University of California Office of the President and the

McConnel Foundation. We draw extensively from this report to suggest ways in which rural students face unique college access dilemmas.

In building our argument about the rural life and its relationship to higher education, we do not position the rural life as a deficit ideology, wherein the struggles for sustainable social mobility would be understood as intrinsic in cultural qualities shared by those who live in rural areas. Rather, we argue that higher education needs to take responsibility for serving rural communities without expecting them to conform or assimilate to dominant cultural practices. We present the metaphor of "the golden cage" to help understand how increased university involvement in the rural life can help address the specific needs of rural student college access.

College Access in Rural Contexts

Among the groups facing underrepresentation in American higher education, students from rural areas have received little attention in research (McGrath et al. 2001; Smith, Beaulieu, and Seraphine 1995; Caldwell and Trainer 1991). Often misunderstood, rural educational goals, needs, and perceptions can be different than their urban and suburban counterparts. Scholars need to better understand the college access dilemmas of rural areas and find ways that colleges and universities can be more responsive to them, with the aim of extending the educational opportunities of rural students (McDonough and McClafferty 2001). Indeed, according to the latest information from the National Center for Education Statistics (NCES) (1999), rural students between the ages of eighteen and twenty-four are enrolled in school at rates over 6 percent lower than the national average, and almost 8 percent lower than their metropolitan counterparts. Further, additional data from the U.S. Department of Education (2003) shows that despite graduating students from high school at higher rates than urban high schools, across race/ethnicity and gender rural high schools still send proportionally fewer students onto four-year and two-year colleges and universities. These statistics and the college-access literature highlight how rural cultures can interact differently with students' educational opportunity than urban and suburban cultures; therefore, what we know about urban and suburban college access might not be applicable in rural contexts.

Although a healthy body of literature continues to develop in the area of college access, most of the attention paid to rural students has focused on the *educational aspirations* of rural students (Ukaga, Yoder, and Etling 1998; Gibbs

1998; Haller and Virkler 1993; Apostal and Bilden 1991) or the *actual attainment* of postsecondary education for rural students (Castaneda 2002; Roscigno and Crowley 2001; McGrath et al. 2001; Smith, Beaulieu, and Seraphine 1995; Philipsen 1993). Few studies have actually focused on the *qualitative differences in educational opportunity* for rural students. Among these, even fewer address the *role of higher education* in addressing rural underrepresentation (Caldwell and Trainer 1991). College access for rural students is an underresearched area with little attention paid to the ways in which rural cultures and higher education intersect and interrelate. One notable exception is Gildersleeve's (2006) study of students from Mexican migrant farm-working families in California. Physical geography was found to influence how students negotiated their postsecondary pathways, and students from rural environments expressed stronger desires to return and serve their communities after college.

The scholarship that does exist points to key variables in rural life that contribute to the underrepresentation of rural students in higher education. These variables focus on what many authors consider the "depressed" environment of rural economies (Roscigno and Crowley 2001; Haller and Virkler 1993). Although we acknowledge that some rural economies are depressed, which helps to highlight the structural disadvantages that many rural communities face in sustaining social and educational opportunities, we caution that viewing rural communities in terms of capital they do not share, but that higher education institutions value, places sole responsibility for the problem on rural communities themselves. According to the logic of deficit perspectives, these are the very communities least likely to have the resources to address their "deficits." Thus a deficit perspective is problematic when working toward a radically democratic goal of increased opportunity. Latino scholars of college choice have well documented the deficit orientation to much of the work done on underrepresented communities (Villalpando and Solórzano 2005; Yosso 2006). Solórzano and Solórzano (1995) point out that deficit orientations ignore larger systemic conditions that perpetuate inequality.

Socioeconomic status (SES), occupational aspirations, and educational resource investment are common themes across the rural education literature (Rosgino and Crowley 2001; Smith, Beaulieu, and Seraphine 1995; Haller and Virkler 1993). What most scholars fail to address, however, are the ways these social constructs interact differently in rural versus nonrural contexts. McGrath and colleagues (2001) point out that status, wealth, and occupational aspirations potentially take on different meanings in some rural areas when compared to urban or suburban counterparts, especially in some rural farming communities. For example, they posit that the rural farming communities in their study signified status as a metric based on a family's prominence in the community, largely connected to their historical participation in civic and farming activity. They illustrated this point by pointing out the different uses of social capital across geographic contexts. Therefore, relying on traditional computations of concepts such as SES has the potential to inaccurately portray the experiences of rural students.

A number of studies have sought to understand rural students' and families' desire to remain in their home community (Gildersleeve 2006; Hektner 1995; Donaldson 1986; Feldman 1990; Hummon 1992; Kasarda and Janowitz 1974). Much of this work supports the idea that some rural students' desire to stay in their close-knit communities affects their educational aspirations, and that their postsecondary planning happens later in high school than for suburban students. This latter note relates to an assumed seamlessness of rural education, where students, families, and school personnel all contribute to a strong ethic of community (Hektner 1995). These studies, however, have not tried to understand ways that higher education institutions might respond to the needs of rural students differently than they respond to the needs of metropolitan students.

In their comprehensive review of research on rural education, Arnold and colleagues (2005) discussed six specific studies that they deemed to meet requirements of medium- to high-quality scientific research related to college access. The work in this area was found to be of mostly medium quality. The topics discussed focus on the influence of SES, students' commitment to remaining in the community, and low occupational aspirations. Most of these studies have already been referenced here, but a major contribution of the review is its argument that research on rural education is not only sparse but also lacks rigor and quality. But the Arnold study privileges quantitative, causal-inference, comparative research; it does not address qualitative, descriptive, or interpretive research studies. This limitation is implicated throughout the article and its discussion of the merits of work.

This chapter hopes to respond to and affirm Arnold and colleagues' call for higher quality and rigorous research on rural education. But we view the distinct lack of culturally contextualized inquiry as an additional drawback to the literature. Higher education cannot respond to the problem of rural access without understanding the processes involved in its manifestation. Culturally driven qualitative inquiry can help unpack how these quantified and comparative findings matter to rurality, and how rurality matters to these quantified and comparative findings in relation to educational opportunity. Thus our chapter meets a clear need in the literature: analysis of rural experiences via culturally driven inquiry, as referenced in the technical report by McDonough and McClafferty, in order to promote higher education responsiveness.

Framing Rural College Access

Our approach is founded in Bourdieuian (Bourdieu and Passeron 1977; Bourdieu 1990) approaches to college access, which situate high school students in their social, organizational, and cultural contexts and demonstrate the essential use of school-level cultural capital and the high school's college structures and cultures (Hearn 1990, 1991; McDonough 1997, 1998). All cultural capital is knowledge and values. The cultural capital that middle- and upper-class families transmit to their offspring substitutes for and supplements the transmission of economic capital as a means of maintaining class status and privilege across successive generations.

McDonough (1997, 1998) has written extensively about the need to examine college access from an organizational culture approach to understand schools' roles in reproducing social inequalities. Her research was the first to identify differences across K–12 schools in their graduates' college enrollment patterns and to link these differences to the schools' structural and cultural arrangements. McDonough's work has shown how a school's culture, in relation to students' postsecondary planning, preparation, and matriculation, consequently structures students' higher education opportunity. McDonough's work also documented how a school's structure (e.g., number of counselors and their expected responsibilities) reciprocally influenced the school's culture. Moreover, her work established the need for developing a college-going culture to improve the college access opportunities for students who are low-income, first-generation, college-bound, and underrepresented minorities. (For more detailed discussion of "college-going culture," see McDonough 1997.) Bourdieuian models of college choice subsequently have been used by numerous scholars (e.g., Kirst and Venezia 2004; Fann 2005; Lareau and Horvat 1999), who have added to the understanding of how specific structural inequalities interact with the individual agency of students and their families.

Fundamentally, any Bourdieuian model of college choice needs to account for individuals' college choices by looking at institutionalized signals that indicate to individuals what is possible and logical. Therefore, this research also investigates the impact of local economic and employment conditions in one rural area in California as they affect high school students' estimations of how much a college education may be worth in terms of projected occupational attainment. We execute this analysis by employing Bourdieu's concept of habitus.

Habitus, according to Bourdieu (1990, 13), exists "as a system of acquired dispositions functioning on the practical level of categories of perception and assessment or as classificatory principles as well as being the organizing principles in action." In other words, objective reality—the material and social facts—determine a range of possibilities from which individuals can take action. This range of known possibilities co-constructs cultural dispositions, the ways of knowing and responding to the world in a given situation. Bourdieu exemplified the habitus as contained within families (1990). McDonough extended the concept of habitus to the organizational level; in college choice, this is understood as school-level habitus (1997). Martyn Lee (1997), a cultural geographer, also has suggested that habitus can be understood in the field of space as belonging to a place, specifically cities. Lee asserts, "A city embodies a habitus: bundles of relatively coherent social dispositions in an ongoing state of generation and regeneration. These dispositions result in *place-specific actions*, the *practice* of the city or, one might almost say, the way a city behaves. This practice appears as the product of the *necessity* to respond to and treat the objective world in particular ways and thus presents itself as a sort of axiomatic logic from which practice is grooved into well-defined responses of habituation, although these are adapted and adaptable to the individual requirements and necessities of different social fields" (133). Lee goes on to identify examples of cultural artifacts, such as land use, budget decisions, historical preservation, welfare practices, and architecture that are conditioned by a city's metaphoric way of viewing the world. He argues that this conditioning transcends the particularities of local governments and indicates habitus's force of logic.

We extend Lee's idea about a city's habitus to the North State area of Shasta and Siskiyou counties in California. As demonstrated by the findings from McDonough and McClafferty (2001), and description (presented in the below section) of these cultural communities, there is a guiding hand that helps shape the possible choices of actions that residents, organizations, and institutions take for granted. Cumulatively, the use of school-level cultural capital, the high school's college cultures, and the North State habitus sheds light on how high schools affect individuals' higher education investment practices and how individuals' strategies for future educational and occupational attainment affect their current investments in education.

College Access in Rural Lives:
The California North State Region

California postsecondary enrollment rates vary by location across the urban-rural continuum. Periodically, California undertakes an eligibility study to assess how closely its enrollment goals, as set forth by the California Master Plan for Education, are met by measuring the actual proportions of public high school graduates eligible for the University of California (uc), the California State University (csu), and community colleges. The last such study (California Postsecondary Education Commission 1997) found that eligibility rates for csu for urban and rural students was exactly the same at 26.7 percent, although both groups of students were below the targeted 33 percent csu eligibility rate set by the Master Plan. uc eligibility rates for both groups were again below the targeted 12.5 percent, but rural students fared worse at 7.1 percent than their urban counterparts at 10.3 percent.

To understand more about the problems of rural college access, the McDonough and McClafferty technical report focused its inquiry in Shasta and Siskiyou counties of the North State area of California. In this rural region, the uc enrollment rates were under 4 percent and the csu enrollment rates averaged 6.3 percent. Also, a recent higher education needs assessment for the North State identified "a significant deficit of bachelor's degree level educated individuals in the area" (mgt of America 2001).

The North State region in McDonough and McClafferty's investigation covered ten thousand square miles, approximately the area of Massachusetts. As the northernmost part of California, bordering Oregon, the North State region is very rural and poses great geographical challenges because of its mountainous terrain and the distances between towns. The region has approximately 210,000 residents. Its school population is primarily poor white students with small numbers of Native American and Latino students. Because of the large number of public parks and forests, federal and state public agencies manage over 60 percent of Siskiyou County land.

Economically, the North State has had difficult times of late, despite major economic development initiatives sponsored by the state and county governments. With serious downturns in the formerly dominant timber industry,

Siskiyou County now relies on a job market of government, services, retail, and farm industries. Experiencing a similar erosion of its former keystone industry, timber, Shasta County has sought a more stable economic base and currently relies on a job market of services, retail, and government.

But recent unemployment trends shape many residents' perceptions of opportunity. For Siskiyou County, unemployment rates have ranged from a high of 13.5 percent in 1996 to a low of 9.5 percent in 2000. For Shasta County, unemployment rates have ranged from a high of 9.9 percent in 1996 to a low of 6.9 percent in 2000. Compared to a statewide unemployment rate of 4.9 percent the North State region has experienced an economic depression, with Siskiyou County being harder hit.

North State Region Technical Report

McDonough and McClafferty had two overarching foci: assessment of current college culture conditions in fifteen rural high schools and assessments of alternative, proposed models of increased outreach in these rural areas. Their report sheds light on major obstacles to increasing college enrollment and schools' capacity for supporting college attendance, as well as attitudes and perceptions of school leaders about ways that higher education institutions can increase outreach in the area. Specifically, the technical report put forth two proposed models of outreach. Model 1 included a university presence in every high school. Model 2 included an outreach center or hub that would work with all the high schools in the area to provide information and support related to college preparation, planning, and culture. A secondary research focus was on the impact of the remoteness of the UC and CSU campuses from both counties on students' college access. The nearest UC is approximately 200 miles away while the nearest CSU is about 150 miles away.

McDonough and McClafferty also made efforts to attend to issues of place and cultural practices intertwined within students' physical location in the North State area of California. They conducted site visits and interviewed the school leadership of all fifteen high schools in the North State area, including principals, assistant principals, and school counselors. Findings from their culturally based, qualitative inquiry are summarized below.

Summary of Findings from the Report

McDonough and McClafferty organized their findings under three main umbrella topics: major obstacles to four-year schools; college advising structures, cultures, and resources; and potential changes in outreach. Major obstacles to four-year university attendance included money, leaving a familiar community, local community colleges, and academic preparation. Many of the findings from McDonough and McClafferty are common in the college-access literature: money, apprehension of and unfamiliarity with new college environments, and lack of academic preparation are issues that many underrepresented populations face in college access. But the specific manifestations of each finding at the micro-level tell specific and nuanced stories of rural students. These stories are qualitatively different than stories that might be told for urban and suburban students.

For example, McDonough and McClafferty reported that money was "the primary obstacle to higher rates of four-year college attendance" (2001, 8). They elaborated on ways that money matters for rural students in college-access deliberations, highlighting that an implicit cost-benefit analysis showed there were no college-educated jobs readily available in students' home communities. Students' desire to sustain their participation in their rural communities reinforced the overall "community college mentality" (13) that McDonough and McClafferty found seduced students into a choice-free college-access deliberation. That is, the economic conditions of the North State, combined with students' desire to remain in their familiar ways of life and the ease of continuing education in the community college as facilitated by both the high schools and community colleges, removed the burden of choice from students' college attendance.

The academic barriers that served as obstacles to rural college access found in McDonough and McClafferty's report related mostly to common problems in rural school–university relations. Specifically, rural schools were not kept in the loop with changes in university admissions standards and nuances about what made an applicant truly competitive, and they did not have the resources to provide the dynamic curricula that students might need to become competitive for university admission. For example, one school in McDonough and McClafferty's study struggled to balance the fiscal and human resources needed to offer both Advanced Placement Spanish and an additional laboratory science course, both of which could benefit students seeking higher education. Moreover, competitive UC campuses virtually require students to complete multiple Advanced Placement courses to ensure admission.

Rural schools generally were found to have strong potential for developing college-going cultures, yet the human and fiscal resources often were spread too thin to make this potential a reality. Although there was adequate counseling available, counselors were neither knowledgeable of, nor inclined to provide, much information or support for colleges outside the immediate geographical area. In discussing potential future outreach, the report overwhelmingly supported increased participation by university-outreach practitioners in the schools and communities of the North State region. Increased presence, in whatever form, was perceived to be an excellent way to focus future outreach efforts.

In response to the McDonough and McClafferty report, an intersegmental collaborative of the University of California and the California State University, local private colleges, the offices of education of the two counties, and the major K–12 school districts in the region created a new clearinghouse for information and services, "College Options," one year after the publication of the report. This center focuses on creating college cultures, helping students better prepare academically for college, increasing the enrollment of high school graduates in four-year colleges and increasing transfers from community colleges to four-year colleges, raising family and community awareness of college opportunities, and building infrastructure support for college and financial aid applications. The staff are out in all the high schools every week, and they work with 1,200 students in an intensive support experience that is essentially a college-preparatory outreach and assistance program. Since they began their full operation in 2003, the community demand for their services has quadrupled.

Extending the Report: Rural Life and the Golden Cage of Rural Access

We argue that McDonough and McClafferty's findings can be linked to an idea of "the rural life." Our discussion and analysis of McDonough and McClafferty's findings center on the constitution of the rural life as an ontological reality facing rural students. By privileging concerns around the rural life, we seek to strengthen our argument that higher education systems and organizations are not attending to the needs of rural students. We make a clarion call for rural college access to be placed on the agendas of higher education governance, outreach, and further research.

Cultural Capital and the Organization of Opportunity

As documented by the technical report's findings of the counseling structures in the North State, these rural schools are excellently positioned to matriculate students into local community colleges. The relationships between high schools and two-year institutions, oftentimes connected by relatives working at each institution, fostered a seamless transition from the twelfth grade to the community college. Further, parents, siblings, and teachers were generally familiar with the community colleges. In this sense, college opportunity was available and accessible. But the ceiling of a community college education is below what students need in today's global, information-based, dynamic economy, and virtually no students matriculate to four-year institutions. Thus the commonly held cultural capital of the area tended to be exercised for immediate entry into the labor force and potentially for community college enrollment.

Since not many of the parents in the North State needed college educations for their present occupations, many of the students in this geography are first-generation college attendees; McDonough and McClafferty's findings echoed the common obstacles that first-generation students face. Scholars have asserted that the cultural capital held by first-generation students' families does not necessarily assist them in successfully navigating pathways to higher education (Nunez and Cuccaro-Alamin 2000). We could consider the cultural capital of first-generation students a counter-capital—that is, capital that effectively helps them survive in their habitus, but that might be counter or dialectically opposed to capital that might help them break into the higher education mainstream. Similarly, the capital students might accumulate from living in a rural area is different than the capital that urban and suburban first-generation students hold.

These differences in cultural capital organize opportunities differentially across geographics. Whereas some of McDonough and McClafferty's findings might be similar to what scholars expect to find in urban areas, there are striking differences to which higher education institutions must attend. First and foremost, the obstacle of money and ability to pay is shaped slightly differently. The literature on ability to pay speaks predominantly to implicit cost-benefit analyses of lower-income families and a distrust of loans (Institute for Higher Education Policy 2005; Heller 2005). This may be true of both metropolitan and rural students, but in the North State, as in many rural environments, students and their families have been conditioned by a depressed economic environment, without a nearby model of economic growth or stability, thus limiting opportunity for higher-paying jobs and the ability to repay loans. Urban areas presumably can be surrounded by more affluent neighborhoods, can draw from their neighboring resources, and have greater mobility to attempt to take advantage of them. Rural students in depressed economic conditions might have only ever known their lower-economic status. It is normalized to them without being challenged by external or competing forces.

Complicating the money obstacle further, as rural students grow up and begin participating in the U.S. economy (e.g., getting jobs, developing consumer tastes) their own perceptions and obligations toward economic stability change. As indicated by McDonough and McClafferty's findings, students earning money from full- or part-time jobs while in community college often become implicated within the North State economy. They become dependent on perpetuating it, and therefore see additional college costs as incompatible with their experience. For example, some students bought new cars from a perceived or real need for transportation to attend community college. Students then became locked into paying off car loans and did not feel that they could afford transferring to a four-year school away from home.

Comparing the academic barriers that rural schools face with those of urban schools also helps illustrate how the different versions of so-called counter-capital can be exercised in ways that steer students away from higher education. McDonough and McClafferty's findings suggest similar obstacles regarding academic preparation: providing a college-prep curriculum and understanding appropriate college knowledge. As noted earlier in this paper, however, rural schools graduate students at significantly higher rates than do urban schools. Some have suggested that rural schools are not plagued by the inefficiencies and complex racialized political economies that bedevil urban schools. This is not to say that rural schools are better at educating their students, but that they are organized differently, and that this organization appears to be graduating students at a higher rate, with strong academic preparations for college but not an inclination to attend four-year college enrollments. Of course, this organization is culturally linked, as fits with our general argument in this chapter. The point here is that the cultural capital found in rural schools, such as a tight-knit community, close relationships between schools and families, and school familiarity with the community, organizes opportunity differently than urban schools, yet in terms of college access comes to a similar outcome— underrepresentation.

A final difference in cultural capital that has negative consequences for rural students is the availability of college and university administrators. Urban schools have long been targets for outreach and precollege, supplemental-preparation programs. But teachers, counselors, and administrators have no such influence on their campuses in the North State. Here, the capital of urban schools has an advantage, whereas the tight-knit community of rural schools lacks a university influence.

The Habitus of Place: The Guiding Hand of the Rural Life

Here, the concept of habitus is helpful. The habitus of rural areas guides the decisions made by institutions and residents of these areas. These decisions are based in a set of possibilities within the parameters of sustaining the cultural practices of the area. For example, the labor force opportunities of the North State area were identified as being largely blue-collar. As cultural capital, the economy of the North State area dictates that higher-educated people go elsewhere for work, with the exception of a small number of teachers, doctors, and lawyers. The guiding hand of the area—its habitus—defines that the rural life is sustainable by taking blue-collar jobs.

Although spread across a vast physical geography, the North State organizes itself within a framework that privileges a tight-knit community where similarities across economic, occupational, and cultural interests are valued. This framework, as demonstrated in McDonough and McClafferty's findings (e.g., the close articulation between schools and community colleges; the reluctance to leave a familiar community), helps sustain the ways of life familiar to rural students. Specifically understanding that students preferred to remain in their familiar environment, we can see the habitus of rurality at work. The predominant view of four-year college in this region was that it meant leaving home—for good. College meant leaving the ways of living in which one is raised. The dearth of college-educated positions in the area, the limited transportation access, and the literal distance between university life and all that it promises afterward is seen as beyond the purview of students' lives. Simply put, college is outside the habitus of many rural students.

Another way to understand the habitus of place at work in the North State is to describe the rural life and link it to the decisions made by students and their families. McDonough and McClafferty's findings suggest that the rural life is characterized as close-knit and in some ways, closed off. By close-knit, we mean that students and their families rely on the community in ways specific to their geographic location. These students had not only gone through school together, but they had gone through their entire lives together. Indeed, the North State rural areas do not have the mobility experienced by many other underrepresented geographies (e.g., urban) (Hobbs 1994; Rieger 1972). By closed off, we mean to affirm that the rural life is experienced as a fulfilling and desirable physical and social location. That many students have never left their home county or travelled to larger metropolitan areas illustrates how part of the rural life can include never needing to experience life outside it. Thus each of the major obstacles to postsecondary education identified in McDonough and McClafferty's findings can be linked to this idea of the rural life.

The habitus of the North State both constitutes and is constituted by the social practices of the region. The expansive space between settlements (which can enforce economic conditions on students that keep them in the region, such as buying a car), the jobs available for high school, community college, and four-year institution graduates (which can affect students' postsecondary aspirations), and the resources available to schools (which structure students' academic preparation) all contribute to the constitution of the North State habitus, but also get constructed and understood within that habitus. Therefore, the decisions around economics, educational aspirations, and educational preparation are all linked in relation to the habitus of the North State—like a guiding hand to reinforce the sustainability of the rural life.

The Golden Cage

We suggest thinking about college access for rural students in terms of a metaphor—the golden cage. As discussed above, the North State area is a desirable location for some students. Leaving it would cause pain and hardship that many students do not feel prepared for, or that they do not feel outweighs the benefits of leaving. But the economies of rural areas like the North State region and the fast-paced changing economies of the postindustrial United States will not be able to sustain the cultural practices of these regions as is. The comfortable living of these students' parents will not be achieved with the same preparation and vocations. Career opportunities will change, and students will need to be more prepared and more flexible than previous generations. All this is to say that the rural life, as fulfilling and sustaining as it is to these students now (or golden, we might suggest), is also trapping them into a low-mobility, low-flexibility, low-socioeconomic status that might very well limit their capacity to obtain and sustain a comfortable rural life experience. Thus the golden cage can be understood as representing the college-going culture of the North State region.

We find this metaphor especially helpful when thinking and theorizing about rural ways of living and educational opportunity. There is incongruence between life in rural areas such as the North State region of California and its institutions of higher education. To understand that incongruence requires a deeper understanding of rural experiences, which is what we have tried to begin doing in this chapter. By thinking about rural students and educational opportunity within the metaphor of the golden cage, we aim to promote an epistemic view of the problem as one with rich resources that benefit students in many ways, and a goal (higher education) that might be made to fit those resources more easily. To this end, we present our analysis of findings from McDonough and McClafferty's report on increased outreach in the North State that speak to how colleges and universities might respond to the problem of the golden cage.

Toward a More Responsive Higher Education

With the golden cage as a metaphorical representation of the college-going cultures of rural areas, we can understand better how increased outreach might have a demonstrable impact on the college access for rural students, particularly in light of the College Options initiative currently underway in the North State. This initiative has not been formally studied, so we can only speak anecdotally about its impact and some lessons that might be gleaned. Broadly speaking, university involvement can fundamentally reorganize the culture of the area. By serving K–12 administrators with assistance in understanding the college preparation and admissions requirements and supporting students' aspiration development, universities can contribute to deconstructing the golden cage and opening up possibilities for students to pursue postsecondary education while retaining their rural lifestyles. Essentially, McDonough and McClafferty's assertion that residents of the North State overwhelmingly favored a university regional center or university presence in every high school voiced a real need for higher education to make itself a vital part of the rural schooling experience.

Incorporating themselves into the rural life by participating in current and new mutually constituted cultural practices, universities can contribute greatly to the organizational cultural capital of the North State region high schools. Consequently, the habitus of rural areas might be challenged or fundamentally reconstituted to allow for the real and informed possibility of four-year postsecondary education. Each and every aspect of the findings presented about increased outreach speaks to this underlying principle. From demystifying higher education, to demonstrating how higher education does not categorically mean disassociating from the community, to supporting the administration in preparing students academically and navigating university bureaucracy, we make a clarion call for universities to respond to rural communities' long-standing heritage and traditions. Increased participation in the rural life is a primary way that institutions can meet this call.

This call extends to educational researchers' involvement in the rural life. Researchers must further attend to the needs of rural college access. Ongoing, longitudinal, holistic studies of rural needs in a P–16 relationship need to keep unpacking the cultural and structural elements of the golden cage. As McDonough and Gildersleeve have argued elsewhere (2005), without making a field corrective that addresses the relationship between different cultural communities and higher education, college-access inquiry might fail to find ways that will substantially alter the current state of inequity across different populations.

All of this is to say that the rural life, being qualitatively different than urban and suburban cultures, is left unattended by higher education. Systems, institutions, and individual organizations need to work toward greater structural and cultural congruence. Higher education's responsiveness to this dilemma must account for the golden cage in order to proactively reconstruct a relationship among rural schools, students, and families that increases participation in four-year postsecondary education.

Conclusion

This chapter sought to promote understanding about the college culture conditions in rural areas like the North State region of California, which was studied by McDonough and McClafferty, and put forth an argument based on the theoretical concept of the golden cage to promote university involvement in rural areas. Our analysis of findings from McDonough and McClafferty's report about high schools' college cultures, curricula, resources, and partnerships was complemented by our attention to issues of place and cultural practices intertwined within the rural life. Our Bourdieuian framework led us to present the metaphor of the golden cage to help understand how higher education opportunity is incongruent with the rural life. We put forth that higher education can move toward a more responsive relationship with rural areas by increased involvement in the rural life. Thus, the door to the golden cage can be opened to four-year postsecondary educational opportunity for rural students.

References

Allen, W. 1992. The color of success: African American college student outcomes at predominantly white and historically black public colleges and universities. *Harvard Educational Review* 62 (1), 26–44.

Apostal, R., and J. Bilden. 1991. Educational and occupational aspirations of rural high school students. *Journal of Career Development* 18 (2), 153–60.

Arnold, M. L., J. H. Newman, B. B. Gaddy, and C. B. Dean. 2005 (April 27). A look at the condition of rural education research: Setting a difference for future research. *Journal of Research in Rural Education* 20 (6), 1–25. Retrieved June 16, 2005, from http://www.umaine.edu/jrre/20-6.pdf.

Bourdieu, P. 1990. *In other words: Essays towards a reflexive sociology* (Matthew Adamson, trans.). Cambridge: Polity.

Bourdieu, P., and J. Passeron. 1977. *Reproduction in education, society, culture* (Richard Nice, trans.). Thousand Oaks, Calif.: Sage.

Budge, K. 2006. Rural leaders, rural places: Problem, privilege, and possibility. *Journal of Research in Rural Education* 21 (13), 1–10.

Caldwell, C. A., and J. F. Trainer. 1991. The campus role in enhancing college participation in a rural community. *Community Services Catalyst* 21 (1), 3–12.

California Postsecondary Education Commission. 1997. *Eligibility of California's 1996 high school graduates for admission to the state's public universities.* Sacramento: California Postsecondary Education Commission.

Castaneda, C. 2002. Transfer rates among students from rural, suburban, and urban community colleges: What we know, don't know, and need to know. *Community College Journal of Research and Practice* 26 (5), 439–49.

Collins, T., E. Flaxman, and L. Schartman. 2001. Perspectives on urban and rural schools and their communities. *ERIC Review* 8 (2), 1–44.

Donaldson, G. A. 1986. Do you need to leave home to grow up? The rural adolescent's dilemma. *Research in Rural Education* 3 (3), 121–25.

Fann, A. J. 2005. Forgotten students: American Indian high school student narratives on college access. Ph.D. diss., University of California, Los Angeles.

Feldman, R. M. 1990. Settlement identity: Psychological bonds with home places in a mobile society. *Environment and Behavior* 22 (2), 183–229.

Gibbs, R. M. 1998. College completion and return migration among rural youth. In R. M. Gibbs, P. L. Swaim, and R. Teixeira, eds., *Rural education and training in the new economy*, 61–80. Ames: Iowa State University Press.

Gildersleeve, R. E. 2006. Toward a college-going literacy: Voices of migrant students coming to know college access. Ph.D. diss., University of California, Los Angeles.

Haller, E. J., and S. J. Virkler. 1993. Another look at rural-nonrural differences in students' educational aspirations. *Journal of Research in Rural Education* 9 (3), 170–78.

Hearn, J. 1990. Pathways to attendance at the elite colleges. In P. Kingston and L. Lewis, eds., *The high status track: Studies of elite schools and stratification.* Albany: State University of New York Press.

———. 1991. Academic and nonacademic influences on the college destinations of 1980 high school graduates. *Sociology of Education* 64 (3), 158–71.

Hektner, J. M. 1995. When moving up implies moving out: Rural adolescent conflict in the transition to adulthood. *Journal of Research in Rural Education* 11 (1), 3–14.

Heller, D. E. 2005. Public subsidies for higher education in California: An exploratory analysis of who pays and who benefits. *Educational Policy* 19 (2), 349–70.

Herzog, M. J., and R. Pittman. 2003. The nature of rural schools: Trends, perceptions, and values. In D. M. Chalker, ed., *Leadership for rural schools,* 11–23. Lanham, Md.: Scarecrow Press.

Hobbs, D. 1994. Demographic trends in nonmetropolitan America. *Journal of Research in Rural Education* 10 (3), 149–60.

Hummon, D. M. 1992. Community attachment: Local sentiment and sense of place. In I. Altman and S. M. Low, eds., *Place attachment,* 253–78. New York: Plenum Press.

Institute for Higher Education Policy. 2005. *How Latino students pay for college: Patterns of financial aid in 2003–2004.* Washington, D.C.: Excelencia in Education.

Kasarda, J. D., and M. Janowitz. 1974. Community attachment in mass society. *American Sociological Review* 39 (3), 328–39.

Kirst, M. W., and A. Venezia, eds. 2004. *From high school to college: Improving opportunities for success in postsecondary education.* San Francisco: Jossey-Bass.

Lareau, A., and E. M. Horvat. 1999. Moments of social inclusion and exclusion: Race, class, and cultural capital in family-school relationships. *Sociology of Education* 72 (1), 37–53.

Lawrence, B. K. 1996. Working memory: An ethnographic case study of the influence of culture on education. Paper presented at the Annual Meeting of the National Rural Education Association, San Antonio, Tex.

Lee, M. 1997. Relocating location: Cultural geography, the specificity of place, and the city habitus. In J. McGuigan, ed., *Cultural methodologies.* Thousand Oaks, Calif.: Sage.

McDonough, P. M. 1997. *Choosing colleges: How social class and schools structure opportunity.* Albany: State University of New York Press.

———. 1998. Structuring opportunity: A cross-case analysis of organizational cultures, climates, and habiti. In C. A. Torres and T. R. Mitchell, eds., *Sociology of education: Emerging perspectives,* 181–210. Albany: State University of New York Press.

———. 2004. *The school to college transition: Challenges and prospects.* Washington, D.C.: American Council on Education, Center for Policy Analysis.

McDonough, P. M., and R. E. Gildersleeve. 2005. All else is never equal: Opportunity lost and found on the P–16 path to college access. In C. F. Conrad and R. Serlin, eds., *The Sage handbook for research in education: Engaging ideas and enriching inquiry,* 59–78. Thousand Oaks, Calif.: Sage.

McDonough, P. M., and K. A. McClafferty. 2001. *Rural college access: Issues and dilemmas.* Technical report submitted to the University of California, Office of the President.

McGrath, D. J., R. R. Swisher, G. H. Elder, Jr., and R. D. Conger. 2001. Breaking new ground: Diverse routes to college in rural America. *Rural Sociology* 66 (2), 244–67.

MGT of America Inc. 2001. *Northern California higher education needs assessment executive summary.* Tallahassee, Fla.: MGT of America.

National Center for Education Statistics (NCES). 1999. *Digest of educational statistics.* Washington, D.C.: U.S. Department of Education, Office of Educational Research and Improvement.

Nunez, A., and S. Cuccaro-Alamin. 2000. *First-generation college students: Undergraduates whose parents never enrolled in postsecondary education.* Washington, D.C.: U.S. Department of Education, National Center for Educational Statistics.

Philipsen, M. 1993. Values-spoken and values-lived: Female African Americans' educational experiences in rural North Carolina. *Journal of Negro Education* 62 (4), 419–26.

Potts, A. 1997. Student university learning environments: An Australian provincial case study. Paper presented at the Annual Conference of Working-Class Academics, Newburgh, N.Y.

Rieger, J. H. 1972. Geographic mobility and the occupational attainment of rural youth: A longitudinal evaluation. *Rural Sociology* 37 (2), 189–207.

Roscigno, V. J., and M. L. Crowley. 2001. Rurality, institutional disadvantage, and achievement/attainment. *Rural Sociology* 66 (2), 268–92.

Smith, M. H., L. J. Beaulieu, and A. Seraphine. 1995. Social capital, place of residence, and college attendance. *Rural Sociology* 60 (3), 363–80.

Solórzano, D., and R. Solórzano. 1995. The Chicano educational experience: A proposed framework for effective schools in Chicano communities. *Educational Policy* 9 (3), 293–314.

Ukaga, O. M., E. P. Yoder, and A. W. Etling. 1998. Rural and urban eighth graders' expectations for completing high school. *Journal of Research and Development in Education* 31 (3), 155–65.

U.S. Department of Education, National Center for Education Statistics. 2003. *The condition of education, 2003.* Washington, D.C.: Government Printing Office.

Valadez, James R. 1996. Educational access and social mobility in a rural community college. *Review of Higher Education* 19 (4), 391–409.

Villalpando, O., and D. Solórzano. 2005. The role of culture in college preparation programs: A review of the literature. In W. G. Tierney, Z. Corwin, and J. Kolyar, eds., *Preparing for college: Nine elements of effective outreach,* 13–28. Albany: State University of New York Press.

Yosso, T. 2006. *Critical race counterstories along the Chicana/Chicano educational pipeline.* New York: Routledge.

11

OPENING THEIR EYES:
E-LEARNING FOR RURAL AND ISOLATED
COMMUNITIES IN AUSTRALIA

Stephen Crump and Kylie Twyford

Introduction

Rural communities and isolated homesteads in Australia have a long and proud history in the culture and identity of all Australians.[1] The exploration and settlement of this vast interior is still seen by many as heroic, though now it is better understood how those events negatively affected the Australian indigenous population. The consequences of the European settlement of Australia's interior are still being addressed through a process of national reconciliation. The aims of this process are to build an understanding across the nation about the value and worth of indigenous peoples and cultures, and thus build a constructive dialogue for changing relationships and material outcomes for the better over the next phase of Australian history. Australians see themselves as rugged individualists, born to the open spaces of the country and actively engaged with the natural environment. The truth is the majority of the population is concentrated on the edges of the island continent, in or near a major city, in suburbs marked by their uniformity and anonymity. Yet in "the bush"

1. The data reported on in this chapter involved contributions from Juhani Tuovinen and Leah Simons while working at the Batchelor Institute of Indigenous Tertiary Education in the Northern Territory, Australia, as part of the National Communication Fund project evaluation. Peter Goodyear from the University of Sydney provided further insights as part of an Australian Research Council Linkage project. Brian Devlin, Charles Darwin University in the Northern Territory, and Alan Anderson, Southern Cross University in New South Wales, are current members of the research team. The views expressed in this chapter are our own.

or "outback" of Australia, families and communities continue to struggle against flood, drought, and fires, isolated by huge distances from one another and from public services and utilities readily available to the rest of the population.

These families and communities, whether black or white, reflect better than any other group in Australia the dilemmas of our time, facing new challenges head on in ways that are rapidly exposing benefits and limitations of the closed identities, isolated spaces, and sense of place of the last two hundred years. Education has been a key element in supporting rural and remote communities through these changes, and the innovative interactive e-learning project reported on in this chapter has done so in a way that helps leap time forward for generations that have been left out of broad technological, social, and economic changes taken for granted by the majority of the population. This chapter, therefore, summarizes research into the theory and practice of "interactive distance e-learning" (IDeL) following the introduction of satellite-supported two-way broadband Internet services for school-aged and adult distance education in the state of New South Wales (NSW) and in the Northern Territory (NT) of Australia (Crump and Goodyear 2005). The aim is to expand and reform educational services to these rural and remote communities to provide greater equity of access and better educational outcomes for the young people and adults involved. Intended and unintended consequences—positive and negative—of the IDeL innovation are explored in our research.

Our project and chapter title, "Opening Their Eyes," refers to the teaching and learning experience of students and teachers involved in IDeL—shifting from post and audio to video and Internet-based communications—but also to the way our research project can use IDeL as a source of fresh insights that will be influential throughout the project's partner organizations (NSW Department of Education and Training, NT Department of Education, Employment and Training, and the IT service provider Optus Networks Pty Ltd). In so doing, we acknowledge the difficulty in arriving at a shared understanding of the rural (Coladarci 2007), and agree that a consistent definition probably is unrealistic. Rather, we focus on a rich description of context using quantitative and qualitative data. Similarly, "community" is not a singular description and can refer to multiple entities. Wenger (1998) argues that while a neighborhood is often called a community it may not be one unless there is mutual engagement, a joint enterprise, and a shared perspective. Whether these elements of community life exist, were enhanced, or were debilitated by the IDeL initiative was an issue left open for the research to explore.

The IDeL service is provided primarily to "School of the Air" (SOTA) students and their families and to remote schools and townships; that is, mostly students and parents on isolated homesteads, students and adults in isolated indigenous communities, and adults seeking vocational education but living on isolated properties or in small towns. In many cases, these communities experience a range of disadvantages, not just in education but also in employment, health services, and transport. Lack of proximity to a school, institution of Technical and Further Education (TAFE), or university appears to contribute to low education or training participation levels for rural, regional, and isolated students, who have fewer options to pursue career goals locally, many having to leave for urbanized areas to find work or pursue other interests. When this occurs, their identity, and that of the community they have left, is disrupted as the modes of belonging and their communities of practice change to alien and unseen connections.

By the end of 2005, IDeL had brought new technology and educational services to nearly four hundred users, broadcasting over millions of square miles using real-time video, shared computer applications, graphics, audio-conferencing, online chat, and e-mail. In 2007, further expansion saw teenage students and more adult learners brought into the program in different locations and for different learning experiences. By linking IDeL to videoconferencing, the program is now accessible by all school and vocational education and training (VET, also known as "further education") students in New South Wales and increasing numbers in the Northern Territory through the use of "virtual" studios. Our research is uncovering data that indicate the potential for the IDeL project to be the catalyst for changing rural identities, reducing the tyranny of distance and reaffirming the sense of place that helps bind and hold rural communities together.

These are global issues. Globalization is changing the nature and purposes of economic and educational development through changing the rules by which nation-states have operated over the last two centuries. Old structures for rural education are being changed not only by national developments but also as a response to global trends in (and shifting sites for) economic production, social organization, and mass culture. This is not a simple or unidimensional phenomenon, but one experienced differently across the globe and containing the contradiction of also fostering an increase in local and specific changes. This chapter will return to the bearing of globalization on educational changes to identity and community in rural and isolated education in Australia without succumbing to what Harvey (1996) calls "globaloney"; that is, "where the globalization thesis can be used to explain almost anything and everything" (Ball 1998a, 120).

Rural and Isolated Education in Australia

Since the colonization and exploration of Australia there has been a concern and commitment to providing a "fair go" to rural and isolated children and schools. Even in the earliest days of the colonies, there were genuine attempts to meet the different needs of colonial and indigenous Australians through schooling. But romantic views of learning from and "civilizing" the "noble savage" gave way to more pragmatic and discriminatory programs as settlement extended beyond the coast into the interior.

The 1866 Public Schools Act in New South Wales set up small schools where twenty-five students could be brought together and part-time schools that had ten students, serviced by itinerant teachers who also visited students in their homes. The other nineteenth-century option was a "provisional public school" that could be set up by a private individual, with no minimum enrollment, and in temporary accommodation. As long as lessons followed the common curriculum and the school passed formal government inspections, provisional schools received taxpayer support and were very popular (Turney, Sinclair, and Cairns 1980).

In the early twentieth century, support for small isolated schools and students was extended through the concept of a "correspondence school." In 1951, this concept was expanded by employing the Flying Doctors' two-way radio equipment to create a "School of the Air," with excited reports of transceivers that had a range of several hundred miles. The first School of the Air was established at Alice Springs in the center of Australia. Other long-standing elements of rural education in Australia include one-teacher schools, central schools, the Country Area Program (a positive discrimination policy still current), and assistance for isolated children, including a boarding allowance and second-home assistance. In many cases Australia led the way in this field.

State and national governments in Australia have thus been active for more than one hundred years in shaping policy and undertaking strategic initiatives to provide equity to rural and isolated students. Communities, driven by concerned parents, have always played a key role, not only in providing much of the face-to-face schooling of their children, but also in pushing for recognition of the problems they and their children face compared to their peers in larger towns and urban centers. Closed identities are associated with ungoverned rural-youth out-migration, decreasing status (and opportunities) for rural employment, the collapse of family businesses and family farms, and, except in idealized pop culture, a disparagement of country music, dance, and stories as boring and irrelevant. Whether satellite delivery of distance education, including the ability to actively interact globally through the Internet, offers the opportunity to open up rural identities for black and white Australians is an open question. Whichever way it goes, asking whose interests are being served was an important consideration for our research. In so doing, we are cautious not to allow metro-centric views to shape our assumptions so that remoteness implies lack, something they are not or do not have. Nor do we assume that justice implies sameness (Christie 2006). Our research balances expanding access to becoming cosmopolitan at least in part through IDeL, with validating the worth of local settings and lives as told to us, without romanticizing the difficulties faced.

Rural and isolated student needs and perspectives have been marginalized in research and policy with regard to pathways into further and higher education and eventual labor market participation (Dwyer and Wyn 1998). Senior secondary school completion and participation rates are significantly lower for these students than for the general population, and deteriorate dramatically the greater the isolation and the higher the indigenous percentage. Of those who do participate in further and higher education experiences, many combine work and study, with the result that 26 percent of students found that work was taking priority over education, and 25 percent would prefer to study without working (Dwyer and Wyn 1998). Rural students often leave for urbanized areas to pursue work and interests because they have fewer options to pursue their aspirations locally. To generate change at the local level it is necessary to actively include and work with communities and schools to identify needs and available resources to strengthen links among schools, vocational training, and employers—a perceived value-added approach for the benefit of communities and businesses.

Researching Technology, Education, and Communities

Extensive research has been conducted into whether new technology adds to positive outcomes in school communities and education systems. Since the 1970s a series of major Australian reports has supported these initiatives, including the 1972 *Senate Standing Committee on the Education of Isolated Children*. In 1981, Darnell and Simpson produced a report on papers compiled from a conference on new directions in rural education titled *Rural Education: In Pursuit of Excellence*, supported by the Western Australian government and the Organization for Economic Cooperation and Development (OECD). In 1991, the National Board of Employment, Education, and Training (NBEET) released *Toward a National Education and Training Strategy for Rural Australians*, which was the first cross-sectoral study of these issues, arguing for better mechanisms for coordination rather than more resources. In 1999, the NBEET Higher Education Council reported on *Rural and Isolated School Students and Their Higher Education Choices*, arguing for the first time that, with 30 percent of Australians affected, a comprehensive government approach was needed if government policy was to have an impact across the range of factors at play. In 2000, the Commonwealth Department of Education and Training released a further report, *Engaging Universities and Regions: Knowledge Contribution to Regional Economic Development in Australia*, which added to the "whole of government" approach: recognition of an inclusive and comprehensive community contribution to change. The Human Rights and Equal Opportunity Commission report *Recommendations: National Inquiry into Rural and Remote Education* (HREOC 2000) provided further evidence of disadvantage and unequal educational outcomes for rural Australia. But new technologies in distance education have been largely overlooked. This is why the IDeL innovation in Australia, and the research into the experiences of the participants, is of such interest.

One of the earliest critiques of increasing the use of Information and Communication Technology (ICT) in education asked whether technology was part of the solution or part of the problem (Apple 1987). The dilemma revolved around the politics of technology (is it independent of social intentions, power, and privilege?), technology and economic realities (is the cost of technology putting teachers out of work?), and social literacy (does new technology embody a form of thinking based on technique rather than substance?). Twenty years later a Demos (2007) report argued in favor of technology being used extensively in education and explained how the current generation is using it to reinvent the workplace and society. Similarly, Fletcher, Tobias, and Wisher (2007, 91) describe "advanced distributed learning," which they argue "is building toward a future in which human knowledge, held in instructional objects, is identified and collected from the global information grid (currently the Web) and is then assembled on demand for real-time interactions tailored to each learner's knowledge, goals, interests and needs."

In contrast, a recent OECD policy brief argues that digital technology has had more impact on educational administration services than on teaching and learning, though it has relaxed time and space constraints (Lane 2006). But not for all. Castells (1998, 129) considered the issue of social inclusion in the "information age" and the experience of social inequality in the United States that occurred during the formative stages of the network society, and warned that this is a sign of what could happen in other countries and communities. Hyslop-Margison (2004, 138–40) points to the claim that the ubiquitous presence of technology in education promotes instrumental rationality and uncritical means-end reasoning, which, according to Habermas (1991), leads to social reproduction protecting prevailing institutional interests. That is, the predominant use of ICT in education stresses information delivery over critical dialogue, though Hyslop-Margison argues that human agency so far continues to play a role in shaping learning experiences in a complex pedagogical relationship. Our research took into account these concerns and reframed the key themes we wanted to explore into a number of issues relevant to the rural context in Australia.

Extensive research has been conducted on distance education in Australia and elsewhere (see Boethel and Dimmock 1997), but not so much on the impact of new learning technologies on distance education outcomes, due in part to the newness of the technologies required to deliver education and training via ICT to rural and remote communities. There is international research, notably from North America, describing isolation from education and training similar to that experienced in Australia. Distance education technologies developed so far do not always contextualize the learning experience in a way that adds meaning, relevance, and authenticity to lessons for rural and isolated students, and includes valued representations of their world. This is a fatal flaw when dealing with groups that have had relatively closed identities and very limited contact with new technologies because of their distance from mainstream services and facilities. McLoughlin (1999) insists that it is essential for educators to accept the cultural identity, participation style, and consumer expectations of the learners, and some research indicates that the level of community involvement in the distance, or distributed (Fletcher, Tobias, and Wisher 2007), learning process is also a critical feature (Searle, Tomaschewski, and Godfrey 2002). These are key issues for considering the extent to which change in rural communities and families is welcome, adopted, and sustainable.

IDeL is an unusually large and complex innovation in the field of education and technology. As noted above, over time, innovative technologies have been incorporated into distance education in an attempt to overcome the disadvantage associated with isolation. The "Bush Talks" consultations conducted by the Human Rights and Equal Opportunity Commission (HREOC 1999) found that access to education of an appropriate standard and quality is a significant concern in rural Australia, as distance creates barriers to the provision of educational services. The commission saw the provision of that access as a social justice issue. In the Australian context, one other imperative was highlighted by the findings of the HREOC inquiry: "For a number of reasons, Aboriginal people have not participated to any meaningful extent in distance education and School of the Air programs. One reason—and this impacts on the delivery of Indigenous education in general—is that many parents perceive their lack of resources and literacy and numeracy skills as barriers to children's participation in such programs" (2000, 10).

There have been earlier attempts to address these barriers. For example, Murray and Gardner (1998) examined the association between the use of technology and collaborative learning in distance education, especially the impact of videoconferencing on the interactivity between geographically isolated students, regardless of race. They argued that videoconferencing increased interactivity between students given the improvements in quality that this technology has experienced (through higher bandwidth, different modes of access, and better-capacity personal computers). Similarly, Crowe (2002) investigated remote indigenous communities using videoconferencing and found that it provided students with "something new" that enhanced their learning experience. But these gains were short-term and ephemeral, so more fundamental changes to educational delivery employing technology were needed to more fully and genuinely engage indigenous communities, including more appropriate pedagogy, culturally sensitive curriculum materials, and teachers trained in teaching English as a second language.

Some research indicates that the level of community involvement in the distance learning process is also a critical feature because of the isolation, space, and identity characteristics of Australia's rural communities (see, for example, Searle, Tomaschewski, and Godfrey 2002). The most important factor for improving outcomes is the total context of learning activities, including all those in the community (teachers, students, technicians, curriculum experts, administrators, and family/parents) using rapidly evolving technology to accomplish their goals (see Crump and Stanley 2000). This is why an interactive distance e-learning context offers scope for significant and far-reaching out-comes for families and communities in remote and isolated locations. Before considering the specific outcomes for participants and communities, an over-view of the IDeL innovation, and the research into this phenomenon, provides a framework for the discussion that follows.

Interactive Distance E-Learning in Australia

In March 2003, students at homesteads in Broken Hill were the first to partici-pate in an IDeL School of the Air lesson. With the Australian government, the school education department, and service-provider project partners invested more than A$17 million (US$14 million) in satellite-based communications infrastructure, together with new studio facilities, hardware, and software applications for students, teachers, and parents, including a program of curric-ulum and teacher development. The students had previously been reliant on two-way radio. IDeL actually refers to the core software package, capable of supporting multicast. This allows two-way audio for up to two students within a classroom at any one time, e-mail within the classroom between teachers and students, interactive whiteboard activities, application sharing (based on Microsoft Windows), document camera, vcr, dvd, PowerPoint slides, con-trolled Internet access, recording and storing lessons for student review, class-room statistical calculation, and pop-up questions.

The IDeL project provides two-way broadband Internet protocol to support interactive teaching and learning for school-aged distance education students, students and adults in isolated Indigenous communities, and adults living in small regional towns and remote communities seeking vocational education. This new infrastructure is being used to deliver primary, secondary, vocational, and community/adult education courses, all accredited through the relevant authorities. The project initially (2002) established teaching studios at existing distance education centers, indigenous homeland centers, and vocational out-reach programs in regional New South Wales (Port Macquarie, Dubbo, and Broken Hill), and in the Northern Territory (Alice Springs and Darwin). In addition, a portable satellite delivery system was set up on a trailer to be taken to remote communities in New South Wales. The services are capable of recep-tion to any location within New South Wales and the Northern Territories as well as other locations nationally.

The project also established a hub at the Optus satellite earth station (ses) at Belrose in Sydney. Terrestrial communication backbones provide links between the studios and the SES, and isolated homesteads and communities have had two-way satellite equipment installed at each defined location (Optus SatWeb two-way VSAT system providing broadband Internet access). The IDeL infrastructure works toward creating more intimate learning relationships, largely through the addition of vision, but also through the immediacy of the educational exchanges between teachers and students. Audio quality has been vastly enhanced, enabling richer and more broadly shared interactions, and this interactivity is a strong foundation for higher order learning interactions achieved through satellite delivery. In 2003, these distance education students *saw* their teachers during the lesson for the first time, instead of just hearing a crackling voice from hundreds of miles away or waiting weeks for their work to be returned by post. Now, students were able to watch demonstrations and view video clips, graphic illustrations, and computer animations; work together on shared software; "chat" over the Web; and get almost immediate feedback on their work via e-mail.

Our research on IDeL builds on a small-scale pilot by Wallace and Boylan (2004), who reported on the NSW trial of satellite delivery. They found that the more consistent service it provided (since radio transmission frequently broke down) resulted in higher levels of participation and a greater sense of community with the School of the Air, as well as between isolated families and communities. They concluded that satellite technologies represented the only truly viable solution for supporting distance education efforts in the Australian outback given the unreliability of telephone and other broadcast systems.

But introducing a full-scale satellite-delivered program meant taking this innovation to a much higher level of complexity. Student and teacher beliefs about good learning have tended to circumscribe what they do with new technology, but new technology also provides a catalyst for appropriating current forms of educational practice into new ones, generating spaces for educational change to occur at each level of intervention. We recognize, also, that not all that happens within ICT and e-learning is educative, in that the veracity of much of the information students can access on the Web is untested and sometimes offensive, abusive, and discriminatory (see Crump 1999).

With a variety of learner needs and teacher strategies brought into play by IDeL, our research asks how learners experience satellite delivery, to what extent is learning dependent on how teachers employ new technology, and does this provide a different appreciation of teachers' pedagogical and professional needs and the educational needs of rural communities? Such research-driven questions are pragmatic in their focus and well contextualized within the education systems and telecommunications-industry partners that have uniquely joined forces to undertake the satellite-delivery innovation.

For isolated learners and communities, the essence of the change being brought about by the technology is the addition of visual modality, fast (and in some cases initial) access to the resources of the Internet, and the opportunity to direct some of their own learning. At a broader level, IDeL changes the experience of place and community for participants, by giving them unprecedented access to the globalizing world.

A focus on changing learner needs and community experiences helps to map ways in which learning is different (or not) from how it occurred using radio/paper technology. It also facilitates an exploration of what this means for the learners, and for the appropriateness of the learning experiences with which they are being asked to engage or generating for themselves.

Methodology and Data Sources

The aims of the research were to gather information from participants (teachers, students, and parents/caregivers) using IDeL technology about how they experience satellite delivery, how they share those experiences, and the impact it has on their teaching and learning. A secondary aim was to analyze the processes of policy development and implementation in the IDeL project through these emerging practices to assess whether there are broader educational and industry applications for the technology. While this chapter reflects the extent and effectiveness of the interactive distance e-learning innovation in New South Wales and the Northern Territories during the development and implementation phases, further research is being undertaken to measure the longer-term effects of IDeL, as well as taking into account rapid changes in the technology and software being used, and the extension of the vision for IDeL into mainstream (metropolitan or large-community) contexts.

Surveys were drawn up for seven groups. These are small cohorts because the groups are very small populations by definition of their isolation and location. Therefore, random sampling was inappropriate and statistically unviable. They are also populations that constantly shift as people (both families and teachers) move in and out of work in rural areas. Surveys were distributed through the School of the Air regular post and returned to the SOTA offices. The seven groups and the response size for each are: School of the Air teachers

(62/44); SOTA students (180/135); SOTA parents (120/86); TAFE students (18/12); TAFE teachers (6/4); remote teachers (in extremely isolated situations in the Northern Territory) (17/13); and IDeL facilitators (15/13). The sample size for TAFE teachers and students, remote teachers, and facilitators was too small even for nonparametric statistical analysis, however these responses provided helpful written comments that have been used to illustrate the findings reported on in this chapter.

Validity was enhanced by triangulation with interview, written, and documentary analysis. Site visits were made to Dubbo and Broken Hill (NSW) and to Darwin, Alice Springs, and Katherine (NT) to collect documentation on the implementation and development of IDeL, interview the SOTA leadership, view the studios, sit in on school and TAFE lessons, and participate in a school staff meeting, IDeL facilitator meetings, and other related events.

Student Sample Profile

1. Girls made up 56 percent of respondents, boys 44 percent. Responses came from students of all ages and in all years/stages of schooling, including two responses from students in secondary education. The highest responses were kindergarten and year 1 (28 percent), and year 5 (19 percent).

2. Ninety-eight percent of students identified themselves as Australian citizens with the remaining 2 percent as Aboriginal or Torres Strait Islander. It is possible that indigenous responses were higher but that indigenous students and parents may have, quite appropriately, identified as "Australian citizen" rather than "Aboriginal or Torres Strait Islander."

3. Eighty-seven percent of students used the IDeL system at home with 9 percent using it at school; the remaining 2 percent indicated "other place," and 2 percent did not respond.

4. Seventy-two percent of student responses came from New South Wales and 22 percent from the Northern Territory, with 6 percent coming from other states or locations (SOTA students using IDeL can be found in South East Queensland, South Australia, East and West Timor, and on boats at sea).

5. Thirty-three postcodes were represented in the student responses.

6. The largest group for "years as a distance education student" was two years with 20 percent, followed by one year (16 percent), five years (9 percent), and seven years (10 percent).

7. The location of the studios students were taught from were: Broken Hill (31 percent), Dubbo (24 percent), Port Macquarie (16 percent), Darwin (14 percent), Alice Springs (11 percent), and Cobar (4 percent).

The results so far from this research are highly instructive in relation to the operations and policy footprint discernible for the IDeL. It has opened our eyes to the changes taking place, and to some of what is being lost and gained by rural and isolated communities in the dismantling of radio—and, to a lesser extent, telephone, print, and post—in the transfer to satellite delivery of lessons. The shift from radio to satellite delivery required radical changes in the way students were learning, yet levels of acceptance are very high for students, parents, and teachers. This is remarkable given all that could have frustrated an innovation of this magnitude and sophistication. The technological, educational, and cultural context was new also for the education system and IT service providers, within which small teams had to manage a large and rapid rollout of infrastructure, software, and backup across huge distances in outback New South Wales and the Northern Territory, as well as in district and head offices.

Changing Identities

Data from the earlier phases of the project suggest that, as a consequence of the introduction of IDeL, SOTA students from a broad social and cultural base are participating more often in their lessons because of the improved technical quality and reliability achieved through the satellite delivery. The simple factor of higher levels of participation is a key to understanding how these new methods are changing community identity and self-worth. One parent explained, "We are now able to be like urban citizens and study via IDeL while living in remote areas."

IDeL appears to have had a significant motivational effect on students from all age groups, socioeconomic statuses, and races. Teachers and parents referred to greater equity arising from the introduction of IDeL. School of the Air students now receive a common and shared educational experience as most groups are "online" every school day compared to an average daily participation rate of about 60 percent "on air" for radio due to variable, poor, and, in some cases, no reception. This significant improvement in IDeL "attendance" has begun to level out social distance as well as geography, especially when participants meet one another in person. Some explanations for this are presented below.

Parents and families feel less remote, and not only in terms of education. Many SOTA radio activities have been redesigned to engage students and families with the broader community, including visual experiences of music, sport, drama, and local government occurring many hundreds of miles away. Students like seeing their friends over the IDeL system, as well as seeing in real time what is happening in the rest of Australia and the world. Students and parents also highly value having e-mail for the same way that it enhances communication and contact with one another as well as the school.

Parents highly value being able to access vocational education and training courses from home to improve IDeL skills as well as gain qualifications for work and career development. The immediate outcome is enhancing the skills base in rural communities, which is important at local, state, territory, and national levels. The success of VET through IDeL can also be measured by the expansion of studios in the Northern Territories and New South Wales, achieved through new national government funding in 2005 to satisfy unmet demand.

Parent use of IDeL has allowed parent and teacher association and other meetings to be interactive and multifaceted compared to using radio. Meetings now include visuals, high-quality documentation, and immediate feedback, which allow parents a better chance to achieve what they want from the meetings. As for their children, technology has increased the capacity for human agency in a way that opens up democratic spaces (Hyslop-Margison 2004) as well as "their eyes." Access to the World Wide Web allows parents to stay more closely in touch with education department initiatives and changes to government policies, syllabi, and related services, as well as to explore easily and quickly educational issues and research around the world. While these are isolated families, their isolation does not mean that they are uneducated or lack savvy; most farm manager families had at least one parent with a university or equivalent qualification.

These findings suggest that remote and isolated communities are opening up to the broader world in ways that are changing identities. Knowledge is a fundamental element in this growth and change (see Wenger 2000). One evocative, if superficial, example is the way many young people learning through IDeL in isolated areas of Australia have abandoned country and western music—and the associated dress codes—to take up more contemporary urban music and dress like their new heroes. Whether these cultural changes are advantageous is most likely a personal judgment, but the key for our research is the way it demonstrates that IDeL has unambiguously "opened their eyes" to what is happening in the rest of the world. IDeL is accelerating the effects of globalization on youth identity in rural and remote areas of Australia. Christie (2006, 34) argues, "We need to produce and maintain spaces where both the local and the global are contextualised, available and relevant, and understand . . . our students' abilities to truly be themselves . . . precisely where they are." On a broader scale, therefore, local versus global knowledges remain a fundamental dilemma in distance education.

As discussed earlier in this chapter, globalization refers to a broad set of economic, social, and cultural relations that are contradictory and incomplete. As Ball (1998a, 120–21) argues, thanks to globalization "things have changed, but not absolutely." Ball uses Harvey (1989) to illustrate how globalization has led to the rhythm and content of daily life becoming more ephemeral and volatile—values and virtues made disposable alongside the mass-produced (in low-wage countries) material products of a globalized economy, engendering a focus on sign systems rather than concrete circumstances or objects. One consequence of this newly disorganized capitalism is the breakdown of social cohesion so that traditional and agreed constructs of community and self begin to lack meaning or relevance for daily experiences.

Yet this is not a one-way street. Young people (urban and rural) seek out cultures beyond their own home turf realizing that regional and national boundaries have given way to global spaces (Gill and Howard 1999). Whether this is a personal or a forced decision is not always clear. Wierenga's (1999) research on young people in a small rural community in Tasmania, the island state of Australia, suggest that young people are focused on an engagement "here" as well as a world "beyond here." The young people in Wierenga's research had a strong sense of connectedness and felt they had more integrated social structures, but what happens next is to a certain extent dependent on individual knowledge of and access to the "opportunity structures" available (see also te Riele and Crump 2003). Wierenga (1999, 189) argues, "Individual life choices are made against a backdrop of local culture." Local culture, in turn, is shaped by social conditions, and people in peripheral geographic locations are more likely to have fewer opportunity structures due to race, low social economic status, and lower school-completion rates. Interestingly, peripheral communities may center on local people and places, or may include different countries and cultures (te Riele 2007). This type of change of identity and sense of place is one that we are detecting for the schools, teachers, families, and communities in our research.

Gewirtz (2003) refers to this as glocal accounts, in our case one that rejects the determinism of some interpretations of globalization in favor of more complex, dynamic, and context-specific explanations. Emphasizing the social and historical context means that everyday experiences and local situations are central. Drawing on Dewey (1916), not only understanding but also action must take place within local and specific situations. Investigating the local and specific is not done for its own sake, but because this can contribute to an understanding of broader issues and thus, potentially, to social change. As Crump (1995, 212) explained, "Local struggles are an expression of what is occurring, or possible, at regional, state, national and even international levels." Ball (1998b) agrees that a focus on the local and specific forces one to adopt a politics of applying ideals of social justice to people's immediate and everyday situations. An immersion in what Shalin (1992, 266) describes as "the practical world, with all its hazards, confusions and unforeseen developments," helps test and clarify meanings and conclusions. In relation to educational innovations, Crump (1995, 213) argued for the inclusion of local contexts and people, suggesting that "under the imposed protection of the state, schools, their teachers, pupils and families need space to express the heterogeneity and dynamism of local communities. Current and future attempts at educational reforms will live or die on their effectiveness to meet practical local problems (to be a context of action) and to provide for community members to be part of the solution (to be agents of action)."

This is important for the analysis of findings in our research, as it explicitly allows for the question of what can be done at the level of individual sites, linked to the context at the structural and systemic level (in terms of the economy and educational policy), and to the question of what happens at the interpersonal level, among teachers, students, parents, and others.

Reducing Disadvantage?

For adults, the change has been just as dramatic as for younger students (mostly their children), especially in relation to the impact on their experienced life chances. In response to the question, "What did you or your family or community gain from participating in the TAFE IDeL program?" one adult respondent answered, "Knowledge of what is out there and how easy it is to access when you know how to." Another adult, who used the schoolroom located at home on a grazing property and took lessons from three different IDeL studios around North South Wales (Broken Hill, Port Macquarie, and Dubbo), responded that IDeL was attractive because of the fast Internet speed, the good range of up-to-date software, ability to share ideas with others, and the fast and efficient way of learning without having to travel, which is costly both financially and in time. The adult learner further explained that the teacher used IDeL to "demonstrate how to do things in real time. Problem areas can be worked on until we 'get it' without having to wait weeks for mail etc. or trying to explain over the phone without visual assistance. It is an excellent way to learn IT skills with the shared application and seeing the teacher's screen."

Another parent and her husband gained recognized qualifications as well as very practical skills and knowledge to assist them in their isolated rural existence: "I have been able to complete Certificate 1 in IT and progress on to Certificate 2 in IT, which I would not have done otherwise. My husband has been able to attend lessons on motorbike maintenance and handyman skills which he would not otherwise have had access to."

The major advantages for most communities can be summarized from the majority of responses as increased computer skills and increased access to further, mostly vocational, education. The novelty of this outcome is expressed in the following quotes:

> It gives me the opportunity to continue learning, it's at my home and I can attend lessons without the worry of a 175 kilometer drive and getting babysitters for my 4 children.
>
> It is because of the IDeL that I can now return to TAFE after nearly 18 years away. Due to the simple fact that it's in my home, the lessons are set out like a virtual classroom without the hassles of driving at night or organizing babysitters. Without this system in place TAFE courses would not be an option for me or for my family to use. So we are very pleased to see this system in place for us and people who live in rural Australia.

While these changes assisted with improving equity for isolated rural students, the challenges faced by communities using IDeL were often ones of a personal nature. When asked what difficulties students encountered, one response was, "Learning to study and learn after a long time. Building up confidence to enroll in all the different courses."

Adults returning to study in urban areas often experience similar difficulties. When asked, "Before you were taught using the IDeL system how did you do your distance education?" this respondent answered, "My children communicated via the radio or telephone. I didn't attempt any TAFE distance Ed courses. . . . Without this system in place myself and my family would not be able to access TAFE courses. Attending TAFE in the nearest town would involve a lot of traveling and money so would not be worthwhile."

Some remote teachers in the Northern Territory felt that IDeL suffered from being designed for "homestead kids" (mostly Anglo-Saxon children of farm managers) thus having limited impact on indigenous students. These teachers pointed out that even with changes to the curriculum, in the Northern Territories it would be hard to achieve the potential of IDeL: for the majority of indigenous students English is a second language, on top of three or four spoken indigenous languages (see Harrison 2005), and indigenous family structures and familial responsibilities mean there is less direct and regular supervision of work (Australian College of Education 2000).

Thus representation from indigenous Australians across the groups has not reached optimum levels, though this also reflects lower levels of participation in SOTA, VET, and in the educational workforce. In addition to the outreach programs from TAFE noted above, the Northern Territory Open Education Centre (NTOEC) has used the IDeL innovation to deliver a range of courses to remote indigenous communities, particularly to 388 secondary students from indigenous community schools and community education centers, 42 "reentry" indigenous students, and VET courses such as the new multimedia music course for remote students, as well as professional development to teachers and community leaders. According to the NTOEC, English as a second language courses for students at three remote areas (Jilkminggan, Minyerri, and Barunga) have been successfully implemented, as has been the development of a new physical education course and an emphasis on art at Numbulwar (the latter of which led to a public exhibition of work). Indigenous students in community schools make up the main component of the increased enrollments for the NTOEC since 1996, and this is the most likely area for future growth (see http://www.ntoec.nt.edu.au/). Teacher comments on the interaction between IDeL and indigenous students included a hospitality and tourism course teacher who wrote, "I used IDeL as part of teaching a course to Indigenous students. The theory components were discussed with the community teacher over the phone/fax, and I demonstrated techniques used in the recipes on IDeL. I filmed the demonstration, then played this back on IDeL, supported by PowerPoint."

But another teacher wrote, "(IDeL is) inappropriate for remote Indigenous context—teaching literacy needs to be hands-on and interactive, and this is problematic with large groups. Time delays compound cultural differences in communication practices, and norms are difficult." The variable experience of indigenous Australians with satellite delivery of distance education is a core area for our further investigations.

Conclusion

"Opening Their Eyes" refers firstly to the teaching and learning experience of students and teachers involved in IDeL—shifting from post and audio to video and Internet-based communications—but also to IDeL as a source of fresh insight that will be influential with respect to future planning of policy, software, and infrastructure development for each of the partner organizations. Already the IDeL is being deployed in urban settings for students isolated by illness or other special needs, as well as to other regions in the Pacific. Our research aimed to help education systems as well as IT service providers understand the possibilities and limits of IDeL for learning in remote communities as well as in the mainstream of educational practice (see also Goodyear and Steeples 1998). In this way, we hoped to extend the metaphor of "opening their eyes" from its origins in the shift from radio to video to encompass all the systemic processes involved in exploiting the lessons learned from IDeL.

As we noted in our introduction to this chapter, Australians see themselves as rugged individualists, born to the open spaces and actively engaged with the natural environment. While this perception is largely a myth, there are vast spaces in Australia that are sparsely populated and, in many areas, primarily indigenous. These peoples and communities are highly resilient and self-reliant—they have to be—but they deserve equal opportunities for education and training as provided by government to the rest of the population. We believe the IDeL project provides a tool for achieving this outcome in a way that recognizes that equality is not "sameness"—and there are many reasons why this has to be so—but that it also can be celebrated and addressed so as to minimize disadvantage. Also achievable are new and more equitable outcomes in other areas of education and community life. These outcomes should not remain peripheral for those too far away to be able to benefit from or participate effectively in what is taken for granted by the rest of the population. The IDeL project in Australia has been the catalyst for rapidly opening up the closed identities, isolated spaces, and sense of place of the last two hundred years, mostly for the better.

References

Apple, M. 1987. *Is the new technology part of the solution or part of the problem?* Canberra: Curriculum Development Centre.

Australian College of Education. 2000. Reconciliation through education and training: Building bridges, confidence, and capacity. *Unicorn* 27 (1), 1–45.

Ball, S. J. 1998a. Introduction: International perspectives on education policy. *Comparative Education* 34 (2), 117–30.

———. 1998b. Educational studies, policy entrepreneurship, and social theory. In R. Slee, G. Weiner, and S. Tomlinson, eds., *School effectiveness for whom? Challenges to the school effectiveness and school improvement movements*. London: Routledge Falmer.

Boethel, M., and K. Dimmock. 1997. *Constructing knowledge with technology: A review of the literature*. Retrieved September 14, 2009, from http://www.sedl.org/pubs/catalog/items/tec27.html.

Castells, M. 1998. *End of millennium*. Oxford: Blackwell.

Christie, M. 2006. Local versus global knowledges: A fundamental dilemma in remote education. *Education in Rural Australia* 16 (1), 27–37.

Coladarci, T. 2007. Improving the yield of rural education research: An editor's swan song. *Journal of Research in Rural Education* 22 (3), 1–9.

Commonwealth Department of Education and Training. 2002. *Engaging universities and regions: Knowledge contribution to regional economic development in Australia*. Canberra: Australian Government Publishing Service.

Crowe, G. 2002. Teaching remote Aboriginal communities using video conferencing. *Literacy Link* 22 (5), 9–11.

Crump, S. J. 1995. Towards action and power: Post-enlightenment pragmatism? *Discourse: Studies in the Cultural Politics of Education* 16 (2), 203–17.

———. 1999. "E-ducation": Electronic, emotionless, and efficient. *Journal of Education Policy* 14 (6), 631–37.

Crump, S., and P. Goodyear. 2005 (June). Interactive distance e-learning in Australia: Replacing radio with satellite technology for School of the Air. In iNet Conference proceedings, Amsterdam. Retrieved June 2006, from http://www.cybertext.net.au/inet/general/g4_25.htm.

Crump, S. J., and G. Stanley. 2000 (December). ICT and learning: Engineering knowledge for the D-Generation. Paper presented to the Annual Conference of the Australian Association for Research in Education, University of Sydney.

Darnell, F., and P. M. Simpson. 1981. *Rural education: In pursuit of excellence*. Nedlands: University of Western Australia Press.

Demos. 2007. *Their space: Education for a digital generation*. Retrieved August 2007, from http://www.demos.co.uk/publications/theirspace.

Dewey, J. [1916] 1944. *Education and democracy*. New York: The Free Press.

Dwyer, P., and J. Wyn. 1998. Post-compulsory education policy in Australia and its impact on participant pathways and outcomes in the 1990s. *Journal of Education Policy* 13 (3), 285–300.

Fletcher, J. D., S. Tobias, and R. A. Wisher. 2007. Learning anytime, anywhere: Advanced distributed learning and the changing face of education. *Educational Researcher* 36, 96–102.

Gewirtz, S. 2003 (January). Recent readings of social reproduction: Four questions and no answers. Paper presented at the International Sociology of Education Conference, London.

Gill, J., and S. Howard. 1999 (November–December). Global citizens/local agents: Repositioning the school at the centre of socio-cultural transformation. Paper presented to the Annual Conference of the Australian Association for Research in Education, University of Melbourne.

Goodyear, P., and C. Steeples. 1998. Creating shareable representations of practice. *Association for Learning Technology Journal* 6 (3), 16–23.

Habermas, J. 1991. *Toward a rational society: Student protest, science, and politics* (Jeremy J. Shapiro, trans.). Boston: Beacon Press.

Harrison, N. 2005. The learning is in-between: The search for a metalanguage in indigenous education. *Educational Philosophy and Theory* 37 (6), 871–84.

Harvey, D. 1989. *The conditions of postmodernity*. Oxford: Blackwell.

———. 1996. *Justice, nature, and the geography of distance*. Oxford: Blackwell.

Human Rights and Equal Opportunity Commission (HREOC). 1999. *Bush talks*. Sydney: HREOC.

———. 2000. *Recommendations: National inquiry into rural and remote education*. Sydney: HREOC.

Hyslop-Margison, E. J. 2004. Technology, human agency, and Dewey's constructivism: Opening democratic spaces in virtual classrooms. *Australasian Journal of Educational Technology* 20 (2), 137–48.

Lane, B. 2006 (April 26). E-learning languishes in the classroom. *The Australian*, 30.

McLoughlin, C. 1999. Culturally responsive technology use: Developing an online community of learners. *British Journal of Educational Technology* 30 (33), 231–43.

Murray, K., and G. Gardner. 1998 (July). Partnership and learning: A case study in video conferencing in West Australian schools. In "EdTech '98, Education and Technology: Planning for Progress, Partnership, and Profit" conference proceedings, biennial conference of the Australian Society for Educational Technology, Perth, WA.

National Board of Employment, Education, and Training (NBEET). 1991. *Toward a national education and training strategy for rural Australians*. Canberra: Australian Government Publishing Service.

———. 1999. *Rural and isolated school students and their higher education choices*. Canberra: NBEET.

Searle, G., R. Tomaschewski, and B. Godfrey. 2002. Managing the learning process: Curriculum, community, and change. In *Linking Learners* (Australian Council for Computers in Education conference proceedings). Belconnen, ACT: Australian Council for Computers in Education.

Shalin, D. 1992. Critical theory and the pragmatist challenge. *American Journal of Sociology* 98 (1), 237–79.

te Riele, K. 2007 (October). Who gets to be cosmopolitan? Young people in peripheral communities. Paper presented at the "Cosmopolitan Civil Societies" conference, University of Technology, Sydney.

te Riele, K., and S. J. Crump. 2003. Ongoing inequality in a "knowledge economy": Perceptions and actions. *International Studies in the Sociology of Education* 13 (11), 57–77.

Turney, C., K. E. Sinclair, and L. G. Cairns. 1980. *Isolated schools: Teaching, learning, and transition to work.* Sydney: Sydney University Press.

Wallace, A. R., and C. R. Boylan. 2002. Outbreak education via satellite. *International Principal Newsletter* 7 (1): 13–16.

Wenger, E. 1998. *Communities of practice: Learning, meaning, and identity.* Cambridge: Cambridge University Press.

———. 2000. Communities of practice: The key to knowledge strategy. In E. Lesser, M. Fontaine, and J. Slusher, eds., *Knowledge and communities.* Boston: Butterworth Heinemann.

Wierenga, A. 1999. Imagined trajectories, local cultures, and social identity. In R. White, ed., *Australian Youth Subcultures.* Hobart, TAS: Australian Clearinghouse for Youth Studies.

12

ADVOCATING FOR ENGLISH LANGUAGE LEARNERS: U.S. TEACHER LEADERSHIP IN RURAL TEXAS SCHOOLS

Rebecca M. Bustamante, Genevieve Brown, and Beverly J. Irby

Texas is the second most populous state in the United States. Statistics reveal that three-quarters of a million children attend rural schools in Texas—more than any other U.S. state (Johnson Strange 2007). Texas has historically experienced economic exchange with Mexico at the state's southern border, as well as international immigration to large urban areas such as Houston and Dallas. However, international immigration to rural areas in central, eastern, and northern Texas is more recent.

In small Texas towns, availability of low-cost land, along with employment opportunities in growing industries such as construction and manufacturing, have increasingly attracted more foreign-born immigrants who want to avoid the high costs of living and hassles of larger urban cities. Further, while many Texas manufacturers participate in the world economy by shipping products overseas, more U.S. companies are choosing to operate out of rural towns to take advantage of lower labor and land costs (Johnson 2006). Enhanced technology and infrastructure have decreased rural isolation in many Texas towns by allowing greater access to information and transportation. Consequently, nearly every small town in the "Lone Star State" now has Vietnamese-owned nail shops (for manicures and pedicures), Mexican restaurants, and national chain retailers that have replaced many of the traditional family-owned businesses that once lined "Main Street."

The impact of these social and demographic changes is also evidenced in the schools. In 2007, English Language Learner (ELL) students made up nearly 8 percent of the rural student population in Texas (Johnson and Strange 2007), and the number of ELL students in rural schools continues to grow at a rapid pace (Texas Education Agency 2009). While demographic trends indicate increases in the number of ELL children in rural schools, little research has been published on teachers' experiences promoting change to support the achievement of culturally and linguistically diverse children in rural school settings. In their research article on preparing rural teachers for diversity, Wenger and Dinsmore (2005, 12) concluded that more research was needed to tell the stories of "how teachers meet diverse student needs while attempting to make 'the connection between pedagogy and the value of place' (Sherwood 2000, 65) in rural communities."

In this chapter, we share stories from teachers of English as a second language (ESL) in rural school districts. These stories are about their perceptions of how they may have influenced change in their schools and communities to better serve the social and academic needs of ELLs. These teachers were identified by their communities as leaders in their schools and selected to participate in Project Triad, a two-year instructional leadership masters program. The particular group of teachers described here were part of a group, or cohort, that was supported by a U.S. Department of Education grant. Like many rural teachers described by Kannapel and DeYoung (1999), teachers in our study (Triad teachers) reported having strong ties to the communities in which they lived and worked. Most of the Triad teachers were originally from these communities and expressed a commitment to remain in the same school districts until they retire.

Triad teachers consistently referred to themselves and their school communities as "rural." Many of their stories also reveal elements that would sharply contrast with the realities of urban settings. For example, two Triad teachers continued taking graduate classes while living in a country barn for two months after their East Texas homes were destroyed in Hurricane Katrina, the major hurricane that devastated parts of Louisiana, Mississippi, and areas of Southeast Texas in 2005.

When they are part of a local community, rural teachers have been found to be naturally interested in maintaining the identity and local traditions of the areas in which they live (Kannapel and Young 1999). Yet, as educators, these teachers often find themselves on the front lines of changing demographics that bring more and more ELLs from other countries into U.S. rural schools. Consequently, rural ESL teachers are in a position to take the lead in developing appropriate curricula, assessments, and professional development to better serve the needs of ELLs at both the school and district levels. To improve curriculum and instruction for culturally and linguistically different "others," teachers are forced not only to examine their own beliefs but also to attempt to influence the attitudes and behavior of others in their communities. Thus, they often take on instructional leadership roles that extend beyond the classroom.

In questioning how well preparation programs equip teachers to take effective leadership roles in rural contexts in the southern United States, Hilty (1999, 169) emphasized, "It is important for rural teachers to begin to articulate those social and cultural phenomena that impact their schools and classrooms, and for us as educators to begin to train teachers to be leaders in rural schools—to empower teachers, students, and parents to articulate a vision of culturally relevant pedagogy that recognizes the unique social and cultural identities of southern schools and communities" (169).

In Hilty's view, teachers in rural southern schools have to be prepared to "teach against the grain" (169), which means being prepared to "alter curricula, raise questions about common [and taken-for-granted] practices, and resist inappropriate decisions" (168). Hilty stressed that this is difficult since "the aims and purposes of [rural] schools are often not congruent with those of the community" (168). This reality is magnified in schools with increasing numbers of ELLs because teachers are required to meet the instructional needs of all students in communities that are typically suspicious of, and often hostile toward, foreign-born newcomers.

This chapter presents select examples of how a group of rural ESL teacher leaders perceived themselves to be influential in reshaping their school and community cultures to better meet the needs of ELLs in the communities in which they live and work. The chapter addresses the notions of identity, place, and community in a globalizing world by sharing ESL teachers' experiences in advocating for the achievement of immigrant students while also negotiating their own personal awareness and identity within their changing communities.

Stories from teachers in three small rural U.S. communities in eastern and central Texas were selected as representative "snapshots" of stories collected from ESL teachers from more than twenty rural Texas school districts. Over a two-year period we collected qualitative data to explore Triad teachers' experiences in working to improve curriculum and instruction for ELL students, as well as their perceptions of change, if any, in their schools, school districts, and communities. Data were triangulated using open-ended questionnaires, interviews, on-site observations, and document analysis. Overall, the Triad teacher stories described in this chapter illustrate how rural ESL teacher leaders may be influential in bringing global perspectives into the unique sociocultural contexts of their own schools and communities.

Project Triad: An Innovative Approach to Teacher Leader Development

Project Triad was designed to enhance the academic performance of ELLs in small, rural school districts in South Central Texas by developing the leadership capacities of ESL teachers in the region. The program was sponsored by a U.S. Department of Education grant and coordinated by the Educational Leadership and Counseling Department at Sam Houston State University, a regional state university located an hour and a half north of Houston.

The program was titled "Project Triad" because the original goal of the program was to train a trio of school professionals in strategies to improve the reading levels of second-language learners in rural Texas school districts. The trio or Triad consisted of a school administrator, a reading specialist, and a bilingual or ESL teacher. Administrators participated in the initial training sessions, but they were unable to continue active participation in Triad due to time and commitment constraints. Since few reading specialists were initially identified to participate in the project, a pool of bilingual and ESL-credentialed teachers and a few reading specialists became the primary program participants. Yet we continued to call the program Project Triad.

Project Triad essentially aimed to offer ESL teachers "state-of-the-art" training in research-based teaching strategies for ELLs, while empowering participants to become change agents in their schools, districts, and communities. Triad teachers were challenged to promote ELL student achievement and overall school improvement through professional development, action research, community outreach, curriculum development, student advocacy, and collaboration with other teacher colleagues in their schools and nearby districts. Throughout the program, Triad Teachers were consistently encouraged to reflect on their own cultural values, as well as examine how their schools and communities were responding to change and the increasing international diversity in their towns.

Over a four-year period, approximately seventy-five rural teachers graduated from Project Triad with master's degrees in instructional leadership. Throughout their participation in the program, Triad teacher leaders shared how they promoted change in their schools and communities to support the achievement of ELL students. They described their own development as leaders, as well as their perceived influence on others on their campuses and in their communities. In several cases, teacher leaders believed they were influential in expanding the perspectives of their local communities from "narrowly exclusive," or unaware of and closed to others' cultural perspectives, to more "universally inclusive," or willing to learn about and accept multiple cultural perspectives in order to create a more inclusive school environment. Triad teachers shared many stories recounting their efforts to reshape their rural school and community cultures.

While Triad teachers represented over fifteen small, rural school districts, we chose to highlight stories from three rural towns where teachers described particularly significant changes in their schools and communities over a two-year period. All three towns reflected the characteristics of changing rural communities in eastern and central Texas, where availability of affordable housing and job opportunities in construction and manufacturing had stimulated the immigration of foreign-born families to traditionally homogeneous rural communities and, consequently, led to greater numbers of ELLs in the schools. The school districts described here well represented the many other rural districts where the Triad teacher leaders worked. We gave pseudonyms to all towns, districts, schools, and teachers described in this chapter.

Representative Profiles of Three Rural Texas Communities

Bison

Bison is a small, rural town located halfway between Houston and Dallas. A population of 1,840 was recorded in the 2000 census, yet there has been observable population growth since then. The town of Bison was established in 1871 and began to grow with the building of the Great Northern Railroad. In the 1900s, when the railroad, cotton gins, and cattle raising fueled the economy, Bison area students attended one-room schools scattered throughout the county. These schools, like many in the southern United States, were segregated. Certain schools were exclusively for white students and others were designated for black students. The current local economy still somewhat depends on cattle ranching and farming, but has expanded to include some large companies, a mining company, a steel pipe factory, three construction companies, and a large feed manufacturer, all of which export their goods to other parts of the world. These businesses have attracted immigrants, primarily from Mexico and Central America, and have led to shifts in the demographic makeup of the Bison community and, consequently, the schools. Recent immigrants have said that Bison provides more jobs, affordable lots, and mobile homes than the larger urban areas. Many immigrants have come to live in Bison at the recommendation of other family members.

At the time of the Triad program, Bison Independent School District (isd) consisted of three schools. In 2007, elementary school enrollment was at 1,325, junior high enrollment at 1,245, and high school enrollment at 1,231. While Bison isd's traditional racial makeup of whites and African Americans has remained relatively stable over the years, with some decrease in the white population, the number of Spanish-speaking ells enrolled in Bison Independent School District has grown rapidly.

Ludson

The community of Ludson is located in central Texas. It has a population of approximately 3,800 people and is primarily residential with few businesses. In 2006, the population was predominately white (78 percent), with an African American population of 5 percent and a Hispanic population of 17 percent. More than 50 percent of the population is of low socioeconomic status.

Officially formed in 1940, Ludson isd evolved from a tiny one-room community school in the late 1800s to a school district of approximately 2,500 students in 2007. Until 1999, all students were housed on one campus. Kindergarten students could walk to the baseball field and watch the high school team practice, and high school students could go next door to serve as mentors for primary and elementary students. Community members expressed a sense of nostalgia about the one-campus district because the close proximity allowed students, staff, and parents to maintain a strong sense of connectedness around what happened at school. In 2006, the original one-campus school had expanded to include forty buildings and over three hundred teachers, many of whom have worked in the district for at least ten years.

New Cally

New Cally, Texas, is larger than Bison and Ludson. The population of New Cally more than doubled over an eighteen-year period, from 8,000 in 1989 to 20,330 in 2007, primarily due to its one-hour proximity to the city of Houston and more affordable housing. Like many central and eastern Texas towns, New Cally's economy traditionally depended on cattle raising and cotton gins. With the coming of the railroad, it became a shipping point for livestock.

Since the 1990s, however, the economy has become more dependent on jobs in nearby cities, making New Cally more residential than commercial. Socioeconomic contrasts are increasingly evident as new gated housing communities are constructed alongside ranches and trailer parks. New Cally's new international diversity is composed of immigrants who represent a variety of countries including Romania, Pakistan, Russia, Vietnam, Mexico, as well as countries in Central America. The socioeconomic and ethnic diversity that has emerged in New Cally over recent years has led to tensions between traditional residents and new arrivals. Resistance from old-timers in accommodating newcomers is evidenced in the scathing local newspaper editorials written by people who had lived in the town for generations. Editorial topics reflect the typically incensed debates over immigration, the value of bilingual programs, and concerns about losing the essence of "the way things used to be." Local newspaper articles frequently feature stories highlighting political and property disputes between wealthier gated communities and the less-affluent ranches and trailer parks.

The New Cally ISD consists of six elementary schools, two middle schools, and one high school. In 2007, the ethnic population in New Cally ISD was 67 percent white, 29 percent Hispanic, 3 percent African American, and 1 percent other groups. Triad teachers from New Cally reported that certain families have produced generations of educators, most of whom have spent their entire careers in the same place.

Changes that supported ELL student achievement were observed in all three towns described above, as well as many other rural communities represented by Triad teacher leaders. We identified five emerging areas in which Triad teachers reported influencing change: (a) teaching and learning, (b) school climate, (c) policy making, (d) parent involvement, and (e) community awareness. Triad teacher reflections also indicated areas of personal and professional development attributed to their participation in the two-year program. The examples of cultural reshaping illustrated below provide "snapshots" of the kinds of changes that were observed.

Teaching and Learning

It is important to note that while the state of Texas has a mandatory bilingual education policy, only one of the districts highlighted here (New Cally) had a bilingual classroom. None of the districts highlighted had special policies, curricula, or training specifically aimed at enhancing the academic achievement of ELLS. In some cases, districts had mandated instructional programs, but these were required for all students and not targeted to ELLs. Additionally, at the time of this Triad program, Texas teachers were not required to obtain special training in teaching second-language learners or certification as English as a second language (ESL) specialists. ESL certification in Texas was obtained by passing an exam and not by completing specific course work or specialized training. Nonetheless, as teachers with ESL specialist certification, the Triad teachers generally were viewed as knowledgeable educators and had a certain degree of freedom in implementing ELL-supportive instructional strategies. It is important to note, however, that through participation in the Triad program, teacher leaders received extensive specialized training in ELL teaching and learning strategies, as well as leadership skill development.

In general, based on the observational and interview data collected in this study, Triad teacher leaders from all three towns appeared to affect teaching and learning in several ways. Their own personal development as master ESL teachers allowed teacher leaders to directly influence ELL student achievement in their own classrooms. In addition, however, they trained other teacher colleagues in effective and appropriate strategies to enhance second-language learning and reading. This was accomplished through in-service training, as well as the informal modeling and mentoring of best practices for making English instruction more comprehensive for ELLs by applying second-language teaching methods and relating academic content to students' prior knowledge and experiences.

Teaching and Learning in Bison

Jan and Maria (pseudonyms) were two of the first teachers to participate in the two-year Triad program. When they first began their program, they were the only two ESL-certified teachers. Maria had come to Bison from an urban district. She and her family had moved in search of a quiet rural setting in which to raise their own children. Jan, on the other hand, was born and raised in Bison. She sought out both ESL certification and Montessori training on her own accord. Through their training in action research, these teachers realized that the ELL students showed significantly poor performance on standardized tests. They also observed that ELL students were not receiving proper instruction in core subject areas, primarily due to the inadequate training of the regular, core-area teachers. They accessed and studied the standards of the association of Teachers of English to Speakers of Other Languages, as well as the state requirements for limited-English proficient students, and found that their schools' instructional practices did not reflect these recommended standards in many areas. They developed an action plan to implement a self-contained classroom for ELL students in grades K–3 to shelter instruction in the content areas. A pullout program was the only option at the time, as no other teachers were certified to teach ESL. Because fourth and fifth grades were departmentalized, the plan stipulated that all teachers in these grades receive training and certification in second-language teaching strategies. They developed a vertical team plan to have an ESL teacher at every grade level to closely monitor students and provide modeling and mentoring for other grade-level teachers. They also adopted a content-based instruction curriculum and the Open Court curriculum to provide structure for new teachers. Content-based curricula aim to make academic content more comprehensible for second-language learners by contextualizing material through greater use of visuals and hands-on instruction. The plan was presented to the school board and approved and implemented in the 2005–6 school year. The Bison Elementary principal reported, "We are seeing monumental improvements in our statewide scores, especially with our limited-English proficient students. I am sure all this is due to the concerted efforts of a few dedicated teachers and it's paying off. We want to have all our teachers ESL certified by the end of next year."

In reference to their efforts, Triad teacher Maria commented, "With the current ESL program, the teachers and administrators have seen the advantages and each year our program will improve. The teachers are open-minded and the administrators are very supportive. The more structure we provide the other teachers, the more comfortable they will feel about teaching our ELLS. They also see that these strategies are beneficial for all students, not just ELLS."

Teaching and Learning in Ludson

Improvements in teaching and learning were also observed in Ludson. When Judy, a Ludson Middle School teacher, first began the Triad program, ELL reading scores were significantly lower than those for the remainder of the student population. While 91 percent of third graders met the state standard in reading, only 60 percent of third-grade ELLS met the standard. Fourth-grade scores showed an even more significant difference, with only 43 percent of ELLS meeting the standard, compared to 86 percent of the total number of fourth graders. Great differences in scores between the ELL students and others could be observed in the areas of reading/language arts and math and science all the way through to the high school level.

For both her action research and curriculum planning courses, Judy decided to investigate barriers and need areas to propose solutions to poor ELL perform-ance. Over the course of two semesters, Judy conducted numerous classroom observations and informal interviews with other teachers in the school. As a result, Judy discovered that most of the teachers were unaware of their stu-dents' English proficiency levels and had no idea how they could help students move to the next level. Based on this information, Judy developed a profes-sional development plan to prepare regular classroom teachers to "shelter" instruction for ELL students. Judy realized, however, that the typical "one-shot," in-service workshop would not be enough to make significant improve-ments in teachers' application of second-language teaching strategies:

> Following one of the Triad workshops, I made a brief presentation to the middle school and high school faculty on an ESL vocabulary teaching strategy I had learned called the "Rule of Three." The workshop was very well received and several teachers reported success when using it in their classrooms. However, a year later, most had completely forgotten about it and were no longer using that vocabulary technique. I realized that the teachers needed more long-term training over time, especially since there is so much to learn about teaching culturally and linguistically diverse [CLD] students . . . and also that implementation had to be monitored until they got it and used strategies consistently until we could see real ELL student improvements. At that point, I thought, if they are given the teaching tools they need, surely teachers will take the initiative to help ALL students learn.

Using the data she had collected, Judy developed a yearlong teacher training program that would prepare Ludson Middle School teachers for "sheltered instruction," or the use of integrated ESL strategies to make regular classroom content more comprehensible and accessible to ELLs. The training involved several all-day summer sessions, followed by periodic in-service trainings, observations, and coaching meetings throughout the next school year. Course content addressed all major areas of ESL teaching theory and methods includ-ing: (a) English proficiency levels in the four skill areas, (b) the importance of authentic assessment and ESL standards, (c) reading strategies for ELLs, (d) the difference between social and academic language, and (e) the importance of contextualizing content using visuals, hands-on activities, and graphic organizers, among many other second-language teaching concepts.

To help teachers empathize more with ELL students in the content classroom, she began the program by showing them a two-minute clip from a French film and asking them to write a short summary of the clip. The teachers shared their feelings and identified what they would need to help them with the assignment. As a respected teacher leader and community member, Judy felt she could guide the teachers in reshaping their attitudes and behaviors toward CLD students: "First of all, I wanted to make sure the teachers understood that CLD students need more than just an adjustment in teaching strategies. In fact, I remembered that Collier and Thomas (2004) suggest that CLD students have more difficulty when skills are addressed in isolation. They found that more progress is made when linguistic, academic, cognitive, and sociocultural areas are addressed and interrelated simultaneously. In order to do this, the teachers needed to first know what it felt like not to understand a language or be immersed in a new culture."

Over the two-year period since Judy initiated the professional development program, ELL achievement scores at Ludson Middle School showed a slow yet steady increase. Many Ludson teachers and administrators believed that Judy's professional development program made a big difference. As a result, the district initiated a formal mentoring program and continues providing regular in-services on ELL teaching and learning for all district schools.

Reshaping of School Culture and Climate

In all three towns, Triad teacher leadership initiatives also appeared to lead to changes in the schools' culture and climate. More inclusive teacher attitudes, greater parent involvement, and more global curriculum and literature all contributed to a more inclusive school culture. In a few cases, Triad teachers directly addressed school-wide cultural competence and proficiency in their schools by conducting "culture audits," or organizational assessments to determine how well a school's policies, programs, and practices address diverse groups in schools (Bustamante 2006).

As a class project, Triad participants conducted culture audits to better understand their school cultures, identify barriers to cultural proficiency, and determine what might be done to create a more inclusive environment where multiple cultures merge to form a new local culture. Audit findings served as data sources for action plans that proposed new programs or practices to respond to increasing school diversity. Many of the action plans included strategies to expand traditional school customs and celebrations to include those of ELL students.

Culture and Climate in Bison

For example, to foster cultural awareness at Bison Elementary, teacher leaders integrated Mexican cultural celebrations such as Las Posadas and Cinco de Mayo. Maria, one of the Triad teacher leaders, initiated the program three years ago by inviting Mexican parents to come in and teach traditional dances to all students: "These are now seen as special, traditional events that are part of our school culture here at Bison Elementary. We try to involve all the teachers and students, not just the ESL students. That way everyone feels included and has an opportunity to learn more. During this time, we also try to tie these celebrations into the curriculum through reading and writing activities. It has also helped our ELL parents feel more included and the number of local community members that attend the event increases every year."

Culture and Climate in New Cally

In New Cally, the Triad teachers' culture audit revealed a lack of culturally relevant resources and literature in both the classrooms and the school library. The teacher leaders began to conduct book talks during teacher in-service meetings to introduce regular classroom teachers to a wide array of culturally appropriate literature that could be used in the classroom. They also demonstrated how the literature could tie into the state-mandated teaching objectives by developing thematic units that teachers could access. They further extended the book talks to parent groups and initiated the school's first multicultural festival.

While cultural celebrations have been referred to as the more superficial "flags, food, and festival" approach to cultural diversity, teachers in these rural communities felt that these newly introduced celebrations provided a great starting place for a more inclusive school culture. By providing something familiar to ELL students and parents and allowing them to be the "cultural experts," other community members were also exposed to new ideas and traditions. Triad teacher leaders viewed cultural celebrations as an important and viable "starting place" in moving toward more diverse school cultures. But evidence revealed that some Triad teachers clearly understood the importance of moving beyond "heroes and holidays" to a more inclusive school culture that reflected culturally responsive policies, programs, and practices. One Triad teacher specifically described this distinction:

> I feel like most teachers here just do not get any exposure to people from other places. There needs to be more emphasis on multicultural education for those new teachers coming in and especially the principals because they have the most to do with how the school is run. We need to not only make sure that parents and students feel welcome, but also see how we can learn from them [immigrant parents] and also make instruction meaningful for the students [ELLS] in the way they can understand it from their own prior experiences. It might take a while to get there.

This Triad teacher's comments suggest a level of conscientiousness about cultural differences that might extend beyond mere tolerance. The model of "cultural proficiency" posited by Lindsey, Robins, and Terrell (2003) provides a useful six-point continuum from the negative characteristics of cultural destructiveness, incapacity, and blindness to cultural competence and proficiency, which involve the value and recognition of other cultural groups in an appropriate and respectful way that also expands individual and organizational knowledge, resources, and behavior. In applying the notion of cultural competence to the Triad teacher stories presented here, it appears that Triad teacher leaders and their schools were at different levels in their development of cultural competence. Participation in the Triad program may have influenced teachers' awareness of their own and others' cultural biases.

Influence on Policy Making

Triad teacher leaders from all three towns perceived that they were instrumental in influencing policy changes. The teachers felt these policy changes were particularly significant in their rural districts where anti-immigration sentiments were generally high and, as one teacher put it, "the good ole boys aren't easy to budge." Some rural sociologists (Israel, Beaulieu, and Hartless 2001) have discussed the role of community social capital in influencing rural student success, with implications of its influence on rural policy making. This community social capital may be accumulated through generalized leadership, community activeness, and supportive interpersonal relationships. Triad teachers appear to have influenced policy making by slowly accumulating community social capital through advocacy and relationship building. They believed they were catalysts in the adoption of policies that specifically supported ELL student achievement at both the school and district levels, as illustrated below.

Policy Influences in Bison

In Bison, one of the Triad ESL teachers proudly described how teacher leaders initiated changes that led to district-wide policy changes. Jan, who was originally from Bison and had lived there her whole life, emphatically stated (while banging on the table for emphasis): "We see ourselves as advocates for children! We go to every school board meeting and advocate for our students. Sometimes we even present research data to show and educate the board about what we need to do for our English Language Learners."

Due to this district-level teacher advocacy, the Bison district has brought in additional resources, reading specialists, professional development on second-language teaching, and English as a second language classes for parents. The district has also required that all teachers in the district become ESL certified within a two-year period.

Policy Influences in Ludson

In Ludson, Triad teacher Judy observed policy making at the school administration level. When she proposed her professional development plan to train other teachers in second language teaching strategies to her principal, he fully supported the idea and obtained extra funding from the district to conduct a one-month summer training institute. As a result of the success of Judy's summer ESL training institute, Ludson ISD decided to extend professional development to all regular classroom teachers. They provided additional funding and required that all elementary and high school teachers complete an ESL certification program within a two-year period. The district also solicited additional training support from a regional education center and acquired curriculum and materials to support reading and sheltered-content instruction for regular classroom settings.

Policy Influences in New Cally

In New Cally, district-level policies were affected by the creation of a parent center at one elementary school. The center received a lot of publicity and was eventually considered a model by the New Cally superintendent. Based on the success of the parent center, the superintendent has proposed that the idea be expanded to other schools in the district.

Parental Involvement

As part of the Triad program, teacher leaders were encouraged to seek ways to increase parental involvement in their schools. The most vivid example of a successful program was initiated by teacher leaders in New Cally. Three New Cally Triad teachers at Queen's Manor Elementary, a pseudonym for the actual school, used their action research project as a basis for establishing a new parent center. The data collected in their research pointed to a great need to reach out to immigrant parents in the school community. In developing the parent center these teacher leaders sought and obtained external funding and volunteer support from various sources.

The parent center idea emerged as a result of findings from an action research project conducted by the three New Cally teachers as part of a Triad research course requirement. Constanza, an ESL teacher originally from a rural Mayan town in Belize, described how the teachers first selected the action research project: "Well, things were really bad, really tense in every way . . . between the school and the immigrant parents, the teachers and the parents, and different groups of parents. Parents of our ELL students would say that they felt unwelcome and intimidated when they came to school. Teachers that have worked here a long time would make mean, discriminatory comments about the ELL students and their parents. So, we decided to look at this for our action research project to get a sense of how people were really feeling . . . perceiving things."

The New Cally Triad teachers used various methods to collect data and triangulate their findings for their action research project. They conducted extensive interviews in Spanish and English with the parents of second-language learners, as well as with the parent groups that traditionally volunteered at the school and led the parent-teacher organization. They also surveyed teachers' attitudes toward parents, parent involvement, and ELLs. By analyzing and aggregating preexisting achievement data, Triad teachers pinpointed trends for various racial/ethnic groups.

Findings from the action research project revealed that newcomer parents frequently felt discriminated against or marginalized in the school environment. Resistance and ethnocentric attitudes were evident on the part of many of the teachers from New Cally who had worked in the district for more than ten years. Some of the ELL parents said they wished they had a welcoming place to gather at school, a place where they could learn more about how to help their children succeed. Based on this parent desire, the Triad teachers developed a plan for a new parent center and began to acquire resources and support.

The teacher leaders also began to apply for grants and external financial aid. They first contacted the Americans for Literacy Project, who were willing to provide two teachers twice a week to teach English as a second language classes for parents. The family center project garnered financial support through grants from various local businesses and the Mexican consulate, who donated literacy materials in Spanish.

Among other programs, the family center now offers a resource library for parents, English as a second language courses, general educational development, parenting classes, translations, résumé assistance, Internet access, and opportunities for socialization. Not only do ELL parents better understand the U.S. educational system and how to better support their children in school, but they help the teachers tremendously. Parent volunteers come to the center to prepare materials (e.g., cut out figures, create game pieces, etc.) for lessons and special activities. Many now also assist teachers in the classroom. Constanza believes that the parent help has contributed to positive changes in teacher attitudes: "Now, the teachers just love these parents. They see what a great help they can be and they are really getting to know them as people. I think the parent center has really helped break down some of the racist and resistant attitudes that the Queen's Manor teachers had toward these parents because now they see that they are people too and that all of this benefits the students in the long run."

The traditional New Cally teachers express more welcoming attitudes toward newcomer parents; overall, greater long-term integration between local New Cally parents and parent groups from different countries is evident. In addition, many parents from the local community now volunteer as English tutors for the parent center. The parent-teacher organization, which was traditionally made up of white, upper-class parents, has become more integrated to include parents representing various socioeconomic classes and ethnic groups including Latinos, Pakistani, East Indians, and Romanians.

Researchers have suggested that parent involvement contributes to greater student achievement. This appeared evident on the Queen's Manor Elementary campus, where ELL test scores, particularly in reading, have substantially increased since the initiation of the parent center.

Community Awareness

In Bison, community attitudes were influenced by the positive changes in teacher attitudes and overall school climate that occurred since the Triad teachers initiated their ELL action plan three years earlier. Since many of the regular classroom teachers who work for Bison Elementary were also active community members, they worked as "ambassadors" in facilitating more openness among their own family and friends. Through education, awareness, increased contact, and relationship building, some teachers reported that the local community was more open and welcoming to the newcomers.

In talking with teachers around the district, it was evident that many saw the "big picture" in talking about globalization and the Bison economy. They expressed a need for the less expensive labor that immigrants provide and also stated that the economic vitality of their town was linked to a global economy, particularly by exports. Most of the teachers also said they were "regulars" at the local Vietnamese-owned nail shop and enjoyed eating at the new Mexican restaurant down the street from the schools. It appears that their gradual openness to ELLs on their campus has helped the traditional community slowly become more accepting of the "new outsiders." When two Bison teachers were asked how they perceived the demographic changes in their community, one responded:

> Well, my husband is a construction supervisor and he says the good thing is that the company doesn't have to pay the workers as much as they would if they get some American guys to do the same job. People get worried about how these people are straining the system on our tax dollars, mostly through health care and schools. As a teacher, I realize these [ELL students] are just kids and their coming here is not their fault. The best thing we can do is try to teach them well so they can be successes and Jan has been showing us ways to do this better.

The other teacher replied:

> Yes, this is just reality and we have to accept it. At first, we just felt suspicious of all these illegal immigrants coming here. Now we realize that they are not ALL illegal and that they are people just like us, even though language is still sometimes a barrier. Now, I feel like I am the one taking up for people when I get together with my own family . . . like I am educating them to be more accepting, like God wants us to for all human beings . . . I guess.

These participant quotes reflect different attitudes toward ELL students, as well as the macro-level economic realities of immigration. The comment about cheap labor reveals how the exploitation of immigrants had affected this community, while the other quote might have indicated a veiled tolerance. Nonetheless, the slowly evolving attitudes of other teachers in the community suggest a greater level of awareness and desire to accommodate to the needs of ELLS. Further, it represents how rural teacher leaders might facilitate greater understanding between newcomers and traditional community members by reframing what it means to be part of the larger human community.

Evolving Considerations

The Need for Research on English-Language Learners in Rural Schools

Research on ELLS in rural schools is limited. In one review of rural education studies conducted between 1991 and 2003 by Arnold and colleagues (2005), no studies were cited on the teaching and learning of ELL students in rural districts. Further, Arnold and colleagues' proposed future research agenda for rural education did not mention the need for research on ELLS in rural schools. Yet within the time period of that review, the number of ELL students in rural schools increased daily, clearly pointing to the need for more research on rural education and ELL students.

There are several areas for future research on ELLS in rural schools. Based on the findings of our study, there is a need to further explore the potentially pivotal role that rural teacher leaders play in influencing changes that improve the academic achievement of ELLS in rural schools. There is a need to gather more community perceptions of ELLS to better understand the unique contextual forces that may support and hinder teacher leadership and student achievement. The Triad study also suggests a need for research on the effectiveness of rural teacher preparation and professional development programs that aim to develop cultural competence and instructional strategies for second-language learners. Essentially, there is a dearth of empirical studies examining nearly every aspect of ELL experiences and achievement in rural settings.

High School Level Considerations

Many of the change strategies initiated by Triad teachers at the elementary and middle school levels eventually led to district-wide improvements for culturally and linguistically diverse students. Ideally, an increasing level of awareness could continue to "filter up" into the high school level, where the drop-out rates of Hispanic and African American high school students in rural areas continues to remain disproportionately high in comparison to those of white rural youth. Because the sense of cultural isolation or "not belonging" can be acute for teenagers, who are particularly sensitive about how well they "fit in," rural teacher leaders could consciously address how to reduce cultural isolation through a multicultural and globally oriented curriculum, intercultural dialogues (Bennett and Bennett 2004), and service-learning strategies (Butin 2003)—all of which have been shown to improve intercultural relationships, particularly among youth.

The Role of Teacher Leaders

Some education scholars clearly link teacher leadership to school reform initiatives (Murphy 2005). Others highlight how teacher leaders can have a sustained, profound impact on student achievement, as well as on schools and communities at large (Crowther et al. 2002; Merideth 2007). Ryan (2006) emphasized that teacher leadership is one key aspect of inclusive leadership that should also involve students, parents, and community members. In small rural towns, teacher leaders are generally also key community members. They frequently know the families in the town and are active in the same religious organizations as their neighbors and colleagues. One of the teacher leaders explained, "I know the superintendent personally because he goes to my church and his wife serves on the ladies auxiliary board with me. I feel like the people in my church listen to what I have to say especially when it comes to school stuff. We all agree that it's all about the children and that helps sometimes in getting more support for our schools. It's something those big districts just don't have."

Harris (2002) suggested that teacher leaders consistently use systematic inquiry (data collection and reflection on practice), and that they also influence practice in schools by empowering and mentoring other teachers by sharing information, resources, and expertise, and forging close relationships throughout the school community: "For teacher leadership to be most effective it has to engage all those within the organization (and the community) in a reciprocal learning process that leads to collective actions" (23).

In describing the challenges of educating ELLs in rural areas, Wrigley (2000, 9) recognized the key roles of leaders coupled with expectations of success: "With optimistic leadership, well-trained teachers, and informed parents who all share expectations of success, the students are likely to reach their potential. Every community, no matter how isolated, has creative people and helpful resources that can improve the quality of education for English Language Learners. A small success can be a start—and each success breeds other successes."

The experiences described by the Triad teacher leaders suggest that they felt they were in a unique position to be catalysts for change within their own local communities, particularly since ESL teachers tended to establish the closest relationships with ELL children and their families. As community members themselves, the Triad ESL teachers worked within their own family and community networks to increase awareness of other cultures and languages, educate others about world geography and history, and facilitate the eventual acceptance of outsiders into the local community. As instructional leaders, Triad ESL teachers shared resources, modeled promising practices in working with ELL students, and mentored other teachers. They worked hard to promote more inclusive policies and culturally responsive instruction and curricula to enhance ELL student learning and reshape their rural school and community cultures.

References

Arnold, M., J. Newman, J. Gaddy, and C. Dean. 2005. A look at the condition of rural education research: Setting a direction for future research. *Journal of Research in Rural Education* 20 (6), 1–25.

Bennett, J. M., and M. J. Bennett. 2004. Developing intercultural sensitivity: An integrative approach to global and domestic diversity. In D. Landis, J. M. Bennett, and M. J. Bennett, eds., *Handbook of intercultural training*, 21–71. Yarmouth, Maine: Intercultural Press.

Bustamante, R. M. 2006. The "culture audit": A leadership tool for assessment and strategic planning in diverse schools and colleges. *NCPEA Connexions*. Retrieved February 3, 2007, from http://cnx.org/content/m13691/latest/.

Butin, D. W. 2003. Of what use is it? Multiple conceptualizations of service-learning within education. *Teachers College Record* 105 (9), 1674–92.

Coladarci, T. 2007 (May 24). Improving the yield of rural education research: An editor's swan song. *Journal of Research in Rural Education* 22 (3), 1–9. Retrieved March 1, 2008, from http://jrre.psu.edu/articles/22-3.pdf.

Collier, V. P., and W. P. Thomas. 2004. The astounding effectiveness and dual-language education for all. *NABE Journal of Research and Practice* 2 (1), 1–20. Retrieved September 14, 2009, from http://njrp.tamu.edu/2004/PDFs/Collier.pdf.

Crowther, F., S. S. Kagan, M. Ferguson, and L. Hann. 2002. *Developing teacher leaders: How teacher leadership enhances school success.* Thousand Oaks, Calif.: Corwin Press.

Harris, A. 2002. Improving schools through teacher leadership. *Education Journal* 59, 22–23.

Hilty, E. B. 1999. Southern schools, southern teachers: Redefining leadership in rural communities. In D. M. Chalker, ed., *Leadership for rural schools: Lessons for all educators,* 155–69. Lancaster, Pa.: Technomic Publishing.

Israel, G. D., L. J. Beaulieu, and G. Hartless. 2001. The influence of family and community social capital on student achievement. *Rural Sociology* 66 (1), 43–68.

Johnson, J., and M. Strange. 2007. *Why rural matters: The realities of education growth.* Arlington, Va.: Rural School and Community Trust.

Johnson, K. 2006. Demographic trends in rural and small town America. *Reports on Rural America* 1 (1). Durham, N.H.: Carsey Institute.

Kannapel, P. J., and A. J. DeYoung. 1999. The rural school problem in 1999: A review and critique of the literature. *Journal of Research in Rural Education* 15 (2), 67–79.

Lindsey, R., K. Robins, and R. Terrell. 2003. *Cultural proficiency: A manual for school leaders* (2d ed.). Thousand Oaks, Calif.: Corwin Press.

Merideth, E. M. 2007. *Leadership strategies for teachers* (2d ed.). Thousand Oaks, Calif.: Corwin Press.

Murphy, J. 2005. *Connecting teacher leadership and school improvement.* Thousand Oaks, Calif.: Corwin Press.

Ryan, J. 2006. *Inclusive leadership.* San Francisco: Wiley.

Sherwood, T. 2000. Where has all the "rural" gone? Rural education research and federal reform. *Journal of Research in Rural Education* 16 (3), 159–67.

Texas Education Agency. 2009. Enrollment in Texas public schools, 2008–09. Retrieved September 14, 2009, from http://ritter.tea.state.tx.us/research/pdfs/enrollment_2007-08.pdf.

Wenger, K. J., and J. Dinsmore. 2005 (October 13). Preparing rural preservice teachers for diversity. *Journal of Research in Rural Education* 20 (10), 1–15. Retrieved March 1, 2008, from http://jrre.psu.edu/articles/20-10.pdf.

Wrigley, P. 2000 (November–December). The challenge of educating English Language Learners in rural areas. *NABE News,* 1–9.

13

GROWING UP RURAL AND MOVING TOWARD
FAMILY-SCHOOL PARTNERSHIPS:
SPECIAL EDUCATORS REFLECT ON BIOGRAPHY AND PLACE

Gretchen Butera and Lisa Humphreys Costello

Introduction

Collaboration between families and schools on behalf of children's success is the focus of numerous programs and policies. Research has established that parental school involvement has a positive influence on academic outcomes for children (Christenson 2004; Epstein 1995; Hill and Taylor 2004; Hoover-Dempsey et al. 2002). It is increasingly clear that both schools and families provide essential contexts for student learning and socialization.

In special education, policy and practice describe a central role for parents that extends beyond what is traditionally considered parent involvement. The rationale for parent partnerships with special educators is important to understand. Students with disabilities often require comprehensive social, educational, and related services both during and beyond the school day to optimize their learning. Because these services often involve multiple professionals and may occur in home and community settings as well as in school, coordination of services is necessary and families are essential participants in that process. As key stakeholders with the best vantage point to view student progress over time, the benefits of an active parental role in both the decision-making process that accompanies special education's Individualized Educational Plan (IEP) process as well as the implementation of the activities identified by the IEP are apparent.

In the past, families have been viewed as contributing to the problems encountered by children with disabilities (Turnbull et al. 2006). This viewpoint was inherently counterproductive in establishing parent-professional partner-ships, and more recently special education researchers have emphasized the importance of parents as partners, the resources and resilience of families, and the value of developing a more reciprocal relationship between parents and educators (Butera, Matuga, and Riley 1999; Christenson 2004; Christenson and Sheridan 2001; Gallagher 2006; Lareau and Horvat 1999; Lightfoot 2004; Sum-mers et al. 2005; Turnbull et al. 2006).

Just as there are considerable ethnic, cultural, and developmental factors that influence parent-school relations for typically developing students (Hill and Taylor 2004), the families of students with disabilities also vary consider-ably and these family characteristics influence how special educators conceptu-alize and actualize family-professional partnerships. In general, though, the extent to which special educators have actually achieved a more reciprocal rela-tionship with families has fallen short of the hoped-for ideal (Hanson et al. 2000; Harry, Allen, and McLaughlin 1995; Soodak and Erwin 2000). Turnbull and colleagues (2006) point out that, while research details how schools comply with local, state, and federal regulations regarding the role of parents in special education processes, educators are seldom active in trying to foster trusting partnerships with the families of the students they teach.

Regardless of developmental status of the student, the relationships between schools and families exist within larger social, political, and economic forces that help shape how teachers understand their roles and live their daily lives as teachers. They do so in an increasingly complex environment. Advances in technology by American economic competitors such as Russia, Germany, and Japan, combined with the low achievement of American students when com-pared to students from other nations, have worked in recent decades to focus the attention of federal policy makers on school reform. Producing students who can safeguard American economic and national security interests is the goal of much of the school reform. The rhetoric reflects the increasing eco-nomic, social, cultural, and technological integration of various regions of the world in recent decades.

Globalization both articulates with and mediates educational reform. Those who study schools as workplaces suggest that globalization has worked to reduce the professional autonomy of teachers. Increased managerial control, accountability, and the use of standards-based tests to improve instruction are viewed as means to transplant lessons about human performance from the business world to schools (Helsby 1999; Ingersoll 2003; Robertson 1997). Under these circumstances, teachers may find their knowledge about their work undervalued. Increasingly, there is evidence that teachers feel stressed and alienated from their work, and believe that it was a mistake to choose teaching as a career (Cochran-Smith and Lytle 2006; Dworkin 1997; LeCompte and Dworkin 1991; Valli and Buese 2007).

For special educators, the impact of increased managerial control, accountability, and the use of standards-based tests to measure instruction may be especially hard on their sense of efficacy. American schools enrolling substantial numbers of students with disabilities face additional accountability demands when disaggregated test scores from subgroups of students with disabilities designate the school as failing to achieve adequate yearly progress, thereby triggering sanctions for the school. There is mounting evidence that the pressure accompanying the threat of such sanctions adds considerable stress to those teachers held responsible for ensuring that their students perform well on standardized tests (Browder et al. 2003; Butera et al. 2007; Cochran-Smith and Lytle 2006; Fore, Martin, and Bender 2002; Kossar, Mitchem, and Ludlow 2005; Thompson, Quenemoen, and Thurlow 2003; Yell, Shriner, and Katsiyannis 2006). Under these circumstances, the relationships between families and special educators may become even more difficult to maintain as the special educators focus on instruction designed to improve test performance at the expense of other aspects of their work (Butera et al. 2007; Kossar, Mitchem, and Ludlow 2005).

Special Educators in Rural Schools

Rural school districts account for a sizeable percentage of students in schools in the United States and a substantial number of students with disabilities (Provasnik et al. 2007). Clearly rural schools are diverse and may have few characteristics in common. But the traditional linkage of rural schools to the community suggests that special educators in rural schools must be cognizant of their local context if they are to optimize the opportunities to partner with families to the benefit of the students they teach (Theobald and Nachtigal 1995). Yet while a great deal of attention is focused on preparing professionals to work in urban environments, there are significantly fewer resources devoted to preparing them to work in rural settings, particularly with respect to the needs of diverse populations (Theobald 2002).

In an analysis of three of the most popular multicultural education textbooks, for example, Ayalon (2003, 30) concluded that "urban-centric views dominate the multicultural education discourse, and, most often, these books neglect to provide information about poverty, racial diversity, or other diversity issues in rural areas." It is not surprising then that personnel preparation programs for special educators not only struggle to infuse situations and dilemmas specific to working with rural children and families (Ludlow 2003), but also overlook the ways in which rural communities can serve as assets for special educators, the students they teach, and the families with whom they may partner.

In fact, Theobald and Howley (1998) describe teacher preparation programs in many universities as accomplices in the deterioration of rural communities when professional preparation programs evade "philosophical study and discussion in favor of cultivating professional expertise" (152). Theobald and his colleagues do not suggest how personnel preparation for rural schools might address the needs of students with disabilities, and this is a concern. Nonetheless, the intradependence of individuals within rural communities (Theobald 1997) is likely to be supportive of special education's ultimate goal of enhancing the quality of life for individuals with disabilities, and rural schools might be especially well situated to partner with families on behalf of their students with disabilities. Given these circumstances, the relationships between special-education personnel preparation and those preparing to work as special educators in rural schools are important to understand.

In this chapter we consider the effects of a professional development course we developed at Indiana University to prepare special educators for parent partnerships with families at the schools where they worked. Students engage in a semester-long field-based Family Project that requires them to partner with the family of an individual with a disability. Throughout the semester the student interviews, corresponds, and interacts with their family in a variety of home and community settings weekly and uses these experiences to consider various issues during class discussions and in weekly written work. In particular, we examine the perspectives of seven rural special educators who participated in this course. All but one were raised in Indiana, all described their current Indiana community as rural, and all described being raised in rural communities. Using the work of Theobald and his colleagues to question our own and our students' apparent assumptions, we discuss the lessons we learned about the professional development of special educators in rural contexts; the role of change in rural schools and communities with respect to the cultural, social, economic, and political change; and the potential role of personnel preparation in relationship to those changes.

Studying Special-Education Personnel Preparation

For this study, we were especially interested in how the sociocultural background of participants influenced their views about and interactions with families with special-needs students (Butera and Dunn 2005). We collected three data types from student participants: artifacts, interviews, and observations. Artifacts included student journals, vignette responses, midterm and final papers, and transcripts of electronic chats. We conducted semi-structured interviews four times at two-month intervals (two of the interviews occurred after the course was completed). Three of the interviews were via telephone with accompanying field notes written on the spot and expanded immediately afterward to capture the essence of the discussion; one interview was face-to-face in the student's home or workplace and was audiotaped. The interviews ranged from thirty minutes to an hour and a half, and through them we sought to examine the perspective of the students on family-professional partnerships and how their personal and professional experiences, beliefs, and attitudes influenced their practice. We observed class discussions in each of the five sections of the course twice during the semester, focusing on the class interactions in which the students we studied actively participated, gathering field notes on the spot and expanding them shortly thereafter.

To analyze the interview, observation, and artifact data, we organized data sets chronologically and read each set several times, jotting down notes in the margins. Employing constant comparative methods, we identified initial themes, categories, properties, and hypotheses and tested them against the cross-case data in each set. A descriptive case study of each student participant was then written, and the students described were asked to review the case studies for accuracy. In three cases the student made minor revisions. Working in teams of two to three, the data sets were then reassembled and coded for the presence of each theme.

In the next section we focus on the data collected from seven of the sixteen student participants in the study who described themselves to us as working within rural schools and as members of rural communities.[1] These rural teachers were enrolled in a graduate program in special education while they worked as special educators, and had had a variety of previous professional experiences. We reassembled their data sets separately from the other (non-rural) special

---

1. Brief biographical descriptions of each rural special educator may be found in the appendix at the end of this chapter.

educators in the course and reanalyzed the data using methods similar to the ones previously described, comparing the data collected from the rural educators to the larger data set. Although there is considerable overlap across the rural and non-rural groups, in general four themes emerged specific to rural special educators. We discuss each briefly in turn.

Growing Up Rural

Across cases, all the special educators described their personal experiences in families as an important framework for how they understood the world around them. This was especially evident for the rural special educators in the study who told vivid stories emphasizing the size or remote location of their upbringing. All seven special educators also reported that they chose to continue to live and teach in rural communities. Although there were several instances where the special educator in question referred to their rural background in a disparaging manner (referring to themselves as "hillbillies" or "hayseeds"), they also displayed a degree of pride about their rural backgrounds. For example, Brittany[2] described growing up in "wide open spaces with beautiful fields of corn and wheat." She compared this to the university town where the course was held, saying, "It's not crowded and chaotic like here." Other rural special educators described the rural communities where they were raised or currently lived as "close" and "caring," and they were proud to report that "folks took care of you if you needed help." They seldom described their rural community as prosperous, however, and sometimes told stories about recent economic decline in their area.

The special educators we studied displayed many of the values often associated with rural America. These values were also evident in the larger sample of students studied, but they were far more pronounced in the data from the rural special educators. Work was highly valued, and all seven rural special educators described their families as hardworking. All seven also placed a high value on self-reliance. They asserted in their journals and in class discussion that families should "take care of their own." In nearly the same breath in which Betsy described her family as hardworking, she reported that they "always helped each other." Margaret wrote that her (also rural) project family was a "nice family [that] takes care of their own," and went on to state that they do not "rely on others a great deal to meet the needs of the family: financially, medi-

---

2. All names used in this chapter are pseudonyms.

cally or emotionally. In fact, they rarely take their problems outside of the home." Like the others, Greg described how self-reliance was valued in his nuclear family, and that if help is needed the extended family is the most acceptable resource for it. He related, "I asked my folks for several thousand dollars to borrow until we sold our other house." But he went on to report being "very embarrassed with initially asking them for that loan."

The special educators we studied also emphasized the importance of faith in their families and in several instances described faith as an asset for their project families. Betsy described her family as "a typical country family who went to church every weekend." Theresa explained that her community growing up had "large churches" and was "very safe." In reflecting about the important resources of communities, Paula explained that churches are "a place to belong and feel welcome." Brittany described belonging to a church volleyball league and called the community in which she lives a "religious town."

Encountering Diversity: Race, Socioeconomic Status, and Disability

More evident than in the larger sample of special educators studied, the rural special educators participating in the study reported lacking personal experience with individuals of color, sometimes encountering them only during their college years. Connie told us, "I'm from a small farming community in southern Indiana. . . . There are no minorities in my town, at least not that I'm aware of. I learned a lot by being around African Americans, Japanese Americans, and more in college." Unlike Connie, however, others in our study reported that they continued to encounter little diversity in college. Brittany went to a small rural college and taught in that community before moving to her current position. Others reported attending state universities with relatively few students of color. They also commented that they lacked the opportunity to get to know individuals of color in their work.

In contrast to their lack of experience with students of color, the rural special educators we studied reported more experience with social-class differences. The relationship of income to social class created an interesting discussion that was particularly evident from the data collected from the rural special educators. Overall, they acknowledged that their families struggled financially, and several reported being the first in their family to attend college. Despite these circumstances, they insisted that their families were decidedly middle class, and several reported themselves as "upper middle class." As they struggled to understand the relationship of income to social class, they continued to assert that it was best not to report that you had financial difficulties. Paula told us that her dad regularly "cussed telemarketers because they asked him how much money he made."

Betsy provided the exception to students' overall reluctance to discuss family finances. She explained that in her family "we always talked about money but there wasn't any." Like Paula, Betsy indicates that her experiences have helped her learn lessons about money as she openly examines her beliefs: "The old adage 'never judge a book by its cover' is very true. I have friends who are financially well-to-do and I have friends who are dirt-poor. . . . My better-off friends do not associate with my poor friends. They do not understand how I can associate with 'those people.' It's actually funny to listen to them. I do not criticize either group for having more than me financially or for having less than me financially." Betsy's openness about financial issues was accompanied by an active concern about how poverty affected the lives of her students and their families. In class discussions, electronic chats, interviews, and journal entries, Betsy frequently pointed out the likely influence of poverty on her students' lives. Her comments were particularly noteworthy because of the relative silence of other rural special educators on the topic.

In common with the larger set of special educators studied, the rural special educators provided details about their family experiences with disability. Betsy explained early in the course that "my cousin lived with muscular dystrophy for fourteen years after being diagnosed with it at age seven. My own family participated actively in his care." Similarly, Margaret reported having a cousin with a disability: "My aunt had Crohn's disease, but did not realize it while she was pregnant. . . . As a result [her son] was incredibly small and slow in physical development. . . . Through a long process and many years of struggle, Jack is now twenty-two and five feet two. I know my cousin blamed my aunt when he was younger and, as a result, she had a lot of guilt."

In many instances, and similar to the larger group of special educators in our study, the rural special educators we studied insisted that individuals with disabilities in their family were treated as every other member. Brittany explained, "My little niece has a communication disorder. We treat her just like everyone else and love to see her picture in the paper. We encourage her to do as much as she can." Theresa talked about her nephew with a disability, stating, "My nephew has a disability and my family treats him like they do any other grandchild. He does the same things that I have watched my other nieces and nephews do when they were his age."

Despite personal family experiences with disability in their biographies, the rural special educators we studied were uncertain about the impact disability might have on their present families.[3] But they report suspecting that the impact might be profound. Asked about how she would feel if she had a child with a disability, Theresa paused and then reflected, "From the experience of my brother and sister-in-law, the hardest thing for them was to accept that their son has a disability." Again, she paused in the discussion and then, with obvious relief, tells us that she is beyond the childbearing years. Similarly, both Paula and Betsy report being relieved when they knew that they had given birth to children without apparent disabilities. Paula explained, "I know it can happen to me. Every day I go to work and witness the life changes people have made due to having a child with disabilities." Yet she goes on to say, "If one of my girls had been born with a disability, I really have no idea how I would have felt."

Teaching as a "Professional"

In common with the larger group of students studied, the rural special educators asserted that active parent participation in school was important. Unlike many of the other students studied, however, the beliefs of the rural special educators did not appear to emanate from their personal family experiences. In fact, they described their own families as not especially involved in their schooling for various reasons. Paula, for example, explains that her parents went to her "athletic events" but were "pretty passive about her school" and expected her "to handle problems on her own." Similarly, Betsy says that her mother "would let us handle situations on our own" unless it "got out of hand," then she "would take over." Brittany describes her family as unable to attend "many school events" because they were "always working."

Also in common with the larger data sets, all seven rural special educators provided details about how they would be (or are) involved in their own children's schooling. Brittany, not yet a mother, explained that she "will be very involved with my kids' education." Similarly, Paula explained, "I think I am a little more involved [than her parents were] just because I am a teacher and I know what is going on. . . . I can call the teacher and we can get more to the point." Betsy, whose daughter is sixteen, wrote in her journal, "I am very active in my daughter's education," although her daughter also "lets me know when I should intervene."

---

3. This was similar to the response of the larger group of students we studied.

Although the rural special educators, like students in the larger data set, described themselves as very involved in their own children's education, they also described how they believed families and special educators should interact from a professional stance. From this viewpoint, they told us that teachers and families each have a distinct role. Communication, when it exists, is proceduralized and formal. They described open houses, report cards, and IEP meetings along with occasional telephone calls or notes home as their preferred ways to communicate with families. Brittany, who described herself as the most active in communicating with parents of all the students in the data set, communicated this proceduralized way of establishing relationships with families of her students: "On a routine basis I communicate with parents through the children's assignment notebook. I also make myself available for the parents an hour before and after school. Once a month I make a phone call to all my parents to discuss their child's progress. I also send home a checklist once every six weeks to let the parents know how their child is doing on their individualized education plan goals that we had set during the case conference."

The rural special educators did not differ from the larger group of students in our study in how they initially described the difficulties they had establishing partnerships with families. It was not their fault, they explained in journal entries and class discussions. School procedures prevented them from having much contact with the families of their students. In several instances, they described circumstances in which school administrators told them they were not to advocate for special education services or discuss student needs with families in order to avoid the costs involved in providing them. They were encouraged to "side with the school corporation rather than the family," according to Connie, and Greg explained that it was important to "cover for school officials when they screw up."

Paula explained that in her school, time constraints keep teachers from more active relationships with families. Both Betsy and Margaret reported feeling restricted in their interactions with the families of their students by the organization in which their school was embedded. The families of their students usually lived at a distance and this made face-to-face contact more difficult. But distance was not the only organizational barrier these two rural special educators reported. Betsy explained that administrators forbade her from contacting parents. Margaret described her disappointment when she learned after she was hired (and contrary to what she was told in her interview) that lack of funding prevented the school from involving families in the design of treatment plans for students with emotional and behavioral disabilities.

Two of the rural special educators we studied, however, described the climate of their school as favorable for family involvement. Their descriptions were notably different in this aspect from the rest of the rural special educators and the larger data sets. In the early childhood center in which Paula teaches, faculty and staff meet regularly to plan curriculum as a team. She reported that parents were "always around, working with us, planning what we'll do next. We have lots of volunteers and they just seem to be an ongoing part of who we are." Greg's school also seemed to promote family involvement. The description of his school in his journal described it as "friendly, rural, like the one I did my student teaching in Kentucky. It's a small, mostly neighborhood school." Under these circumstances both Greg and Paula reported that families were welcomed in their schools, and in most instances they thought the administrators they worked with encouraged them to establish partnerships with families in planning and implementing IEPs.

With the exception of Paula and Greg, data from the rural special educators were similar to the data from the larger group in that special educators reported that opportunity for parents to participate in school events was limited. Most reported that parents came to their school for athletic events, PTA meetings, and open houses. But the educators reported that parents were seldom invited to participate in program planning or evaluation and they were not encouraged to volunteer in classrooms, although they were asked to help their child at home.

Moving Toward Partnership

At the end of the course and in interviews conducted after the course was over, it was evident that the personnel preparation activities designed to support the development of family partnerships resonated strongly with the rural special educators. They described themselves as far more likely to actively involve families in program planning and classroom activities than previously. They also reported feeling better prepared to advocate for the families of the students they taught. In this regard, their data differs from the other special educators more in its intensity than its content. For example, Betsy wrote in her final paper, "It is IMPORTANT to connect with the families of my students." Paula told us in an interview that families and teachers are "essential parts of each other's lives." Brittany explained herself with conviction, writing in her final reflection, "I feel it is particularly important to develop and maintain a *strong* relationship with parents. Communication between parents and myself is *very essential* in my classroom."

The seven rural special educators also ended the course emphasizing their increased understanding about partnership itself in that they reported relishing opportunities to get to know the families of the students on a more personal level, a finding that differed from their peers in urban settings. Greg provides a good example of this, explaining in his final journal entry that when he sees the parents of his students "at McDonalds or in town . . . now I feel very comfortable in conversing with them about school or otherwise." He thinks this helps him discuss matters that were previously difficult to talk about with families, and he tells us in his final interview that he has come to view the families of the students he teaches as "semi-close acquaintances." He also tells us that he now calls families on a regular basis to "just talk about" school as often as he does to discuss specific problems. Finally, he acknowledges that families may have different attitudes than he does about what it means to work hard, spend money, or how to be an effective parent, and says, "That's okay, I think."

Like Greg, Theresa explained in her final interview that she now knows the project family as "friends," and she thinks there is value in this more equitable relationship. She tells us that she began the Family Project believing she knew the family well but quickly realized that there was a lot "going on for them I did not understand." Having spent time getting to know the family's perspective and their goals for their child, she has changed her perspective about the value in "just listening" to others talk. And she also says, "It's okay that they think differently than I do. . . . I know the common goal that both Rachel and I have is for Sam to finish high school. I know Sam wants this too. We will all work together to reach this goal."

As a final example, Paula, writing in her final paper, reported that "spending time with this family brings their perspective to a higher priority during my decision-making as a teacher." She thinks that she will continue to place a high priority on uncovering family priorities for their children when she engages with them to plan. This is new to her and she elaborates about it in her final interview, telling us that the Family Project allowed her to "form a real connection with Scott, my student, and his family. By [my] asking meaningful questions, Lisa [the mother] shared some priorities with me. As a result, we were able to set up some programs at school for Scott that helps their family."

Margaret has had fewer opportunities to interact with the families of the students she teaches than many of the other rural special educators in the study because many of her students' families live a considerable distance away.

Nevertheless, she provides us with evidence that she has different attitudes about her relationships with families. In the final class discussion, Margaret spoke about the barriers to partnerships with parents in her especially challenging setting as follows: "Because my students are in a residential setting and their parents live all over the state, currently there is very little participation by parents in their child's education. . . . In the past I might have only attributed it to a lack of caring on the part of the parents. However, I now believe that this lack of involvement is due to many factors. . . . After closely analyzing the level of participation, I believe that it could be due in part to my own interaction with and expectations of the parents." In her final interview, Margaret tells us about the influence that course activities have had on her as she reflects about the value of considering on biography and place: "I learned to delve into myself and figure out who I was and figure out what made me that way. It made me more complete. I can talk to my students and their parents better because I understand where I'm coming from. . . . It's about reflection."

In addition to her growing awareness of the potential assets in the community for meeting student and family needs, Brittany ended the course anxious to bring about more systemic change at her school, as demonstrated by her extensive list of ideas about how to do this in her final paper. In general, data from the rural special educators and the larger data set strongly suggested that study participants ended the course more likely to advocate for families and to attempt to bring about change in school procedures on their behalf. In his final paper Greg discussed talking about an upcoming IEP meeting with a family. He reported urging them to be aware of their son's needs and to protect needed services. He reflected on this in his final interview and commented that he is far less likely to "go along with that." Recalling his comments in earlier class discussions, Greg laughed and concluded, "We sometimes cover for school officials . . . even if we don't agree with what they have done. I didn't do that in this case . . . I don't think I will again."

Lessons Learned

Our study of rural special educators provided evidence that the personnel preparation activities we employed were effective in supporting the development of family partnerships. Across the data sets, there was substantial evidence that the personal experiences of rural special educators related to biography and place influenced their views of parent-professional partnerships. Their beliefs and cultural values about families, schools, and communities were evident in the stories they told of their lives. Often these beliefs helped to explain how they viewed families, schools, and communities and why partnerships with families were sometimes problematic. Valuing hard work, self-reliance, and faith, they had difficulty understanding other perspectives, and this influenced their practice in ways they did not always recognize. For example, they had been taught a degree of shame associated with financial difficulties and they were reluctant to discuss these matters. This made it difficult for them to acknowledge that families may struggle with the added financial burdens associated with disability and they avoided discussions about it both in class and with families. They also seldom acknowledged that lack of resources might interfere with a family's ability to help their child with a disability and tended to think that families could overcome obstacles if they worked hard enough to help their child. It was interesting to note that Betsy, who provided the exception to this common pattern of response, reported that financial issues were openly discussed in her family. Betsy also appeared to be the most aware of the likely influence of financial difficulties on families and was most likely to raise it as an issue in class discussions.

There were other ways that personal family experiences tended to influence how the rural special educators thought about families. Because they valued self-reliance and were reluctant to seek help outside their family, they had a degree of disregard for families who needed to seek help from others. Although they were reluctant to admit that this attitude might affect how they interacted with families, after considering it they acknowledged that it probably did not facilitate partnerships. Similarly, their ideas about the value of hard work and faith sometimes resulted in assumptions that families were not doing enough with their children when student progress was slow. Class activities provided the impetus to examine their beliefs and consider how they had acquired them. As they became more aware of their own cultural assumptions, they were also better able to consider how their beliefs may work to hinder or facilitate family partnerships.

Initially the rural special educators we studied provided examples of what Theobald and Howley (1998) and Graue (2005) describe as the professionalization of teachers. Acting within traditional, role-based boundaries, they described relationships with families in which they maintained a degree of distance. In doing this, they unknowingly undermined the balance needed for reciprocity in the relationship. Through course activities, they were able to examine and challenge the roles they typically assumed with families, in essence providing an opportunity for role reconstruction.

Moving from teacher to student during the Family Project provided the opportunity for prospective professionals to "deprofessionalize" the relationship. These field-based experiences allowed the special educators to engage with families on a more personal level, infusing what Theobald and Howley (1998) refer to as humanity and context into their professional preparation. The significance of physical and psychological proximity in breaking down role-based barriers is clear and explains why merely reading about families (in a case study, for example) is insufficient to bring about change. The data suggest that greater physical proximity in face-to-face interactions leads to increased psychological proximity, facilitating a breakdown of traditional roles. Through the process of getting to know families, perceptions about families often changed and the special educators we studied assumed a more active role in their relationships with families, compelled to take action or advocate for them if needed.

The closer relationship the study participants were able to assume with their project families also afforded them the opportunity to examine preconceived notions and misconceptions they held. This was especially valuable for the rural special educators who reported that they lacked experience with diversity. Under these circumstances, the Family Project provided an important venue to challenge their assumptions about how families "should be," and acted to broaden their tolerance for families who differed from their own. But it is important to note that only Greg and Brittany elected to work with families who differed from their own in substantive ways. In this way, the rural special educators did not differ from the other students studied or in the course at large. Although they were urged by their instructors to pick diverse families to work with for their projects, they seldom did so, usually explaining that the time commitments required of the project made it necessary for them to pick a family that they could easily access (in their neighborhood, for example). As most were working full-time as special educators and also had families of their own, no doubt time was a problem for them. But providing students with access to diverse families is clearly crucial for personnel preparation, given the increasing diversity of students they will teach. In this regard, it should be noted that the definition of diversity must include consideration of the full range in which students and their families may vary, including family structure and membership, as well as disability status and cultural or ethnic background.

The attitudes of the rural special educators about disability are puzzling. In their biographies they tended to minimize the impact of disability on their family of origin, yet they acknowledged that, should they experience disability in their current family, the impact was quite likely to be profound. They seemed unaware of this apparent contradiction early on in the class. We noted that the rural special educators we studied initially lacked ongoing opportunities to interact with the families of their students, save the usual parent conferences and IEP meetings. Under these circumstances, it may be that their experience as special educators provided them with an idea of the challenges involved in parenting a child with a disability, without providing them with an opportunity to appreciate the rewards. Invariably, the opportunity to view the daily life experiences of families with disabilities and discuss those experiences during the Family Project helped them acquire a more balanced view of the impact of disability on the family.

Theobald and Howley's (1998) description of the university's role in professionalization provides another explanation for the rural special educators' attitudes about disability. In their description of the university's role in the professionalization of teachers, the authors point to the emphasis on rationality in the university's preparation of professionals. A knowledge base is taught that is common to the profession, and problems are reduced so that they can be readily understood. Meanwhile, rationality tends to "diminish the scope and force of such enduring human concerns as justice, beauty and even truth. In this process, the relevance of intellect to emotion—to compassion, empathy and delight—is broken and often denied" (153). The professional stance our students initially assumed with families suggests that they had already been socialized into thinking about professional problems in the ways Theobald and Howley describe. Their difficulty relating to the complexities of family experiences related to a child with a disability illustrates how an emphasis on professionalism acts to "subvert intellect and feeling" (155). Under these circumstances, the importance of direct experience with families as a means to teach prospective special educators how to establish family partnerships can scarcely be overemphasized.

While the rural special educators we studied valued hard work and described an active role for themselves as special educators, this did not correspond to active involvement with families in the beginning of the course. Frequently, they explained this by describing school settings that prevented them from being more active. These sorts of explanations were less common by the end of the course as they increasingly took responsibility for assuming the initiative in relationships with families. In this way, examining their own perspectives about families helped them cultivate the ethic of responsibility for the benefit of others in the rural communities in which they teach. While this falls far short of assuming the responsibility for the health and well-being of the community, at large as Theobald and Howley (1998) describe it, it is an important first step and may be quite important in establishing authentic partnerships with their students' families. Under these circumstances, cultivating relationships with families made it more possible for them to have discussions about topics that before may have been uncomfortable for both the special educators and the families.

It is important to note that the schools in which the rural special educators we studied worked differed in school climate. There was evidence that some rural schools appeared more connected to the community than others, and when this was the case, the special educators viewed family-professional partnerships as easier to establish and maintain. This speaks to the power associated with renewing community within schools and suggests it as a powerful way that schools can support special education practice. We take note of our data in the context of Beeson and Strange's (2000, 84) description of Indiana as a state where "consolidation has left many large rural schools." No doubt school size and the consolidation of rural schools have had a deleterious impact on school climate. It may be that many of Indiana's rural schools have lost the advantages that Theobald and his colleagues suggest are important for renewing school-community connections.

But it is also important to note that the sort of school climate likely to be favorable for family partnerships was only described in the data from rural special educators, lending support to the assertion by Theobald and his colleagues that rural schools are places where the renewal of community might begin. It is also heartening that, as the course ended, the rural special educators were more likely to recognize assets available within the community for families than were the special educators from less rural places, despite the fact that rural communities may lack many of the formal community resources typically described as central to multidisciplinary practice in special education and more frequently found in more urban and suburban settings.

The stories told to us by the rural special educators we studied often illustrated the impact of school reform on the rural communities in which they lived and taught. In particular, the loss of teacher autonomy was widely lamented throughout course discussions and students' written work. In schools where the numbers of students with disabilities enrolled required that their test scores be examined as data disaggregated from the rest of the school's scores, the pressure for special educators to conform to standardized curriculum in an effort to raise the test scores of students with disabilities was especially intense. They see themselves as unable to meet the individualized learning needs of their students as a result, and report feeling overwhelmed by the demands placed on them. Under these circumstances, they report having too much to do and family-professional relationships therefore suffer. These circumstances are of concern and have been noted elsewhere (Butera 2005; Cochran-Smith and Lytle 2006; Gallagher 2006). Particularly troubling is the manner in which increased accountability envisions teachers' work as technical, "divorced from their decision making processes, ideas, beliefs, theorizing and analyses" (Cochran-Smith and Lytle 2006, 685).

We have noted the relative absence of commentary in our data about the broader economic, social, cultural, and political forces at work in the rural communities in which the special educators we studied teach and live. Their silence suggests that they are relatively unaware of how the forces of globalization help to define the circumstances of their work. We also acknowledge that we were not purposeful in eliciting consideration of these important factors influencing school change. Rather, like our students in the process of reflecting and interpreting their experiences, we were guided more by their immediate experiences than by any broader understanding of the global realignment of work in general, with teaching as a part of a larger process (Helsby 1999; Ingersoll 2003; Robertson 1997). We have challenged our own assumptions as a result and are considering ways to expand our activities so that students have opportunities to examine how economic, social, and political forces influence schools locally and how change might occur. Using reflection in a macro sense and expanding the discussion beyond teaching strategies and classroom and school practice will be important if we are to help teachers participate in renewing connections between schools and communities.

In this way, our data serve as a commentary on the role of personnel preparation in bringing about change that can begin in rural communities as Theobald (1997) suggests. We believe that the lessons we have learned here have broad implications for the professional preparation of others who work with families, particularly in rural communities. In this chapter, we note that in many ways the perspectives of the rural special educators we studied did not differ from those of special educators from urban or suburban settings (although we also made note of instances in which they did). Therefore, heeding the admonitions of Coladarci (2007, 3), we hesitate to "speak unequivocally to the rural circumstance." We also emphasize that cultural characteristics are seldom static and vary greatly, depending on the individual and circumstances.

The point is that an individual's culturally embedded experiences influence the way that person understands the world. To effect change, it is essential to help teachers and other professionals examine their assumptions and beliefs about those with whom they work (Butera 2005; Kalyanpur and Harry 1999; Turnbull et al. 2006). If rural schools are to play a role in the renewal of community as Theobald and his colleagues envision, personnel preparation must be purposeful in helping those who work in them understand the broader forces that work to change schools and communities. Such discussion will no doubt better prepare rural schools to renew the connection to community. Doing so will ultimately support family-professional partnerships in special education.

Appendix: Brief Descriptions of the Special Educators in the Study

Paula, a teacher and administrator in an early childhood center, has eleven years of teaching experience. Her undergraduate education was in early childhood education with a minor in special education.

Margaret is a teacher in an alternative program for junior/senior high school students with emotional behavioral disorders, many of whom come from outside the immediate community. She has eight years of teaching experience entirely in this setting.

Brittany is a teacher certified in elementary education and is completing course work to be fully certified in special education. She teaches fourth- and fifth-grade students with learning disabilities and mild mental retardation in a resource room in a large rural school. She has six years of teaching experience.

Greg is in his second year of teaching. Although he attended college several years ago, he worked in a factory after graduating because it paid more than teaching and he had difficulty finding a teaching position near his home. He teaches functional life skills in an elementary school setting to students with moderate or multiple disabilities.

Connie has been a teacher in a middle school for the past four years. She teaches in a seventh-grade resource room for literature and English and co-teaches in an inclusion class for three periods. The majority of the students she works with have learning disabilities or mild mental retardation.

Betsy has over fifteen years of teaching experience. Currently she teaches children with emotional and behavioral disorders in a correctional facility and is completing course work for full certification in special education.

Theresa has ten years of teaching experience and works at an alternative high school, having taught both high school and junior high school previously. She received her undergraduate degree in elementary education and is pursuing a master's degree in special education.

References

Ayalon, A. 2003. Why is rural education missing from multicultural education textbooks? *Educational Forum* 68 (Fall), 24–31.

Beeson, E., and M. Strange. 2000. Why rural matters: The need for every state to take action on rural education. *Journal of Research in Rural Education* 16 (2), 63–140.

Browder, D., F. Spooner, R. Algozzine, L. Algrim-Delzell, C. Flowers, and M. Karvonen. 2003. What we know and need to know about alternative assessment. *Exceptional Children* 70 (1), 45–61.

Butera, G. 2005. Collaboration in the context of Appalachia: The case of Cassie. *Journal of Special Education* 39 (2), 106–16.

Butera, G., and M. Dunn. 2005. The case of cases in preparing special educators for rural schools. *Rural Special Education Quarterly* 24 (2), 22–27.

Butera, G., S. Eckes, R. Weir, and V. Vasquez. 2007. At the crossroads: A case study of the impact of standards-based reform on special education. Paper presented at the Annual Conference of the American Educational Research Association, Chicago, Ill.

Butera, G., K. Matuga, and S. Riley. 1999. Doing as we do: Guiding student development in family-focused early intervention using family stories and parent co-instruction. *Infant-Toddler Intervention* 9 (2), 107–24.

Christenson, S. L. 2004. The family-school partnership: An opportunity to promote the learning competence of all students. *School Psychology Review* 33 (1), 83–104.

Christenson, S. L., and S. M. Sheridan. 2001. *Schools and families: Creating essential connections for learning.* New York: Guilford Press.

Cochran-Smith, M., and S. Lytle. 2006. Troubling images of teaching in No Child Left Behind. *Harvard Educational Review* 73 (4), 668–97.

Coladarci, T. 2007. Improving the yield of rural education research: An editor's swan song. *Journal of Research in Rural Education* 22 (3), 1–9. Retrieved March 1, 2008, from http://jrre.psu.edu/articles/22-3.pdf.

Dworkin, A. G. 1997. Coping with reform: The intermix of teacher morale, teacher burnout, and teacher accountability. In B. J. Biddle, T. L. Good, and I. F. Goodson, eds., *International handbooks of teachers and teaching,* 459–98. Dordrecht, Netherlands: Kluwer.

Epstein, J. L. 1995. School/family/community partnerships: Caring for children we share. *Phi Delta Kappan* 76 (9), 701–12.

Fore, C., C. Martin, and W. N. Bender. 2002. Teacher burnout in special education: The causes and recommended solutions. *High School Journal* 86 (1), 36–44.

Gallagher, J. J. 2006. *Driving change in special education*. Baltimore: Brookes Publishing.

Graue, E. 2005. Theorizing and describing preservice teachers' images of families and schooling. *Teachers College Record. Special Issue: A Symposium on the Implications of the Scientific Research in Education Report for Qualitative Inquiry* 107 (1), 157–85.

Hanson, M. J., P. J. Beckman, E. Horn, J. Marquadt, S. R. Sandall, D. Greig, and E. Brennan. 2000. Entering preschool: Family and professional experiences in this transition process. *Journal of Early Intervention* 23 (4), 279–93.

Harry, B., N. Allen, and M. McLaughlin. 1995. Communication versus compliance: African-American parents' involvement in special education. *Exceptional Children* 61 (4), 364–77.

Helsby, G. 1999. *Changing teachers' work*. Buckingham: Open University Press.

Hill, N. E., and L. C. Taylor. 2004. Parental school involvement and children's academic achievement: Pragmatics and issues. *Current Directions in Psychological Science* 13 (4), 161–64.

Hoover-Dempsey, K. V., J. M. T. Walker, K. P. Jones, and R. P. Reed. 2002. Teachers Involving Parents (TIP): Results from an in-service teacher education program for enhancing parental involvement. *Teaching and Teacher Education* 18 (7), 843–67.

Ingersoll, R. M. 2003. *Who controls teachers' work? Power and accountability in America's schools*. Cambridge: Harvard University Press.

Kalyanpur, M., and B. Harry. 1999. *Culture in special education: Building reciprocal family-professional relationships*. Baltimore: Brookes Publishing.

Kea, C. D., and C. A. Utley. 1998. To teach me is to know me. *Journal of Special Education* 32 (1), 44–47.

Kossar, K., K. Mithchem, and B. Ludlow. 2005. No Child Left Behind: A national study of its impact on special education in rural schools. *Rural Special Education Quarterly* 24 (1), 3–8.

Lareau, A., and E. M. Horvat. 1999. Moments of social inclusion and exclusion: Race, class, and cultural capital in family-school relationships. *Sociology of Education* 72 (1), 37–53.

LeCompte, H. M., and A. G. Dworkin. 1991. *Giving up on school: Student dropouts and teacher burnout*. Thousand Oaks, Calif.: Corwin Press.

Lightfoot, D. 2004. "Some parents just don't care": Decoding the meanings of parental involvement in urban schools. *Urban Education* 39 (1), 91–107.

Ludlow, B. 2003. Riding fences. *Rural Special Education Quarterly* 21 (4), 28–33.

National Center for Educational Statistics. 2003–4. Status of education in rural America. Retrieved October 7, 2007, from http://nces.ed.gov/pubs2007/2007040.pdf.

Provasnik, S., A. KewalRamani, M. M. Coleman, L. Gilbertson, W. Herring, and Q. Xie. 2007. *Status of education in rural America*. Washington, D.C.: National Center for Education Statistics.

Robertson, S. 1997. Restructuring teachers' labor: "Troubling" post-Fordisms. In B. J. Biddle, T. Good, and F. Goodson, eds., *International handbook on teachers and teaching*, 621–70. Dordrecht, Netherlands: Kluwer.

Soodak, L. C., and E. J. Erwin. 2000. Valued member or tolerated participant: Parents' experiences in inclusive early childhood settings. *Journal of the Association for Persons with Severe Handicaps* 25 (1), 29–41.

Summers, J. A., L. Hoffman, J. Marquis, A. Turnbull, D. Poston, and L. L. Nelson. 2005. Measuring the quality of family—professional partnerships in special education services. *Exceptional Children* 72 (1), 65–81.

Theobald, P. 1997. *Teaching the commons: Place, pride, and the renewal of community*. Boulder: Westview.

———. 2002. Preparing teachers for our nation's rural schools. *Basic Education: A Monthly Forum for Analysis and Comment* 16 (5), 7–14.

Theobald, P., and C. Howley. 1998. Public purpose and the preparation of teachers for rural schools. *The Teacher Educator* 33 (3), 150–64.

Theobald, P., and P. Nachtigal. 1995 Culture, community, and the promise of rural education. *Phi Delta Kappan* 77 (2), 26–33.

Thomson, S. J., R. F. Quenemoen, and M. L. Thurlow. 2003. The status of large-scale assessment practices for students with disabilities in rural America. *Rural Special Education Quarterly* 22 (4), 3–9.

Turnbull, A., R. Turnbull, E. Erwin, and L. Soodak. 2006. *Families, professionals, and exceptionality: Positive outcomes through partnerships and trust* (5th ed.). Upper Saddle River, N.J.: Pearson.

Valli, L., and D. Buese. 2007. The changing roles of teachers in an era of high-stakes accountability. *American Educational Research Journal* 44 (3), 519–58.

Yell, M. L., J. G. Shriner, and A. Katsiyannis. 2006. Individuals with disabilities education improvement act of 2004 and IDEA regulations of 2006: Implications for educators, administrators, and teacher trainers. *Focus on Exceptional Children* 39 (1), 1–24.

CONCLUSION:

ECONOMICS, COMMUNITY, AND RURAL EDUCATION:
RETHINKING THE NATURE OF ACCOUNTABILITY
IN THE TWENTY-FIRST CENTURY

Kai A. Schafft

One of the principal dilemmas for rural schools and communities—and a central theme woven through the chapters of this book—is how local identities and the lived realities of rural communities are reconciled against the backdrop of global social, cultural, political, and economic change. As we note in the introduction to this volume, this is not a new dilemma, but rather one with roots extending as far back as the late nineteenth and early twentieth centuries (see, e.g., Cubberley 1922; Sherman and Henry 1933; Theobald 1995; Tyack 1972; Vidich and Bensman 1968). Then, as now, education was understood as a primary point of policy intervention for addressing the needs of rural people and communities, both of which, more often than not, were seen as backward and deficient within a rapidly changing and urban-oriented society (see, e.g., the chapters by Butera and Humphreys, Howley and Howley, and Theobald and Wood in this volume). Then, as now, public policy enacted through educational reform pushed for greater expert control, standardization, and professionalization within schools. And then, as now, there was substantial debate over the role of education and its broader social purposes. As sociologist Newell Sims wrote in 1946, "There has been much disagreement among students of country life over the aims of rural education. Opinion has revolved around two poles, one holding the school to be an agency for conserving country life, the other for making it the agency for adjustment to general society" (537).

This, for many scholars, has represented the primary and longest-standing tension of educational reform with regard to rural schools and communities.

As Kannapel and DeYoung argued over half a century later, echoing Sims's observations, "At the heart of the (rural school) problem is the conflict over the purpose of schooling, with state and national reform leaders typically calling for schools to prepare students to contribute to national interests, while rural education scholars (and probably many rural parents) believe rural schools should also serve local community interests" (1999, 72). This tension is ultimately one of accountability. To whom is education accountable? Whose purposes does it serve?

Sims goes on to conclude, "Since many born and bred in the country are certain to migrate to the city, since the country itself is being urbanized and integrated with the wider world, and since vocational training is being provided by extra-school agencies, it would seem that the country school's aim should indeed be the fullest development of the child's personality in relation to the general culture" (537).

Sims's "general culture" in the mid-twentieth century was, of course, a thinly veiled reference to "urban society," his conclusion a tacit acknowledgement that the spatial and cultural subsumption of the rural by the urban was a fait accompli. And in many ways this subsumption has indeed seemed nearly inevitable as schools have become ever more distanced from their communities by school consolidation,[1] the standardization of curricula (regardless of the particularization of local context), and the radical restructuring of education through high-stakes testing mandates such that, as one administrator from a school in rural Pennsylvania once bluntly told me, "if it doesn't raise test scores, it's just not relevant to my job."

Now Sims's "general culture" is more likely to be understood as not just urban but also *global*, and not just cultural in nature but also implicitly *economic* as the role and purpose of education has drifted ever more in line with national priorities and the requirements of the global marketplace, and ever further from the needs, contexts, and lived realities of local communities (Budge 2006; Corbett 2008a; DeYoung 1995; Engel 2000; Eppley 2009; Foster 2004; Gruenewald 2006; Gruenewald and Smith 2008; Howley 1991; Jo 2005;

---

1. In 1930 there were approximately 130,000 school districts in the United States. By 2000, due to consolidation, that number had shrunk to 15,000 (Lyson 2002). Consolidation efforts continue despite evidence from multiple sources suggesting that the expected efficiencies and economies of scale argued to result from consolidation in many or most cases do not bear out (Bard, Gardener, and Wieland 2006). At the time of this writing governor Edward Rendell of Pennsylvania has proposed a legislative commission to examine the possibilities of further reducing Pennsylvania's 501 school districts to 100, a move that would increase the average district student enrollment size from 3,480 to 17,400.

Spring 1998; Theobald 2006, 2009; Theobald and Rochon 2006; Woodrum 2004).

As the briefing book from the 2005 National Education Summit on High Schools somewhat alarmingly states, "High school is now the front line in America's battle to remain competitive on the increasingly competitive international stage" (Achieve Incorporated and the National Governors Association 2005, 9). This language mirrors the same discourse and imagery used over twenty years earlier in *A Nation at Risk*, the report issued by the National Commission for Excellence in Education, which stated, "If an unfriendly foreign power had attempted to impose on America the mediocre educational performance that exists today, we might well have viewed it as an act of war" (1983, 7).[2] Again, to whom is education accountable? Whose purposes does it serve?

Education and the Social Technology of Economic Narratives

Foster (2004, 179) argues that "much of our social reality is constructed through established narratives. Such narratives enter into mainstream consciousness because those who tell them are the inheritors of power. The power displayed, in turn, reinforces the truth of those narratives." Finlayson and colleagues have referred to these narratives as "social technologies" (2005, 519), sociocultural discursive mechanisms that structure what might be imagined as possible. These mechanisms play a direct role in shaping social processes by providing particular conceptual and discursive possibilities, and denying others. They act to naturalize and transform to "common sense" what are in fact far from neutral positions. The hegemonic narrative of the late twentieth and early twenty-first centuries has been that of neoliberalism and the language of the "free market," a narrative that has fundamentally shaped global economic and social systems as well as that of education itself.

Neoliberalism can be understood as a framework of social and economic practices based around an interrelated set of assumptions. Among these are the following: Society is structured by the instrumental choices made by rational, economically maximizing individuals who are guided principally by self-interest. At the aggregate level, the sum of individual choices and behaviors, when

2. See Berliner and Biddle (1996) and Gabbard (2003) for critiques of *A Nation at Risk* and the crisis narratives it employs. See Saltman and Gabbard (2003) for a discussion of neoliberalism, the militarization of civil society, and the relationship to education.

unconstrained by government regulation,[3] result in the most efficient distribution of labor and resources, and consequently the most efficient means of creating wealth.[4]

Hence, the well-being of society is most effectively achieved by enhancing entrepreneurial individualism and maximizing individual freedom of choice vis-à-vis privatization and "the ongoing and unrestricted exchange of goods and services among producers and consumers in competition with each other" (Engel 2000, 19). These social and economic practices are dependent on institutional structures at both national and international levels in the form of public policy, trade agreements, and so forth that not only create but *guarantee* strong private property rights, and therefore protect the economic free market (Harvey 2005). Within this paradigm, the role of education then is to produce members of a labor force who have the flexibility, adaptability, and mobility to respond to the shifting imperatives of the national-level and indeed *global* labor market and economy (Apple 2001; Corbett 2007; Jo 2005; Spring 1998). The function of education is therefore largely structured around the economic roles that students will play later in life (Theobald 2006).

Market-based transactions require access to information, necessitating the creation, analysis, and dissemination of large quantities of data (Harvey 2005; Leys 2003). Within education this translates into the dependence on standardized, quantifiable indices that can be used to assess and evaluate the performance of educators and educational institutions (Corbett 2008b; Downey, von Hipple, and Hughes 2008). Educational reform efforts emphasizing market-based solutions thus privilege regulatory standards, high-stakes testing (e.g., in the case of the United States, the No Child Left Behind Act), strict accountability measures, school choice, and privatization. This, in turn, creates strong incentives for schools to show "improvement" vis-à-vis these indices, indices

---

3. Under neoliberalism, the primary role of the state is to create and protect the institutional structures that guarantee the proper functioning of markets, as well as to establish new markets where previously they did not exist or existed only in a weak form. This includes social/collective goods such as health care, social security, welfare, education, and the environment (e.g., the issuing of "pollution vouchers") (Harvey 2005; Polanyi 1957; Speth 2008).

4. These assumptions are in large part rooted in Adam Smith's notion of the "invisible hand" of the market. Smith writes, "By directing that industry in such a manner as its produce may be of the greatest value, [the individual] intends only his own gain, and he is in this, as in many other cases, led by an invisible hand to promote an end which was no part of his intention. . . . By pursuing his own interest he frequently promotes that of society more effectually than when he really intends to promote it" (1796, 423). See Finlayson and colleagues (2005) for a critique of the "invisible hand" as an organizing metaphor for understanding economy and society.

that function as *proxies* for academic achievement but quickly become fetish-ized as academic outcomes in and of themselves.[5] In the United States under No Child Left Behind, educators and administrators face unprecedented pres-sure—both formal and informal—to regulate their actions in strict accordance with testing and assessment mandates. Failure to "perform" can result in sig-nificant institutional penalties (e.g., school reorganization or closure), informal public censure (see, e.g., the Schafft, Killeen, and Morrissey chapter, this vol-ume), or the risk of enrollment decline as students and their parents (acting as individual utility maximizers) weigh the option of leaving for higher perform-ing schools.

This has radically altered the role and mission of educators and educational administrators. The notion of the school as a community institution implies that the school and those who work within it have some fundamental moral or social accountability to the community itself (Furman 2004). In fact, some of the earliest rural school reform efforts, such as those advocated by Theodore Roosevelt's Country Life Commission around the turn of the twentieth century, were based around enhancing the connection between rural education and the lived realities of rural life, ensuring that curricula maximized the chances that rural areas would retain their young people.[6] Other earlier qualitative and eth-nographic studies have likewise demonstrated how deeply embedded schools are within the structure of rural communities (Peshkin 1978; Vidich and Bens-man 1968).

Educational reforms shaped by neoliberal narratives however, have dramati-

5. See Schoenfeld (2006) for an illuminating discussion of these issues. Schoenfeld worked briefly as a content advisor for the U.S. Department of Education's Institute of Education Sci-ences What Works Clearinghouse (WWC), a database of educational programs and products that, through the use of "rigorous" experimental or quasi-experimental studies, were found to be educationally "effective" (that is, they raised standardized test scores). Schoenfeld was asked to help assemble a protocol for WWC staff to evaluate mathematics curricula at the middle school level. Raising substantive questions in the protocol about the narrowness of WWC criteria in evaluating and determining educational "effectiveness," Schoenfeld's work was ultimately cen-sored by the Institute of Education Sciences. See also Gruenewald's (2006) commentary.

6. While the recommendations made by the Country Life Commission were sensitive to rural context, they were no less oriented toward "expert" social engineering than the economic agendas of education one hundred years hence. They promoted efforts to enhance the social and economic vibrancy of rural communities, but were also motivated by the desire to curb patterns of selective rural-to-urban migration that some feared would leave rural communities, as one commentator said at the time, "fished out ponds populated chiefly by bullheads and suckers" (Theobald 1997, 104). As Corbett has argued, rural schooling has long been an assimilatory proj-ect, conducting "the missionary work of cultural elevation" in rurality's "backwards space" (2007, 258).

cally weakened this relationship, and along with it reconfigured the nature of accountability. As Corbett (2007) has written elsewhere, this reconfiguration is connected to "the idea that education is fundamentally about learning things that someone, somewhere decides to be important. . . . In the end, accountability will come to mean that children and teachers will be forced to render accounts to distant, powerful others, not to their parents, their communities and even to themselves" (273). Educators and administrators must answer to the test, not to the community.

Structurally, these reform measures have not only changed the roles played by educators and administrators, but similarly have weakened schools themselves along with the school-community bond through school closures; the cutting of "nonessential" (i.e., untested) classes such as art, history, and physical education in the effort to increase math and reading scores; decreased local control and local parental involvement; and the implementation of curricula disembedded from place, local context, and community experience (Nichols and Berliner 2007). These changes have also transformed educators and educational leaders from autonomous, responsive practitioners of a living craft to technocrats enacting sets of prescribed, rationalized tasks. That is, "if it doesn't raise test scores, it's just not relevant to my job."

While it is ironic given the comprehensive educational reforms based around achievement and accountability, it is also perhaps little wonder that the interest that high school students have placed in their studies—as well as the perceived relevance of these studies to their later lives—has steadily declined in the last few decades. An annual survey of U.S. high school seniors conducted through the University of Michigan found that 34.6 percent of students in 1983 reported that their courses were "quite or very interesting," while 19.8 percent found their courses "slightly or very dull." By 2005 only 21.2 percent found their courses "quite or very interesting" and 33.3 percent found their courses "slightly or very dull." In 1983 over 40 percent of seniors found their course work "often or always" meaningful. By 2005 that figure had dropped to 27.5 percent. In 1983 50.5 percent of high school seniors believed their schooling would be "quite or very important" later in life, while by 2005 that figure had dropped to 37.1 (Wraga 2009).

Building School and Community: A Counter-Example

As nearly all the chapters in this volume suggest, rural schools hold enormous symbolic, cultural, and economic importance to the communities in which they are located. Yet schools cannot survive long if the communities they serve are experiencing unchecked economic decline and social fragmentation. Therefore it is in the best interests of both school and community to work toward mutual enhancement and well-being (Schafft, Alter, and Bridger 2006; Schafft and Harmon, forthcoming).

Despite the multiple ways in which the social, cultural, and economic histories—and *fates*—of rural schools and communities are intertwined, however, educational reform of the type we have discussed has increasingly led rural school administrators to see community improvement and educational improvement as competing and opposing priorities: a zero-sum game. While community-building efforts may hold *intrinsic* value to educators and administrators, if the bottom line is the test score (and this may be particularly the case in smaller, resource-poor rural communities where low test scores are more likely, and consequently pose greater threats), community building may seem like an unwise expenditure of time and effort. Instead, many educators are inclined under these circumstances to operate conservatively, hedge their bets, and focus instead on academic assessments (Nichols and Berliner 2007).

Regardless of the institutional rationalities that militate against active school-community engagement, multiple exceptions exist, although they too often go unnoticed and unrecognized. These exceptions are worth paying attention to, though, because they provide instructive counter-examples and demonstrate how rural school and community improvement can be viewed not as a zero-sum game, but rather as *complementary and fundamentally interconnected* priorities. They also provide critical educational leadership models at a time when institutional circumstances would seem to pose dangerous opportunity costs for pedagogical risk taking.

The Center on Rural Education and Communities (CREC) within Penn State University's College of Education was conceived as both a research and outreach effort to focus explicitly on the intersection between rural schools and communities. As part of this effort, and in collaboration with the Pennsylvania Association of Rural and Small Schools, a statewide nonprofit organization that advocates and lobbies for rural schools, the center issues an annual Building Community Through Rural Education award. This award recognizes a rural school or district that has distinguished itself through strengthening education while building connections between school and community. Each year CREC receives multiple applications from schools and districts across the commonwealth that describe the many ways in which rural schools and communities coordinate efforts for mutual benefit. Local needs, community identity, and

area resources nearly always directly shape these efforts. They are neither standardized, nor do they fit prescribed formulas for community building. Rather,
they are tailored, necessarily, to local context and circumstance.

St. Marys Area Middle School, the 2008 Building Community award winner,
is one such example. Located in the heavily forested, sparsely populated north-
central part of Pennsylvania, the school has an enrollment of about 550 students
and is situated on a multiple-acre tract, much of it wooded. There are strong
traditions of hunting and fishing, and forestry provides an important part of
the area's economic base. Because of this, it is little surprise that a significant
share of the school's efforts and activities reflect this identity and contain a
strong emphasis on natural sciences and environmental stewardship.

Over the past several years, St. Marys Middle School has spearheaded a set
of coordinated environmental education initiatives that draw from local context and dovetail with curricula in ways that speak directly to the lived local
experience. The centerpiece is the development of a regional Environmental
Learning Center funded through a series of grants, sponsorship, and student-
led fund-raisers, in many cases the result of partnerships developed with local
and state organizations like the Pennsylvania Conservation Corps, the Pennsylvania Department of Environmental Protection, the Workforce Investment
Board Youth Council, and the Pennsylvania Fish and Boat Commission.

Originating from microbiology lessons conducted in a stream flowing
through the school's campus, it occurred to St. Marys educators that there was
an important untapped opportunity to adapt the science curriculum in ways
that would take direct advantage of the natural environment literally at the
school's doorstep and immediately familiar to its students. Several teachers,
with the support and encouragement of the principal and the district superintendent, began plans to construct an aquaculture facility on the middle school
campus.

Raising funds from a variety of local- and state-level sources and making
use of student and community volunteer labor, the school designed and constructed what has become a student-managed trout nursery that currently
raises and releases over one thousand trout into local streams each year. Integrated into the local curriculum (as well as responsive to state academic standards), students are completely responsible for managing water quality,
feeding, stocking, controlling for disease, and monitoring the production of
effluent. Students record data on trout health, feeding habits, stress levels, and
appearance, and they assist in maintaining tanks and fish raceways.

The aquaculture project has also been coupled with the building of an all-season outdoor classroom and accompanying greenhouse complex. The construction of the complex was supported in part through a grant sponsoring a crew of local at-risk youth employed through the Pennsylvania Conservation Corps. The school has since created additional youth-employment opportunities during the summer months at the site through the Regional Workforce Investment Board.

The greenhouse complex was developed as a natural extension of the aquaculture project and provides a hands-on opportunity for students to investigate hydroponics and aquaponics as a means of addressing water quality. Through the greenhouse complex, students discharge nitrogen-rich wastewater from the trout nursery. This wastewater then is filtered through soils that in turn support the plants raised in the greenhouse. The students are further involved in efforts to use this waste water to grow niche plant species that can be used in the environmental remediation of acid drainage at local mining sites, an effort coordinated with the Elk County Conservation District and a local campus of Penn State University.

There are additional plans to expand the greenhouse efforts in the form of an intergenerational gardening project linking middle school students with seniors from the community who have expertise in horticulture to create additional community mentoring opportunities. "Many within our senior population were born or raised on farms and many others had productive subsistence gardens for most of their lives," the award application materials stated. "Transition to assisted living facilities often means that they must give up their gardens. We will link these 'master gardeners' with our eager adolescents in a program that cultivates the best in both groups."

The Environmental Learning Center additionally has a strong focus on alternative and renewable energy. A grant-funded 1.5 kilowatt wind turbine helps to provide energy used in the outdoor classroom and for the trout nursery. This is coupled with three mobile solar labs for use in science instruction. Additional fixed solar panels are planned for the outdoor classroom, with plans for students to monitor the output, which will be used to power the batteries for a "green" golf cart used for transport across the school campus. The middle school is also pursuing plans to produce biodiesel from waste cooking oil.

In total, it is difficult not to be struck by these efforts—how they address community issues in a variety of practical, applied ways; their thematic integration; how they link the school and students with the broader community; the ways in which social and institutional networks, both formal and informal, have developed through these efforts; and the way in which academic instruction has been seamlessly superimposed onto multiple hands-on, student-driven, and locally relevant learning opportunities. It is not business as usual, though perhaps it should be.

Conclusion: The High-Stakes Tests Ahead

The beginning of the twenty-first century has not been a hopeful one. This century has been indelibly marked by the terrorist attacks of 9/11 in New York City and Washington, D.C., as well as other equally devastating acts of violence elsewhere across the globe. Over the course of the last decade the United States has been embroiled in tragic and intractable wars in both Iraq and Afghanistan, causing enormous suffering, death, and destruction, obliterating scarce resources, and wasting precious opportunities. In the case of Iraq it's clear that the war was both initiated and perpetuated under false pretenses and deliberate distortion of information by the Bush administration, abetted by a largely uncritical public cowed by the threat of further terrorist attacks. The reputation of the United States suffered further damage from its indiscriminate use of torture, extraordinary renditions, as well as the well-documented abuse of human rights at Abu Ghraib, Guantanamo, Bagram, and scores of other places, actions that were widely interpreted as indicative of this country's (and by extension the West's) antagonistic stance toward the Muslim world as a whole.

Meanwhile, the twin specters of global climate change and peak oil loom ever larger, with the spikes in gasoline prices during the summer of 2008 a harbinger of further fuel shortages and price increases in the near future. We are already seeing the effects of climate change, a climatic phenomenon that no longer entertains any serious doubt within the scientific community, and one that will have dramatic effects on global economies, demographic patterns, food production, and environmental conditions for generations to come (IPCC 2007).

Finally, as this chapter is being written, we face the greatest global financial crisis since the Great Depression with the bankruptcy of major financial institutions, massive housing foreclosures, job layoffs, rising unemployment, and increasing numbers of people both in the United States and around the world facing new and severe forms of insecurity. Testifying before Congress in October 2008, Alan Greenspan, the former Federal Reserve chair and lifelong advocate of free trade policies and limited government regulation, was forced to admit that the financial collapse had left him in a "state of shocked disbelief" because recent events had appeared to so fully contradict conventional economic wisdom.

Shocked disbelief. These are daunting, and in many respects, unprecedented problems. It is far from clear how we will fare. But most of the problems that we face globally—*and* locally—are not individual, but *collective* in nature. They affect all of us and likely defy solutions that do *not* involve collective resolve, understanding, commitment, and action. This suggests that this historical moment represents a critical opportunity in which to challenge the conventional wisdom that has guided the practice of education these last few decades.

This chapter has discussed the ways in which educational institutions, using market-based models, and emphasizing competition, individual achievement, and standardized curricula, have weakened schools, alienated educators, and disengaged students. It has also discussed how in certain respects these practices have had disproportionate effects on rural people, schools, and communities by devaluing place-based knowledge and disregarding the value of community-based inquiry. Education has become placeless, the "quintessential institution of disembedding" (Corbett 2007, 251). But "placelessness erodes our ability to commit to much of anything other than our own self-interest," Theobald writes. "And as a result, we have become a society marked by few allegiances and almost no propensity to shoulder mutual obligations" (1997, 120). This is despite the fact that the social, economic, and environmental problems we face at both local and global levels have *everything* to do with mutual obligations.

Again, to whom is education accountable? Whose purposes does it serve?

It is beyond the scope of this chapter to enumerate a set of prescriptions to transform the state of rural education. Others elsewhere have made strong arguments and compelling suggestions about the ways education might be a force for civic reengagement and community revitalization, rural and otherwise.[7]

Two points are worth making, however. The first is that, as I hope I have made clear in this essay and as others have argued, the market-based model of education reform has implications that are strongly antithetical to community, to place, and to civic engagement. Economic narratives have further derailed any meaningful discussion of education—what it should constitute, what its goals should be, how it might be done—in favor of a commonsense discourse

7. See, among others, Corbett (2007, 2008b); Edmondson (2001); Foster (2004); Gruenewald and Smith (2008); Schafft and Harmon (2010); Sobel (2005); Starrat (2002); and Theobald (1997, 2006, 2009). Also in this volume see contributions by Edmondson and Butler, Faircloth and Tippeconnic, and McDonough and colleagues.

of "accountability" that reduces the practice and experience of education to a test score (Apple 2007). The global economic crisis, coupled with the enormous, social, political, economic, and environmental challenges that we face, should lead us to challenge the conventional wisdom of market-based educational models.

Second, it is worth rethinking the "rural school problem," which similarly is at its root a question of accountability. While the dilemma has often been posed as one of preparing students for rural society versus urban society, or global versus local, the formulation of this dichotomy is a distraction from the real question, which is how we prepare ourselves and our children to live lives that are local *and* global, to understand local phenomena as connected to larger regional-, national-, and global-level processes—and simultaneously to understand how the ways in which lives that are lived locally have *precisely* global social, political, economic, and environmental implications. In the end the issue is not *which* community education prepares students for, but rather that education is able to equip people to live *in* community, regardless of where that community might be (Corbett 2007).

We *are* in a new era of high-stakes testing. But these high-stakes tests bear no resemblance to those mandated by the federal government. And yet they have *everything* to do with the way in which education as a public institution is envisioned and conducted.

Of the many high-stakes tests that I see facing us, consider the following:

How do we ensure not only the future social, economic, and environmental viability, but the agency and self-determination of our rural communities in the face of economic globalization and unprecedented environmental change and degradation?

How do we rethink public education in ways that are fundamentally inclusive of the values of community, democracy, peace, and tolerance as principal indicators of academic achievement and prosperity?

How can we continue to identify and address the structures that reinforce and reproduce poverty and inequality as they occur over space, over time, across gender, and across race, ethnicity, and cultures?

Beyond the narrow goals and assumptions of the "war on terror," how can we help to bring about *true* security by fostering equitable, just, tolerant, and sustainable societies?

These are the *true* tests of our times, and the stakes couldn't be higher.

References

Achieve Incorporated and National Governors Association. 2005. *National Education Summit on High Schools 2005 Briefing Book*. Washington, D.C.: Achieve Incorporated and National Governors Association. Retrieved January 15, 2010, from http://achieve.org/files/Achievebriefingbook2005.pef.

Apple, M. W. 2001. Markets, standards, teaching, and teacher education. *Journal of Teacher Education* 52 (3), 182–96.

———. 2007. Ideological success, educational failure? On the politics of No Child Left Behind. *Journal of Teacher Education* 58 (2), 108–16.

Bard, J., C. Gardener, and R. Wieland. 2006. Rural school consolidation: History, research, summary, conclusions. *Rural Educator* 27 (2), 40–48.

Berliner, D., and B. Biddle. 1996. *The manufactured crisis: Myths, frauds, and the attack on America's public schools*. New York: Addison-Wesley.

Budge, K. 2006. Rural leaders, rural places: Problem, privilege, and possibility. *Journal of Research in Rural Education* 21 (13), 1–10. Retrieved February 2, 2009, from http://jrre.psu.edu/articles/21-13.pdf.

Corbett, M. 2007. *Learning to leave: The irony of schooling in a coastal community*. Halifax: Fernwood Publishing.

Corbett, M. 2008a. Captain Beefheart's piano: Confessions of an unrepentant illiterate. *International Journal of Critical Pedagogy* 1 (2), 148–59.

———. 2008b. The edumometer: The commodification of learning from Galton to the PISA. *Journal for Critical Education Policy Studies* 6 (1). Accessed February 1, 2009, at http://www.jceps.com/index.php?pageID = article&articleID = 125.

Cubberley, E. 1922. *Rural life and education: A study of the rural-school problem as a phase of the rural-life problem*. Boston: Houghton Mifflin.

DeYoung, A. J. 1995. Constructing and staffing the cultural bridge: The school as change agent in rural Appalachia. *Anthropology and Education Quarterly* 26 (2), 168–92.

Downey, D. B., P. T. von Hippel, and M. Hughes. 2008. Are "failing" schools really failing? Using seasonal comparison to evaluate school effectiveness. *Sociology of Education* 81 (3), 242–70.

Edmondson, J. 2001. *Prairie town: Redefining rural life in the age of globalization*. Lanham, Md.: Rowman and Littlefield.

Engel, M. 2000. *The struggle for control of public education: Market ideology vs. democratic values*. Philadelphia: Temple University Press.

Eppley, K. 2009. Rural schools and the highly qualified teacher provision of No Child Left Behind: A critical policy analysis. *Journal of Research in Rural Education* 24 (4), 1–11. Retrieved February 2, 2009, from http://jrre.psu.edu/articles/24-4.pdf.

Finlayson, A. C., T. A. Lyson, A. Pleasant, K. A. Schafft, and R. J. Torres. 2005. The "invisible hand": Neoclassical economics and the ordering of society. *Critical Sociology* 31 (4), 515–36.

Foster, W. P. 2004. The decline of the local: A challenge to educational leadership. *Educational Administration Quarterly* 40 (2), 176–91.

Furman, G. C. 2004. The ethic of community. *Journal of Educational Administration* 42 (2), 215–35.

Gabbard, D. 2003. A nation at risk: Reloaded, part I. *Journal of Critical Educational Policy Studies* 1 (2). Accessed February 1, 2009, from http://www.jceps.com/index.php?pageID = article&articleID = 15.

Gruenewald, D. 2006. Resistance, reinhabitation, and regime change. *Journal of Research in Rural Education* 21 (9), 1–7. Retrieved February 2, 2009, from http://jrre.psu.edu/articles/21-9.pdf.

Gruenewald, D. A., and G. A. Smith, eds. 2008. *Place-based education in the global age.* New York: Lawrence Erlbaum Associates.

Harvey, D. 2005. *A brief history of neoliberalism.* Oxford: Oxford University Press.

Howley, C. 1991. The rural education dilemma as part of the rural dilemma: Rural education and economics. In A. J. DeYoung, ed., *Rural education: Issues and practices,* 73–145. New York: Garland.

IPCC. 2007. *Climate change, 2007: Synthesis report. Contribution of working groups I, II, and III to the fourth assessment report of the Intergovernmental Panel on Climate Change* (core writing team, R. K. Pachauri and A. Reisinger, eds.). Geneva: IPCC.

Jo, T. 2005. Neoliberalism as a social ideology and strategy in education. *Forum for Social Economics* 35 (1), 37–58.

Kannapel, P., and A. DeYoung. 1999. The rural school problem in 1999: A review and critique of the literature. *Journal of Research in Rural Education* 15 (2), 67–79.

Leys, C. 2003. *Market-driven politics: Neoliberal democracy and the public interest.* New York: Verso.

Lyson, T. A. 2002. What does a school mean to a community? Assessing the social and economic benefits of schools to rural villages in New York. *Journal of Research in Rural Education* 17 (3), 131–37.

National Commission on Excellence in Education. 1983. *A nation at risk.* Washington, D.C.: Government Printing Office.

Nichols, S. L., and D. C. Berliner. 2007. *Collateral damage: How high-stakes testing corrupts America's schools.* Cambridge: Harvard Education Press.

Peshkin, A. 1978. *Growing up American: Schooling and the survival of community.* Chicago: University of Chicago Press.

Polanyi, K. 1957. *The great transformation: The political and economic origins of our time.* Boston: Beacon Press.

Saltman, K. J., and D. Gabbard, eds. 2003. *Education as enforcement: The militarization and corporatization of schools.* New York: Routledge.

Schafft, K. A., T. R. Alter, and J. Bridger. 2006. Bringing the community along: A case study of a school district's information technology rural development initiative. *Journal of Research in Rural Education* 21 (8), 1–10.

Schafft, K. A., and H. Harmon. 2010. Schools and community development. In J. W. Robinson, Jr., and G. P. Green, eds., *Introduction to community development: Theory, practice, and service learning,* 245–59. New York: John Wiley.

Schoenfeld, A. H. 2006. What doesn't work: The challenge and failure of the What Works Clearinghouse to conduct meaningful reviews of studies of mathematics curricula. *Educational Researcher* 35 (2), 13–21.

Sherman, M., and T. K. Henry. 1933. *Hollow folk.* New York: Thomas Y. Crowell.

Sims, N. L. 1946. *Elements of rural sociology.* New York: Thomas Y. Crowell.

Smith, A. [1776] 1965. *An inquiry into the nature and causes of wealth of nations.* New York: Modern Library.

Sobel, D. 2005. *Place-based education: Connecting classrooms and communities.* Great Barrington, Mass.: Orion Society.

Speth, J. G. 2008. *The bridge at the end of the world: Capitalism, the environment, and crossing from crisis to sustainability.* New Haven: Yale University Press.

Spring, J. 1998. *Education and the rise of the global economy.* Mahwah, N.J.: Lawrence Erlbaum Associates.

Starratt, R. J. 2002. Community as curriculum. In K. Leithwood and P. Hallinger, eds., *Second international handbook of educational leadership and administration,* 321–48. Dordrecht, Netherlands: Kluwer.

Theobald, P. 1995. *Call school: Rural education in the Midwest to 1918.* Carbondale: Southern Illinois University Press.

———. 1997. *Teaching the commons.* Boulder: Westview.

———. 2006. A case for inserting community into public school curriculum. *American Journal of Education* 112 (3), 315–34.

———. 2009. *Education now: How rethinking America's past can change its future.* Boulder: Paradigm.

Theobald, P., and R. S. Rochon. 2006. Enclosure then and now: Rural schools and communities in the wake of market-driven agriculture. *Journal of Research in Rural Education* 21 (12), 1–8. Retrieved February 2, 2009, from http://jrre.psu.edu/articles/21-12.pdf.

Tyack, D. B. 1972. The tribe and the common school: Community control in rural education. *American Quarterly* 24 (1), 3–19.

Vidich, A. J., and J. Bensman. 1968. *Small town in mass society.* Princeton: Princeton University Press.

Woodrum, A. 2004. State-mandated testing and cultural resistance in Appalachian schools: Competing values and expectations. *Journal of Research in Rural Education* 19 (1), 1–10. Retrieved February 2, 2009, from http://jrre.psu.edu/articles/21-13.pdf.

Wraga, W. G. 2009. Toward a connected core curriculum. *Educational Horizons* 87 (2), 88–96.

Contributors

Genevieve Brown is Professor of Educational Leadership, an experienced public school administrator, and Dean of the College of Education at Sam Houston State University, Huntsville, Texas. Her research focuses on leadership preparation, development and evaluation, leadership theory, and issues of equity and social justice as related to educational leadership.

Rebecca M. Bustamante is an assistant professor in the Department of Educational Leadership at Sam Houston State University in Texas. Her research interests include culture and leadership, intercultural communication, organizational theory, leadership for social justice, English Language Learners, and international education.

Gretchen Butera is an associate professor in special education at Indiana University, where she also serves as an associate chair of the Department of Curriculum and Instruction. Her research interests include young children in poverty, particularly in rural settings. She is coinvestigator of Children's School Success, a large, multisite research investigation of a curriculum designed to address young children at risk for school failure due to poverty, disability, or English as a second language.

Thomas Butler is the superintendent of Ridgway Area School District, a small district in western Pennsylvania. He has a doctorate in Educational Leadership from Penn State University. His dissertation focused on the relationship between rural schools and communities, and he continues his involvement in a variety of rural educational leadership initiatives.

Michael Corbett teaches in the School of Education at Acadia University following a nineteen-year career as a public school teacher in Manitoba and Nova Scotia. His research focuses on the dynamic and ambivalent relationship between life in Atlantic Canadian coastal communities and the structures and processes of schooling. He is interested in the way that questions of identity and education articulate with understandings of place and space.

Lisa Humphreys Costello is a nationally certified school psychologist and a Postdoctoral Fellow at the Early Childhood Clinical Research Center at Bradley Hospital and Warren Alpert Medical School of Brown University.

Stephen Crump is the Pro Vice-Chancellor and Director of the Central Coast Campuses and a professor in education at the University of Newcastle, New South Wales, Australia. He is currently chief investigator for an Australian Research Council project on interactive distance e-learning. He has led two major reports and an ARC project on Vocational Education and Training for the New South Wales and the Australian national governments as well as a task force into New South Wales matriculation certificate reforms.

Jacqueline Edmondson is Associate Dean for Undergraduate and Graduate Studies at Penn State University's College of Education. She is author or coauthor of several books and journal articles, including *Prairie Town: Redefining Rural Life in an Age of Globalization* (2003, Rowman and Littlefield).

Parfait Eloundou-Enyegue is an associate professor of development sociology at Cornell University. His work on the sociology of education addresses differences in access to education for vulnerable groups, including children from low-income, rural, or large families, as well as girls in sub-Saharan Africa.

Susan C. Faircloth is an associate professor of education at Penn State University, where she is the codirector of the Center for the Study of Leadership in American Indian Education. Her research focuses on the education of American Indian and Alaska Native students. Prior to joining the faculty at Penn State, she served as the Director of Research and Policy Analysis with the American Indian Higher Education Consortium.

R. Evely Gildersleeve is an assistant professor in educational leadership and policy studies at Iowa State University. His research investigates the social contexts of educational opportunity for migrant communities and other marginalized groups, focusing primarily on college access. He has received fellowships funded by the Lumina Foundation for Education and the Spencer Foundation. Gildersleeve received his Ph.D. in education from UCLA and is a graduate of Occidental College in Los Angeles.

Sarah Giroux is a graduate student in the department of Development Sociology at Cornell University. She is broadly interested in the demography of inequality, especially with regard to the relationship between fertility change and inequalities in children's health and schooling outcomes.

Susan L. Groenke is an assistant professor at the University of Tennessee in Knoxville, where she advises and teaches in the graduate English education program. Dr. Groenke's research interests include the roles that language plays in the negotiation of student identities in and out of school.

Aimee Howley is Associate Dean for Research and Graduate Studies at Ohio University's College of Education. She teaches research and evaluation courses in the Educational Studies Department. Her most recent book, with Craig Howley, is *Thinking About Schools* (2007, Lawrence Erlbaum Associates).

Craig Howley is an adjunct professor in the Educational Studies Department in the College of Education at Ohio University. Currently he codirects the research initiative of a consortium of Appalachian universities involved in rural mathematics education.

Beverly J. Irby is a professor in and Chair of the Department of Educational Leadership and Counseling at Sam Houston State University in Huntsville, Texas. Her research focuses on leadership and social justice issues related to bilingual and English as a secondary language teachers and administrators within the school context.

Alecia Youngblood Jackson is Associate Professor of Educational Research in the College of Education at Appalachian State University. Her research interests bring feminist and post-structural theories of power, knowledge, language, and subjectivity to bear on a range of overlapping topics: deconstructions of narrative and voice, cultural studies of schooling (with an emphasis on the rural), and qualitative method in the postmodern.

Fatou Jah is a Ph.D. candidate in the department of Development Sociology at Cornell University. Her areas of specialization include applied demography, population, (reproductive) health, and international development. Currently, she is examining the relative contributions of educational and demographic transitions on the recent changes in employment inequalities in African labor markets and their implications for women and their families' well-being.

Karen McClafferty Jarsky holds a Ph.D. and M.A. in education from UCLA, where she also completed a postdoctoral fellowship. She is currently an independent researcher and writer. She has published on college culture, rural college access, culturally diverse learners, P-16 collaboratives, higher education curriculum, and sociology of education.

Kieran M. Killeen is an associate professor of education at the University of Vermont. His research interests include school finance, rural education, and the implications of student mobility for effective school reform.

Patricia M. McDonough is a professor in the higher education program at the University of California, Los Angeles. Her research is in the areas of college access, and she has conducted research on students' choice of college, college costs and financial aid, high school counseling, college rankings, African American and Latino students, rural college access, private college counselors, and college admissions officers.

John Morrissey recently retired as a school counselor after working in upstate New York school districts for over thirty years. He has a long-term interest in highly mobile students and the effects of poverty on youth social and academic outcomes. He has made numerous presentations regarding these issues to school personnel, boards of education, and at academic and professional meetings.

Jan Nespor is a professor in the Cultural Foundations, Technology, and Qualitative Inquiry program at Ohio State University.

Kai A. Schafft is Assistant Professor of Education at Penn State University, where he directs the Center on Rural Education and Communities and edits the *Journal of Research in Rural Education*. Dr. Schafft's research examines the relationship among social inequality, spatial inequality, and rural development, with current work focusing on the interrelationships between rural schools and communities.

Paul Theobald holds the Woods-Beals Chair in Urban and Rural Education at Buffalo State College. He has published widely in the area of community-based and place-based education and is probably best known as the author of *Teaching the Commons: Place, Pride, and the Renewal of Community* (1997, Westview).

John Tippeconnic III is a professor of education and Director of the American Indian Leadership Program at Penn State University. Leadership development and the implementation of educational policy in American Indian and Alaska Native communities and schools are among his research interests. He is currently Chair of the Governing Board of Comanche Nation College.

Kylie Twyford works at the University of Newcastle as the senior research associate on the Australian Research Council Linkage project "Interactive Distance E-Learning for Isolated Communities: Opening Our Eyes." Dr. Twyford previously worked for many years as a distance education teacher and manager in the vocational education and training sector in Australia, focusing in the area of ICT in distance education and its influence on student motivation.

Kathy Wood is the Director of the Center for Excellence in Urban and Rural Education and an associate professor in the Elementary Education and Reading Department at Buffalo State College. She earned her M.A. and Ph.D. from the State University of New York at Buffalo in Educational Administration, and her B.A. (in Elementary Education) from Howard University. Her research interests include urban and rural education, pre-service teachers' dispositions in diversity, and professional development for in-service teachers.

Index

Page numbers in *italics* refer to figures; those followed by "t" refer to tables; those followed by "n" refer to notes, with note number.

Rural Studies Series

STEPHEN G. SAPP, *General Editor*

LaVergne, TN USA
27 June 2010
187437LV00001B/1/P